YOUR GUIDE TO PASSING THE

AMP REAL ESTATE Exam

3RD EDITION

Joyce Bea Sterling

Dearborn™
Real Estate Education

Vice President: Roy Lipner
Publisher: Evan Butterfield
Development Editor: Anne Huston
Senior Managing Editor: Ronald J. Liszkowski
Art and Design Manager: Lucy Jenkins
Typesetter: Janet Schroeder

Published by Dearborn™ Real Estate Education,
a division of Dearborn Financial Publishing, Inc.®
30 South Wacker Drive
Chicago, IL 60606-7481
(312) 836-4400
http://www.dearbornRE.com

Library of Congress Cataloging-in-Publication Data

Sterling, Joyce Bea
    Your guide to passing the AMP real estate exam/Joyce Bea Sterling. — 3rd ed.
        p. cm.
    Includes index.
    ISBN 0-7931-4513-9
    1. Real estate agents—Licenses—United States—Examinations, questions, etc.   2. Real estate business—Licenses—United States—Examinations, questions, etc.   3. Real property—United States—Examinations, questions, etc.   I. Title: AMP real estate exam.   II. Title

HD278 .S85   2001
333.33'076—dc21   2001028809

Contents

Preface

It is with pride that we present the third edition of *Your Guide To Passing the AMP Real Estate Exam*. This was the first exam guide on the market that was designed specifically for the licensing exam administered by Applied Measurement Professionals, Inc. The AMP exam questions are complex, and we believe this book will provide you with the testing edge to help you pass the exam.

Other than attending class, one of the most effective ways to prepare for your state exam is by studying exam topics and answering practice questions. *Your Guide To Passing the AMP Real Estate Exam* contains a streamlined review of the areas covered on the exam and more than 700 questions for you to answer.

In writing the exam guide, the author has assumed that the reader is attending a real estate prelicensing class and that this book is being used as a review of the material covered in class. Specific state information regarding fair housing, transfer of deeds and so on should be obtained from your classroom instruction.

TEXT FEATURES

Each student taking the AMP exam receives a candidate's handbook from his or her state. This handbook contains a detailed outline of the material on the AMP real estate exam. *Your Guide To Passing the AMP Real Estate Exam* has been organized to parallel this content outline. Chapters 1-6 in this guide correspond to the six subject areas covered on the examination, while Chapter 7 is a math refresher. Also, prior to the chapter discussion of each topic in this guide, the appropriate section of the AMP content outline from the candidate's handbook has been reproduced for your convenience.

At the end of each section, the information just covered is summarized in a list format called **Key Point Review.** This has been included for two reasons. First, to provide a review of the material covered, because repetition of the material will help you learn it. Second, because most students feel they should study the night before the exam but are overwhelmed with so much review. The key points are designed to give a very focused, detailed review of the important material when you are down to the final days or hours before your exam. The number of points per section varies, as does the length of the individual points because some sections cover more topics than others.

Reminder light bulb icons are strategically placed throughout the book near important points to remember.

A 60-question quiz concludes each chapter. Each quiz indicates broker-level questions for easy identification, and provides a detailed answer key. The **Math Review** also contains 60 questions pertaining to brokerage, financing, appraising, area and settlement math.

This Guide concludes with **sample salesperson and broker examinations,** each offering 100 questions and rationales.

NEW TO THIS EDITION

This third edition is based on the **latest AMP national exam outline.** The author has added/ expanded topics, updated questions and answers, and changed the content order as appropriate to the new outline. In addition the **Key Point Reviews** have been updated wherever necessary.

There have been **five new broker questions,** along with rationales, added to each chapter, offering additional practice opportunity.

Appendix I features a Web-Site Directory, with important real estate related sites for additional research and information. **Appendix II** contains IRS Form 8300, which is now included in the AMP content outline.

The **Glossary** has been expanded to include new topics covered in the AMP outline.

A CD-Rom containing a 50-question salesperson practice exam and a 50-question broker practice exam is packaged with this edition to provide additional computer practice. The total package now contains more than 700 questions, making it the most complete program available to help students pass the exam!

ACKNOWLEDGMENTS

We wish to thank those who participated in the preparation of the third edition of *Your Guide to Passing the AMP Real Estate Exam* by serving as reviewers. We appreciate their insight and suggestions.

Susan S. Barron, Oakton Community College, Des Plaines, Illinois
Diane Silver Berryhill, Ben Farmer School of Real Estate, Savannah, Georgia
Vincent De Paul, College of DuPage and the Illinois Academy of Real Estate, Glen Ellyn, Illinois
Sarah Love, Century 21 Real Estate Academy, Des Plaines, Illinois
Roger Meade, Meade and Associates Appraisal, Fort Mitchell, Kentucky

Our gratitude also is extended to those who contributed questions or submitted reviews for the second edition of the book. These include:

Frank W. Anderson, American Real Estate Institute, Montgomery, Alabama
Patricia A. Bean, Southeastern Institute of Real Estate, Southfield, Michigan
Gene Bergan, Dakota West Institute, Rapid City, South Dakota
Robert J. Connole, PhD., DREI, Connole-Morton Real Estate School, Missoula, Montana
Robert E. Hart, MLS Training Institute, Tucker, Georgia
Thomas L. Meyer, Cape Girardeau Missouri School of Real Estate, Cape Girardeau, Missouri
Del D. Nordstrom, Pro-Ed, Sioux Falls, South Dakota
Dave A. Toorenaar, Greenridge Realty, Inc., Grand Rapids, Michigan
Don W. Williams, Alabama Courses in Real Estate, Homewood, Alabama
Avery Yarbrough, DREI, Avery Yarbrough & Associates, Inc., Birmingham, Alabama

A special thanks is extended to John Muething, Keating, Muething & Klekamp, Cincinnati, Ohio.

ABOUT THE AUTHOR

Joyce Bea Sterling has been teaching real estate principles, practices and law since 1986, and has helped thousands of students pass their exams. Currently, she teaches prelicensing classes as an adjunct Professor at Northern Kentucky University (previously an AMP state), continuing education classes at Northern Kentucky Real Estate School, and exam review courses in Ohio. She has a Bachelor of Arts in Education from Northern Kentucky University and a Suggestive Accelerated Learning and Teaching Certificate from Iowa State University.

Her experiences as an instructor include teaching every grade level from kindergarten through college, and she is considered a specialist in learning. Her credentials also include loan origination, public speaking and stress management consultation. She is the coauthor of *Modern Real Estate Practice in Illinois*, 3rd Edition, and of exam review audiotape sets for the states of North Carolina, New York and Pennsylvania, all published by Dearborn™ Real Estate Education. She's also the coauthor and on-camera cohost of the *Mastering Real Estate Math* video, also published by Dearborn™ Real Estate Education.

REQUEST FOR FEEDBACK

We have taken every precaution to produce an accurate book to help you pass your exam. We welcome any feedback, and your comments will be used to evaluate the current edition and to formulate changes for future editions. Please direct all comments to Joyce Bea Sterling, c/o Editorial Group, Dearborn™ Real Estate Education, 155 N. Wacker Dr., Chicago, IL 60606–1719, or e-mail comments to RealEstate@Dearborn.com.

Introduction

ABOUT YOUR TEST!

Knowledge is power . . . and knowledge of real estate can make you or save you thousands of dollars in the future. Congratulations on your decision to secure a real estate license! To get started, you must pass the AMP exam; then you can begin your career as a real estate licensee.

Applied Measurement Professionals, Inc. (AMP), of Lenexa, Kansas, began in 1990 with the goal of supplying professional testing for future real estate agents. This introduction will help you review basic reading and study skills, understand the format of the questions and develop an exam strategy. The remaining chapters will guide you through a review of the six areas covered on your real estate exam.

AMP provides a candidate's handbook that contains your exam application. It is available through your school or the real estate commission and provides you with specific information regarding your own state exam. It is also available at www.goamp.com. Please read it carefully.

This guide was written to be a streamlined review of the material presented in the classroom. Should you need more in-depth information about a subject, please refer to the textbook used in your class.

WHAT'S ON YOUR TEST?

The national examination content outline for brokers and salespeople is as follows:

	Number of Items	
	Broker	**Salesperson**
1. Listing Property	17	22
2. Selling Property	16	20
3. Property Management	13	9
4. Settlement/Transfer of Ownership	15	13
5. Financing	18	21
6. Professional Responsibilities/Fair Practice/Administration	21	15

More specific information on each of these areas can be found at the beginning of each chapter. A booklet will be used when testing in Alabama, Michigan and Montana.

A computer will be used when testing in Georgia, Illinois, Missouri, Nebraska, North Dakota, Nevada, South Dakota and Wyoming.

LISTENING EFFECTIVELY

Most real estate students have work, family and many other responsibilities. That's why it is so important to concentrate intently on the information the instructor presents in class.

Here are three basic rules for listening effectively.

Rule 1. Listen to what the instructor is saying, as well as to the inflections in the instructor's voice. An instructor's voice will change as important material is presented.

Rule 2. Instructors do not know what will be on any given test. However, some material is more important than other material. Listen carefully for the material that the instructor indicates you must know for the state and national exams.

Rule 3. Your time is valuable. Make the most of it while you are in class. A student who doodles, reads other material or goes on a mental vacation during class time is missing valuable information.

READING EFFECTIVELY

Comprehensive reading is a skill that takes practice. Here are some steps to help you develop this essential skill for studying and passing the test.

Step 1. Begin preparation for your exam with your textbook or other instructional materials. Most text authors provide a preview of the material, as well as a summary at the end of each chapter. Read the preview, skim the headings and read the summary to grasp the author's plan of presentation of the material. Then, with an understanding of what is to be learned, read the chapter.

Step 2. Highlight important words and terms while you are reading. Be sure to learn the words that you do not understand or ask your instructor their meanings. Be sure you learn the vocabulary words. This is essential for passing your exam.

Step 3. If possible, relate the material to your own life experiences. Recall listing your property with an agent, as well as what occurred during the real estate transaction. Read the important material at least three times. Then take the test at the end of the chapter. Read the material until you understand why you missed any of the questions.

Step 4. Next, use this guide to help you review the important material until you sit for your exam. Even if you have only a few minutes to review, it will help keep the material fresh in your mind. Remember . . . *repetition is the key to learning.*

Step 5. When you have completed your classes, read the most important material in this guide at least three times, then answer as many test questions as you can. You will find test questions at the end of every review area and sample salesperson and broker tests at the end of this guide. Go ahead and take the broker test, even if you're sitting for the salesperson exam. The more questions you can answer, the easier the state exam will be.

OTHER STUDYING TIPS

Read the class assignment before attending class to help you identify the areas in which you want to ask questions.

Find a quiet place to study. If you are studying at home, resist answering the phone or engaging in any other activities that can be distracting, such as having the television or radio on in the background. Most schools have a library or classroom available for study. If you make the effort to go to the library, you will probably be able to better focus on learning the material.

Consider forming a study group or finding another individual with whom you can study. Each individual should commit to reviewing the material independently before attending the study session. Determine your goals for each group meeting, and appoint a group leader to keep you on target.

Sometimes one person may try to dominate the study group. Be aware of any person who wants to control the entire group or who thinks he or she has all the right answers. Studying in groups should be a joint effort.

UNDERSTANDING THE FORMATS OF THE QUESTIONS

The following question formats can be found on your AMP exam. Many students miss questions because they do not take the time to read carefully.

When approaching a question on your state exam, read and answer each question three times. Read the first time to identify the format of the question being asked and its content. Read the second time to create in your mind a scenario of what the question is asking. If possible, underline key words and phrases. Then, read each question a third time to make sure that you understand exactly what is being asked.

Answer the question in your mind, then read the answers to find that answer. Read each answer three times. There may be a key word or phrase in one of the answers or in the question that indicates the right answer. There should be ample time to read each question and each answer three times, but pace yourself. Keep track of the time and complete the test.

Let's explore some of the types of questions that you may encounter on your exam.

The EXCEPT Format

When the word *EXCEPT* appears at the end of the question, it means you are looking for the *opposite* of what your logic tells you is correct.

"All of the following are true EXCEPT" means you are looking for the one answer that is false.
"All of the following are false EXCEPT" means you are looking for the one answer that is true.

The NOT Format

When *NOT* is found in a question, it means you are looking for the one answer that should not be included. This format is used to see if you really understand what is involved in a certain law or principle.

The SITUATIONAL Format

With a *SITUATIONAL* format, a scenario is created and the possible answers may include two Yes answers and two No answers. Questions in this format test your comprehension of the material, as well as your ability to analyze each answer. There may be only one word or phrase in the answer that will make it correct.

A situational format question can be very long. Read it carefully and create the situation in your mind before answering the question.

The DEFINITION or RECALL Format

These test questions are easy . . . as long as you know the definitions of the vocabulary words. A definition is given in the question, and you must match it with the answer.

The MOST IMPORTANT Format

In questions of this type, a key word or concept makes one answer more important than another.

The LEAST Format

The *LEAST* format could include the terms *LEAST INFLUENCE* or *LEAST LIKELY*. Look for the answer that is least probable.

Example:

Which of the following would LEAST LIKELY be found in an abstract of title?

The BEST Format

The word *BEST* means the most advantageous or, as it relates to the test question, the better choice. This format also can be used for recall questions.
Example:

> A tenancy in common interest that grants the right to interval ownership of the property would BEST describe a(n)

The key words in this question are *interval ownership,* which would be best described as a time-share.

The TRUE Format

"Which of the following is *TRUE?*" means there are three wrong answers and one true answer. This format may be combined with the situational format to test your understanding of the meaning of a concept.

The FALSE Format

"Which of the following is *FALSE?*" means there are three true answers and one false answer.

The DIFFERENCE Format

With the *DIFFERENCE* format, you will make comparisons or look for the distinction between two words or concepts.
Example:

> The MAJOR DIFFERENCE between actual eviction and constructive eviction is

Knowing the definitions of actual and constructive eviction, as well as the proper process for each eviction, is essential to correctly answer this question.

The HAVE IN COMMON Format

Questions using this format ask what a group of words have in common.
Example:

> What do the terms *possibility of reverter, right of reentry* and *remainder* have in common?

To correctly answer this question, you must know the definitions of *possibility of reverter, right of reentry* and *remainder.*

The MOST LIKELY Format

The MOST LIKELY format is asking for what would normally happen in a given situation.
Example:

> In a real estate transaction, the agent would MOST LIKELY represent whom?

The APPLICATION Format

The APPLICATION format tests to see if you can apply the information you have learned.
Example:

> If the net income on a property remains constant and the cap rate increases 1 percent, the value of the property will. . .

This question is testing your knowledge of an appraising formula.

The ACCOUNTABLE Format

This question will set up a scenario or a situation and then ask who can be held accountable or if a certain party is accountable.

Example:

> A broker was asked to list a property by the executor of an estate. When the broker asked if the property was zoned commercial, the executor replied, "I think so." Without additional verification, the broker listed and sold the property as having commercial zoning. The purchaser hired an architect to design a building and attempted to secure a building permit. The buyer was informed that the property was zoned residential. Who can be held ACCOUNTABLE for the damages?

To correctly answer this question, you must understand the law of agency.

HOW TO USE THIS BOOK

Chapters One through Six in this guide follow the six subject areas presented on the national AMP exam outline found in the candidate's handbook (available at www.goamp.com), while the seventh chapter is a math review. After you have read a chapter, review the key points and then answer the questions.

Take the time to review the material on the questions you missed, and if necessary, also review your principles book. The key points are to be reviewed in the final days before taking your exam.

The "reminder icon" is found throughout the text. It is placed next to material that is important for you to know.

You will also notice that some of the headings throughout the book are bracketed by black bullet points (•). This means that the particular topic appears on the broker examination only.

1

Listing Property

This chapter covers the following information regarding the listing of property: listing, appraisal of property value, methods of property valuation, the nature of real property and services provided in the agency relationship with the seller.

Content Outline—Listing

I. Listing Property

   A. Listing

      1. Hidden defects
      2. Listing agreement signatures by all parties
      3. Tax assessment and tax rate
      4. Deed restrictions and covenants
      5. Legal descriptions
      6. Lot size
      7. Physical dimensions of structure
      8. Appurtenances (for example, easements and water rights)
      9. Utilities
      10. Type of construction
      11. Encumbrances (for example, liens and restrictions)
      12. Compliance with health, safety and building codes
      13. Ownership of record
      14. Homeowners' association bylaws and fees
      15. Brokerage fee

HIDDEN DEFECTS

An agent must be aware of two types of defects in a property:

- **Latent defects** are hidden structural defects not easily discovered by inspection.
- **Patent defects** are easily visible when inspecting a property.

Misrepresentation occurs when property defects are not disclosed to the buyer. The buyer may be able to rescind the sales contract or receive **compensatory damages,** which are **actual damages** for the repair of the defect. An agent is liable for not disclosing known defects and may be liable for defects the agent "should have known" about.

LISTING AGREEMENT SIGNATURES BY ALL PARTIES

The signatures of all parties named on the deed are required on the listing agreement. If this is not possible, owing to the death of the owner or one of the owners being absent, then a party with legal authorization to perform must sign the listing. An administrator, executor or a person with a proper power of attorney could sign the listing. Both spouses should sign the listing agreement, even if the property is held in the name of only one of them.

TAX ASSESSMENT AND TAX RATE

Property taxes also are called **ad valorem taxes.** Computation of property taxes is shown in detail on page 174.

DEED RESTRICTIONS AND COVENANTS

Deed restrictions are provisions placed in deeds to control the future uses of the property. The restriction may be either a deed condition or a deed covenant.

A **condition** creates a conditional fee estate, which means that if the condition is breached, the title may revert to the grantor or the grantor's heirs.

A **covenant** is a promise between two or more parties in which they agree to perform or not to perform specified acts on the property. If a deed covenant is breached, there can be a suit for money damages or injunctive relief. Deed restrictions normally "run with the land," meaning they transfer from one owner to the next.

LEGAL DESCRIPTIONS

In some states, a street address is sufficient to identify the property in a listing and sales contract. Other states require the legal description in these contracts, as well as in deeds, mortgages, notes and other real estate documents. Metes-and-bounds, lot-and-block and the rectangular or government survey are the legal descriptions commonly used.

Metes-and-Bounds

The **metes-and-bounds** survey method or the **boundary survey** involves describing land by the **metes (distance)** and **bounds (direction).** A starting point must be identified that future surveyors

FIGURE 1.1 *Reading a Bearing*

can use, and it is known as a **point of beginning (POB)** or a **point of commencement (POC).** The surveyor travels around the property being described until the lot closes, that is, the surveyor returns to the point of beginning.

A metes-and-bounds legal description uses feet as the unit of measurement to describe the distance between monuments; direction is given by the bearing of one monument in respect to another monument, described by using north, south, east and west, in relationship to degrees, minutes and seconds.

For example, imagine a circular clock with a line drawn from 12 to 6 and another line from 9 to 3. North is 12 o'clock, east is 3 o'clock, south 6 o'clock and west 9 o'clock. The four quadrants then are NE, NW, SE and SW. A legal description reading N45°E means that a surveyor is moving 45° eastward from due north. On the imaginary clock, the surveyor is facing the position of the hour hand at 1:30 P.M. (See Figure 1.1.)

Other survey terms are

- **Monuments**—used to physically identify the POB and the intersections of the boundary lines of the area being surveyed;
- **Benchmark**—a permanent reference point used to establish elevations and altitudes above sea level; and
- **Datum**—a point, line or surface from which elevations are measured to determine such things as the heights of structures or grades of streets.

Lot and Block

The **lot-and-block** method of legal description is used on maps and plats of recorded subdivided land (also known as a *recorded plat* or a *recorded map*).

When a developer subdivides a tract of land for the development of a subdivision, the surveyor's plat map is recorded in the county courthouse where the property is located. Each **parcel (lot)** of land is assigned a lot number and each group of contiguous lots is given a **block number.** A description might read, "Lots 5 and 6 of Block 9 of the Brentwood Subdivision." Because all states use this method, a description must include the county and state to distinguish it from another area.

Government, Rectangular or Geodetic Survey

The **government** (*rectangular* or *geodetic*) **survey** is based on a system of imaginary lines called **principal meridians,** which run north and south, and **base lines,** which run east and west.

- The largest square is called a *check* and measures 24 miles by 24 miles. Each check has 16 townships.

FIGURE 1.2 *Sections of a Township*

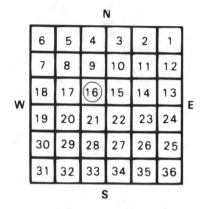

- A **township** measures 6 miles by 6 miles. Each township has 36 sections. (See Figure 1.2.)
- A **section** measures 1 mile by 1 mile and contains 640 acres.
- **Correction lines** are used to compensate for the earth's curvature.
- **Oversized** or undersized sections are called fractional sections.

A government survey description could read: The NW¼ of the NE¼ of the SW¼ of Section 32, Township 12 North, Range 3 West of the tenth Principal Meridian. When asked to locate the legal description of a parcel of land using the government survey, read the description backward. Using Figure 1.3 as an example, to locate the N½ of the SE¼ of the SW¼, begin by locating the SW¼; then locate the SE¼ of the SW¼; then the N½ of the SE¼ of the SW¼.

To compute the acreage of the N½ of the SE¼ of the SW¼, remember there are 640 acres in one section of land. Divide 640 by the denominators. 640 ÷ 4 ÷ 4 ÷ 2 = 20 acres of land.

Suppose a question asks for the numbers of acres in the SW¼ of the NE¼ of the NE¼ and the N½ of the SE¼ of the SW¼; the words *and the* indicate that there are two parcels of land, as shown in Figure 1.4. Again, divide 640 acres by the denominators, but compute the acreage for the two tracts separately. Thus, 640 ÷ 4 ÷ 4 ÷ 4 = 10 acres and 640 ÷ 4 ÷ 4 ÷ 2 = 20 acres. 10 + 20 = 30 acres of land.

FIGURE 1.3 *Locating a Parcel of Land in the Government Survey*

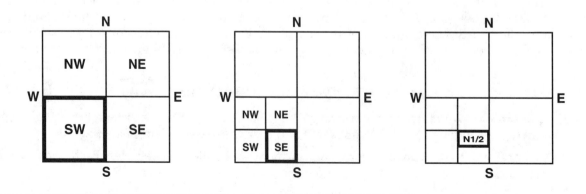

FIGURE 1.4 *Locating Two Parcels of Land in the Government Survey*

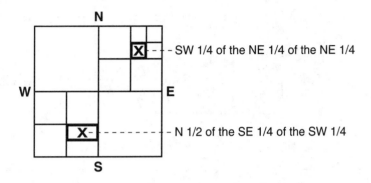

LOT SIZE

The accuracy of the lot size is essential in both residential and commercial properties. If there is a discrepancy between the lot size quoted in the listing contract or deed and the actual lot size, the *actual lot size* found by the survey will prevail.

Other terms associated with lot size are

- **floor area ratio**—the ratio of the floor area to the land area on which the building sits;
- **livability space ratio**—requires a minimum square footage of nonvehicular outdoor area in a development for each square foot of total living area;
- **front footage**—the linear measurement of a property along the street line or water line, always given first when dimensions are stated (if a lot measures 100' x 200', then the first dimension given [100'] refers to the front footage); and
- **setback**—the amount of space required between the lot line and the building line.

PHYSICAL DIMENSIONS OF STRUCTURE

The **foundation walls** are masonry or concrete walls below the ground level that serve as the main support for the frame structure. If the house has a basement, the foundation walls form the basement.

Unless custom dictates otherwise, the general rule of thumb is that when an agent or appraiser measures a building to compute the **gross living area (GLA),** only the area above grade (ground) level is used. The external dimensions of the building are measured, excluding the garage, porch or patio. The square footage of foundation related walls or the basement is included in the appraiser's description of the property. It has a different square footage calculation than the square footage calculation for above grade level.

APPURTENANCES

Listing contracts and sales contracts usually state which appurtenances are sold with the property. The word **appurtenant** in real estate means attached to the land or deed.

- **Tangible** (touchable) **property,** such as any physical improvements on the property, and fixtures, such as lighting, heating and plumbing equipment, are appurtenances. A listing con-

FIGURE 1.5 *Appurtenant Easement*

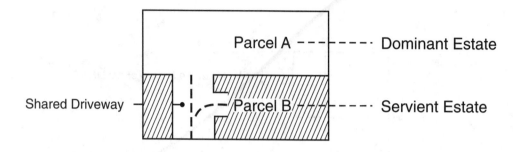

tract should identify fixtures that "go with the property" and fixtures that a seller intends to take with him or her after the sale.
- **Intangible** (cannot touch) **property** includes rights and privileges that belong to and pass in the deed from the grantor to the grantee. Easements and water rights are intangible appurtenances. An **easement** is the right to use the land of another, but it does not include the right of possession. Amont the various types of easements are the following:

Appurtenant Easement

- Benefits a parcel of real estate
- Involves two tracts of land owned by two different people
- The dominant estate benefits from the easement
- The servient estate is burdened by the easement

Easement in Gross

- Benefits a person or a legal entity
- Involves one tract of land
- Personal gross easements terminate on the sale of the property or death of the easement owner (e.g., the billboard)
- Commercial gross easements are usually assignable when the property is sold or on the death of the easement owner (e.g., a utility)

FIGURE 1.6 *Easement in Gross*

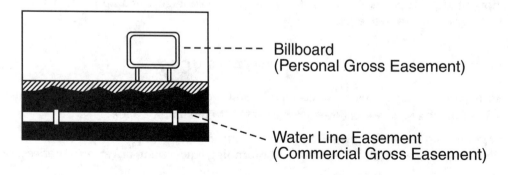

Easement by Necessity

- Created when a buyer purchases a landlocked property
- Buyer must be given the access rights to ingress (enter) and egress (exit) the property

Easement by Prescription

- Created when a claimant uses a property for a statutory period of time
- Use must have been open, notorious, continuous, exclusive and without the owner's approval

---

LICENSE

A license is the *personal privilege* to enter the land of another and use it for a specific reason, such as hunting, fishing or entering a building to go to the movies. A license *can be revoked* at any time and terminates on the death of either party or the sale of the land.

UTILITIES

A **utility** is a service provided to a property, such as supplying gas, electricity, telephone service and water. Depending on the custom in the community, the company providing the service may be able to place a lien on the property if fees for such services are not paid.

TYPE OF CONSTRUCTION

Agents should have a working knowledge of construction to help determine the quality, upkeep and flaws of a property. This includes such details as identification of the type of foundation, exterior structural walls and framing, interior walls and finishing, style and type of roof, windows and doors.

ENCUMBRANCES

An encumbrance is any claim, lien, charge or liability that affects the value or the use of a property. Encumbrances that affect the *title:* liens, mortgages and judgments. Encumbrances that affect the *use:* deed restrictions, encroachments and easements.

COMPLIANCE WITH HEALTH, SAFETY AND BUILDING CODES

To ensure health, safety and welfare of homeowners, there are local, state or municipal building and construction standards that must be met. These standards include the regulation and control of design, construction, quality, use, occupancy, location and maintenance of all buildings and structures.

A *building permit* must be issued for the construction of a new building or other improvement, any substantial repair of an existing structure or the demolition of a building. The purpose of the permit is to ensure compliance with the **building code,** or *minimum standards of construction.* A violation of code and failure to disclose violations may constitute misrepresentation and make the contract voidable. When the building "meets code," a **certificate of occupancy** is issued.

OWNERSHIP OF RECORD

When a property is purchased, most buyers record their deed and title at the courthouse, or at the Torrens office if the property is registered land. Recording the deed in public records gives notice to the world of ownership of the property.

NOTICE

Constructive notice or *legal notice* gives the buyer protection by preventing a previous owner from selling the property to a third party.

Actual notice is express or direct knowledge acquired because the information has been read, heard or seen.

HOMEOWNERS' ASSOCIATION BYLAWS AND FEES

Bylaws are established by condominiums and subdivisions for the administration and management of the community. The bylaws also establish the homeowners' association, the power given to the board and the responsibilities of each homeowner. (See Ownership in Real Estate and Conveyance later in this chapter for more detailed information.)

BROKERAGE FEE

The fee that an owner pays a brokerage company for the services of marketing, advertising and securing a ready, willing and able buyer is negotiated between the broker and the seller. Should a contract be entered into with a buyer, the payment of commission also should be established in that agreement. The *Sherman Antitrust Act* is a federal law that prohibits price-fixing. Most states also have antitrust laws.

Listing—Key Point Review

1. A latent defect is a hidden defect; a patent defect is obvious.

2. The signatures of all parties named on a deed or the signature of a party legally authorized to perform must be on the listing agreement.

3. Property taxes, also known as *ad valorem taxes,* and special assessments take priority over all other liens on the property.

4. A deed condition creates a conditional fee estate. If the condition is breached, the title may revert to the grantor or the grantor's heirs.

5. A covenant is a promise between two or more parties in which they agree to perform or not to perform specified acts. Breach of a deed covenant can result in a suit for money damages or injunctive relief.

6. The metes-and-bounds legal description involves describing the land by metes (distance) and bounds (direction). Degrees, minutes and seconds are used in the legal description.

7. Every metes-and-bounds survey must start and end (close) at the point of beginning. Actual distance between monuments takes precedence over other descriptions when a discrepancy exists. A bench mark is a permanent reference point placed by a government survey team to establish elevation or altitude above sea level.

8. The lot-and-block method of legal description is used on maps and plats of recorded, subdivided land. *Contiguous lots* means lots that adjoin one another.

9. The government, rectangular or geodetic survey is based on a system of imaginary lines: principal meridians, which run north and south, and base lines, which run east and west.

10. The largest area in the government survey system, called a *check,* is 24 miles by 24 miles. Checks are divided into townships, which are 6 miles by 6 miles. Townships are divided into sections, which are 1 mile by 1 mile. Each section contains 640 acres. Oversized or undersized sections are called *fractional sections.* Correction lines are adjustments for the earth's curvature.

11. The measure of a property along the street or water line is called the *front footage.* It is important to know if a required setback is measured from the center of the street or the curb line.

12. In computing the gross living area or GLA of a building, only the area above grade or ground level is used. The external dimensions of the building do not include a garage, porch or patio.

13. The word *appurtenant* means attached. Tangible (touchable) appurtenances include personal property or fixtures that may or may not pass in the deed. Intangible (cannot touch) appurtenances include rights and privileges that belong to the land and pass in the deed.

14. An easement is the right to use the land of another; it does not include the right of possession.

15. The parcel of land that benefits from an appurtenant easement is known as the *dominant estate.* The parcel of land burdened by the easement is known as the *servient estate.*

Listing—Key Point Review (Continued)

16. An easement in gross is a personal or commercial interest in or right to use the land of another. Personal gross easements normally terminate on the death of the easement owner and do not pass with the deed when the property is sold. Commercial gross easements, such as a utility easement, generally transfer when the property is sold.

17. An easement by necessity is created for a landlocked property to provide the access rights of ingress (entry) and egress (exit).

18. An easement by prescription is created when a claimant uses another's property for a statutory period of time and follows the proper legal proceedings to secure the easement. The claimant's use must have been open, notorious, continuous, exclusive and without the owner's approval.

19. A license is a personal privilege to enter the land of another and use it for a specific purpose. It can be revoked at any time and terminates on the death of either party or the sale of the land.

20. An encumbrance is any claim, lien, charge or liability that affects the value or the use of a property.

21. Building codes are established to ensure the health, safety and welfare of property owners.

22. A building permit must be issued for construction of a new building or other improvement, substantial repair of an existing structure or demolition of a building.

23. Constructive or legal notice gives notice to the world of the ownership of property. A recorded deed provides constructive notice and protects the owner in regard to third parties.

24. Actual notice is express or direct knowledge gained by reading, hearing, or seeing the information.

25. Commission rates are negotiable between principals and the brokers. The Sherman Antitrust Act and state laws prohibit collusive acts designed to restrict competition.

Content Outline—Assessment of Property Value

I. Listing Property

    B. Assessment of Property Value

        1. Location
        2. Anticipated changes (for example, in zoning or use)
        3. Depreciation
        4. Deterioration
        5. Obsolescence
        6. Improvements
        7. Economic trends

LOCATION

The location of a property is one of the major factors in determining its value. *Location*, or **situs**, is the preference people have for a certain area. When determining the value of a property, an adjustment may be necessary to compensate for locational differences within the neighborhood.

ANTICIPATED CHANGES

The *principle of anticipation* says that the value of a property will adjust with any anticipated change. If the anticipated change is considered positive, such as a change of zoning from residential to commercial, the value of the property generally increases. If the anticipated change is considered negative, such as the expansion of an airport that will increase the noise level within the neighborhood, the value of the property generally decreases.

DEPRECIATION

Depreciation is a loss of property value due to any cause. This could include ordinary wear and tear, damage caused by fire or vandalism, or by acts of nature such as hurricanes, floods, earthquakes, etc. The three types of depreciation that the appraiser determines are physical, functional and external. Please remember that *land does not ordinarily depreciate;* only the improvements are depreciated.

Terms Associated with Depreciation

- **Depreciation** causes a loss of property value.
- **Curable depreciation** is reasonable and economically feasible to correct.
- **Incurable depreciation** is not economically feasible to correct.
- **Physical depreciation** may be curable or incurable and is caused by lack of maintenance and ordinary wear and tear.
- **Functional obsolescence** may be curable or incurable and occurs because of poor design or changes in technology.
- **External obsolescence** is incurable and occurs because of factors located outside the property (e.g., a nearby nuclear power plant, pig farm or drive-in theater). External obsolescence may be referred to as *economic, locational* or *environmental obsolescence.*

DETERIORATION

Depreciation of the property can occur through deterioration, which is the effect of normal wear and tear or of natural elements.

OBSOLESCENCE

To be *obsolete* is to be *outdated;* thus, **obsolescence** can occur due to functional or external depreciation of the property.

IMPROVEMENTS

Improvements are added to the land for the purpose of increasing the value of the property. Improvements *to* land include buildings, additions such as a family room, or the replacement of a roof. Improvements *of* land include streets, sidewalks and utilities.

ECONOMIC TRENDS

The life cycle of a community includes *growth, stability, decline* and *restoration.* An appraiser evaluates the community to determine which cycle the property is in and how that affects the value of the property.

Assessment of Property Value—Key Point Review

1. Situs, area preference or location is one of the major factors in determining the value of a property.

2. The principle of anticipation says that the value of a property will increase or decrease with any anticipated change.

3. Depreciation causes a property to lose value. Depreciation may be curable (reasonable and economically feasible to correct) or incurable (not economically feasible to correct).

4. Physical depreciation, either curable or incurable, is caused by lack of maintenance or the effects of ordinary wear and tear.

5. Functional obsolescence, either curable or incurable, occurs because of the absence or inadequacies of features in design or construction.

6. External or environmental obsolescence is incurable and occurs because of factors located outside the property.

7. Improvements to increase property value may be either *to* land (buildings, building additions, etc.) or *of* land (streets, sidewalks, etc.)

8. The life cycle of a community includes growth, stability, decline and restoration. An evaluation of the community determines which cycle the property is in and how that affects its value.

Content Outline—Property Valuation

I. Listing Property

    C. Property Valuation

        1. Comparative market analysis using the sales comparison approach
        2. Property valuation using the income approach
        3. Appraisal terms
        4. Appropriate listing price recommendations

An appraisal is the process of developing and communicating an objective opinion of a property's value, and different methods are used for different types of property. Table 1.1 on page 14 summarizes the different approaches to appraising.

The purpose of the appraisal is to determine the market value of property. The **market value** is the most **probable price** a buyer will pay for the property in an arms length transaction. That is a transaction wherein the buyer doesn't have to buy, the seller doesn't have to sell, both have a knowledge of the market, and there is no other relationship between them (such as being relatives). **Market price** is the actual selling price of the property. **Cost** is the actual dollars spent to produce an asset. Value, price and cost could be the same, but they are usually different.

When using the Sales Comparison method, an appraiser will compare the amenities of the subject property to at least three like-kind properties that have recently sold. For example:

Comparable 1–Sale price–$250,000—Plus adjustment of $2,500 for a smaller lot
Comparable 2–Sale price–$255,000—Minus adjustment of $5,000 for a remodeled kitchen
Comparable 3–Sale price–$248,000—Minus adjustment of $3,000 for a poorer location

The appraiser would use the comparable property with the fewest adjustments, so the subject property would be valued at $250,000.

APPRAISAL TERMS

The principles of value that an appraiser will use in the appraisal process are:

- **competition**–the interaction of supply and demand wherein excess profits attract competition;
- **conformity**–the maximum value is achieved when the property is in harmony with its surroundings.
- **contribution**–the value of any part of the property is measured by its effect on the value of the whole;
- **highest and best use**–the most reasonable, probable and profitable use of the property.
- **increasing returns**–when money spent on an improvement increases the property value;
- **decreasing returns**–when adding improvements to the land does not produce a proportional increase in property values.
- **plottage**–the value that is created when two or more tracts of land are merged into a single, larger one; assemblage is the process of merging the parcels of real estate;
- **progression**–when a small structure is placed in an area of larger more expensive structures, the value of the smaller structure will increase;
- **regression**–when a large structure is placed in an area of smaller less expensive structures, the value of the larger structure will decrease;
- **substitution**–the foundation for all approaches to appraising; the maximum value of a property tends to be set by the cost of purchasing an equal substitute property; and
- **supply and demand**–the amount of goods available in the market to be sold and the demand or need for the good.

An appraiser is paid based on the time spent and cost of doing the appraisal.

The steps in the appraisal process are:

1. State the problem;
2. List the data needed and the sources;
3. Gather, record and verify the necessary data;
4. Determine the highest and best use;
5. Estimate the land value;
6. Estimate the value by the three approaches;
7. Reconcile the estimate of value received from the direct sales comparison, cost and income approaches to arrive at a final value estimate for the subject property;
8. Report the final value estimate.

TABLE 1.1 *Approaches to Appraising*

Name	Used To Appraise	Also Known As	
Sales Comparison	Residential property and vacant land	*Market Approach* or *Direct Sales Comparison Approach*	• The value of the subject property is determined by comparing it with at least three comparable properties that have recently sold. • If the comparable has an amenity the subject does not have, the appraiser subtracts the value of the amenity. • If the comparable does not have an amenity the subject does have, the appraiser adds the amenity's value to the value of the comparable. • The appraiser reconciles the information and estimates the **market value** or the most probable price a buyer will pay. • **Market price** is the selling price of the property. • **Cost** is the actual dollars spent to produce an asset. Market value, market price and cost can be the same, but seldom are.
Income Approach	Investment or income-producing property	*Capitalization*	The appraiser capitalizes or determines the present worth of the future rights to the income the property generates by converting the net income of the property into a value. See the appraisal section of Chapter 7, Math Review, for more details.
Cost Approach	Special-purpose properties (houses of worship, libraries) or new properties used at their highest and best use	*Replacement Cost Estimate*	• **Reproduction cost** is the dollar amount required to construct an *exact duplicate* of the subject property. • **Replacement cost** is the dollar amount required to construct improvements of *equal utility using current materials*. • The value of land is determined by the sales comparison approach to appraising. See the appraisal section of Chapter 7, Math Review, for more details.
Gross Rent Multiplier	Single-family house or duplex being purchased for investment purposes	*GRM* (Uses monthly rent to determine value)	The appraiser uses the market, or economic, rent to determine the value. The *market rent* is a property's rent potential, or what should be charged for the rental of the property. The *contract rent* is what the owner is currently charging for rent. See the appraisal section of Chapter 7, Math Review, for more details.
Gross Income Multiplier	Small income-producing properties, e.g., shopping strip	*GIM* (Uses annual rent to determine value)	See the appraisal section of Chapter 7, Math Review, for more details.

APPROPRIATE LISTING PRICE RECOMMENDATIONS

A competitive, or comparative, market analysis (CMA) is used to determine the appropriate list price of the property. Unless there are unusual circumstances, the CMA should give the seller the factual information necessary to determine an appropriate list price.

NEED FOR INDEPENDENT APPRAISAL

When an agent lists a property with unusual circumstances, an independent appraisal should be recommended. For example, there has been major growth in a community within the past three years. The agent is listing a 100-acre farm surrounded by this growth. Determining the highest and best use of the farm, or the use that will generate the greatest net return to the land and/or building over a given period of time, requires an appraisal.

Also, some sellers may seek an independent appraisal before a property is listed because they want to know the estimated value before contacting an agent. This could happen if the property has historic value.

Property Valuation—Key Point Review

1. The purpose of an appraisal is to determine the market value, or most probable price that a buyer will pay for the property in an arms length transaction. An appraiser is paid according to the time spent and cost of doing the appraisal, not the price of the property.

2. Market price is the actual selling price of the property. Cost is the actual dollars spent to produce an asset. Value, price and cost could be the same, but they are usually different.

3. Competition is the interaction of supply and demand wherein excess profits attract competition.

4. Conformity is the maximum value achieved when the property is in harmony with its surroundings.

5. Contribution is the value of any part of the property, measured by its effect on the value of the whole.

6. Highest and best use is the most reasonable, probable and profitable use of the property.

7. Increasing returns is when money spent on an improvement increases the property value (such as remodeling the kitchen, which will usually increase the property's value.)

8. Decreasing returns is when adding improvements to the land does not produce a proportional increase in property values (such as in-ground swimming pools that may not produce a proportional increase in property value).

9. Plottage is the value that is created when two or more tracts of land are merged into a single, larger one; while assemblage is the process of merging the parcels of real estate.

Property Valuation—Key Point Review (Continued)

10. Progression is when a small home is placed in the area of larger more expensive homes, the value of the smaller home will increase.

11. Regression is when a large home is placed in an area of smaller home, the value of the larger home will decrease.

12. Substitution is the foundation for all approaches to appraising; the maximum value of a property tends to be set by the cost of purchasing an equal substitute property.

13. Supply and demand is the amount of goods available in the market to be sold and the demand or need for the good.

14. The steps in the appraisal process are: state the problem; list the data needed and the sources; gather, record and verify the necessary data; determine the highest and best use; estimate the land value; estimate the value by the three approaches; reconcile the estimated values for the final value estimate, and report the final value estimate.

15. In the sales comparison approach to appraising, the value of the subject property is estimated by comparing it with similar properties that have recently sold. The value of an amenity present in the comparable but lacking in the subject is subtracted from the sale price of the comparable. If the amenity is present in the subject property but absent in the comparable, its value is added to the sale price of the comparable. The property with the fewest adjustments is used to determine the market value. Adjustments are always made in the comparable properties.

16. The income or capitalization approach is used to appraise investment property. The appraiser estimates the present worth of future rights to the income the property generates.

17. To determine value using the cost approach to appraising, the appraiser determines the replacement or reproduction cost of the improvement, subtracts the depreciation, then adds the value of the land to determine the value of the property.

18. Replacement cost is the dollar amount required to construct improvements of equal utility using current materials. Reproduction cost is the dollar amount required to construct an exact duplicate of the subject property.

19. When using the GRM or GIM to estimate the value of a property, the market rent is used. The market, or economic, rent is an estimate of the property's rent potential, or what should be charged for rent. The contract rent is what the current owner is charging for rent.

20. An agent uses a CMA to determine the appropriate list price of a property.

21. An agent who lists a property with unusual circumstances should recommend an independent appraisal.

Content Outline—Nature of Real Property

I. Listing Property
    D. Nature of Real Property
        1. Property subdivision and selling of parcels
        2. Real and personal property included in, or excluded from, the sale
        3. Differences between personal and real property
        4. Ownership in real estate and conveyance
        5. Methods of land description
        6. Interests in real property
        7. Planning and zoning

PROPERTY SUBDIVISION AND SELLING OF PARCELS

The control of land use and development is influenced by public (government) and private (nongovernment) restrictions and public ownership of land by federal, state and local governments. Public controls include state regulations aimed at protecting the public health, safety and welfare.

A developer places private restrictions on real estate to control and maintain the desirable quality and character of a subdivision or property. This is done through the use of deed restrictions and restrictive covenants.

REAL AND PERSONAL PROPERTY INCLUDED IN OR EXCLUDED FROM THE SALE

The definitions of *land, real estate, real property* (see Figure 1.7), *personal property* and other important terms are summarized as follows:

- **Land** is defined as the earth's surface including air rights, surface rights and subsurface rights.
- **Real estate** is defined as land and anything permanently attached to it.
- **Real property** is defined as real estate plus the bundle of legal rights that are inherent in the ownership of real estate. This includes the physical surface of the land (surface rights) and what is permanently attached to it (bundle of rights).
- Real property can be a *divided interest;* that is, one party can own the air and surface rights while another party owns the subsurface or mineral rights. Unless a contract stipulates otherwise or mineral rights have been previously sold or leased, air, surface and subsurface rights are purchased with the property.
- **Personal property,** also known as *personalty* or **chattels,** is all property that does not fit the definition of real property. It includes movable items not attached to real estate, such as furniture, cars and clothing. It also includes items that were once attached but have been severed from real estate, such as trees, crops and chandeliers.

Physical and Economic Characteristics of Real Estate

The physical characteristics of real estate can be remembered by the acronym *HID.*

H—Heterogeneity or nonhomogeneity—means that every parcel of land is different;

I—Immobility—the geographic location of a parcel of land can never be changed; and

D—Durable—land is indestructible, meaning improvements can depreciate or be destroyed but the land still remains.

The economic characteristics of real estate can be remembered by the acronym *DUST*.

D—Demand is the amount of properties (goods) that people are willing and able to buy at a given price.
U—Utility asks the question, "How has the land and improvement been utilized?" (A one-bedroom home versus a three-bedroom home)
S—Scarcity means that when the supply is limited, the price will increase.
T—Transferability means that there must be a good and marketable title to the property.

Fruits of Nature and Emblements

Trees, grasses and perennial shrubbery that do not require annual cultivation are considered real property (*fructus naturales* or fruits of nature).

Emblements, or crops that require annual planting, are considered personal property. Unless a contract stipulates otherwise, as long as an annual crop is growing, it will be transferred as a part of the real property. However, former owners or tenants are entitled to harvest the crops that are a result of their labor.

Deed restrictions or conditions place certain limits on the right to sell or the right to use the property.

Restrictive **covenants** set the standards for all the parcels within a defined subdivision. These restrictions are available in the public records, so any potential buyer has the right to review them before purchasing a property.

Fixtures and Trade Fixtures

A **fixture** is an item that was once personal property but has become affixed to the land or improvement so that the law construes it to be a part of the real estate. Most items that are a permanent part of a building are considered fixtures.

A **trade fixture** is an item that is owned by the tenant and attached to a rented space. Trade fixtures are used in conducting a business and are also known as *chattel fixtures*. If a tenant leaves the property in good repair, trade fixtures usually can be removed from the property before the lease expires. If trade fixtures remain on the property after the lease expires, they generally belong to the landlord.

A fixture can be excluded from the sale of the property. "What goes" and "what stays" should be discussed in detail with the seller when the property is listed. To reach a meeting of the minds, the buyer must have an understanding of the contents of the listing agreement.

Water Rights

Riparian rights are water rights granted to owners of land along the course of a river, stream or lake. **Flowing water rights:** Land adjoining navigable rivers is usually owned to the water's edge, while land adjoining nonnavigable streams and lakes is owned to the center of the stream or lake.

Littoral rights are water rights of owners whose land borders on large, navigable lakes, seas and oceans. **Non-flowing water rights:** Ownership ends at the mean high-water mark.

The action of water may affect the quality of land ownership. An owner is entitled to all land that is accumulated by **accretion** or the increase in land resulting from the deposit of soil by water's action. The deposits are called **alluvion** or *alluvium*.

FIGURE 1.7 *Land, Real Estate and Real Property*

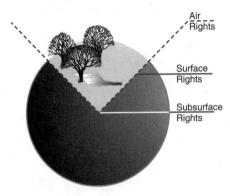

Land
Earth's surface to the center
of the earth and the airspace
above the land, including the
trees and water

Real Estate
Land plus permanent
man-made additions

Real Property
Real estate plus "bundle
of legal rights"

When water recedes, new land is acquired by **reliction. Avulsion** is the loss of land as a result of a sudden or violent act of nature, such as an earthquake. The gradual wearing away of land is called **erosion.**

DIFFERENCES BETWEEN PERSONAL AND REAL PROPERTY

Should a question arise as to whether an item is real or personal property, the courts use four tests to determine the status of the property. The acronym **MARIA** will help you remember the tests to determine if an item is real or personal property.

M   Method of annexation: Was the item permanently attached? Can it be removed without causing damage?

A   Adaptation to real estate: Is the item being used as personal or real property? For example, house keys are movable but are considered to be real property because of their adapted use to the property.

R   Relationship to the parties: Emblements are considered the personal property of the tenant, but in the purchase of farm emblements, could belong to the seller or buyer depending on what is negotiated.

I   Intention: What was the intention of the owner when the item was installed? Did the owner intend it to remain permanently or to be removed when the property sold? (Courts have ruled that this is the most important factor in determining if an item is real or personal property.)

A   Agreement: What was the agreement in the sales contract?

OWNERSHIP IN REAL ESTATE AND CONVEYANCE

The three basic types of ownership in real estate are *severalty, co-ownership* and *trust.* (See Table 1.2 on page 21.) Because the interpretation of these forms of ownership varies from state to state, specific questions regarding ownership should be directed to an attorney.

Trust

A *deed in trust* is established to manage a property for an owner. The three parties in a trust agreement are the **trustor** (grantor), the **trustee** (holds legal title and manages the property) and the **beneficiary** (party benefiting from the trust).

If the trust is established during the lifetime of the owner, it is known as a *living trust*. A trust established by will or after the death of the owner is known as a **testamentary trust.**

Community Property

In **community property** states the laws are based on the idea that a wife and husband are *equal partners* in a marriage. Thus, any property acquired during the marriage is deemed to have been obtained by mutual effort. Listings, deeds and mortgages require the signatures of both spouses. When a spouse dies, the surviving spouse automatically owns one-half of the community property, and the other half of the estate is inherited by the decedent's heirs.

Separate Property

Separate property is owned solely by either spouse before marriage, but also includes property inherited before or during marriage or received by gift. Separate property can be sold or mortgaged without the signature or permission of the nonowning spouse.

Partnership

A **partnership** is an association of two or more persons who establish a business for profit as co-owners. A *general partner* is personally liable for business losses and obligations and is responsible for the operation and management of the business.

A *limited (passive) partner* is liable for business losses only to the extent of his or her investment. A limited partner does not participate in the operation of the business.

Many states have adopted in whole or in part the *Uniform Partnership Act*, which provides that realty may be held in the name of the partnership. It also establishes the legality of the limited partnership form of ownership and provides that realty may be held in the name of the limited partnership.

Condominiums

Condominium ownership is a way of owning real estate that blends severalty and tenancy in common ownership. (See Figure 1.8.)

- A *master deed* conveys the land to condominium use.
- The *declaration* allows the developer to create a condo community.
- *Bylaws* govern the operation of the homeowners' association, which manages the community.
- Each condo owner must pay a *maintenance fee* for the expenses of managing the community; a lien can be placed against individual units, which may be foreclosed if this fee is not paid.
- *Special assessments* are improvements to the property that are not covered by the maintenance fee and must be paid by the owners.
- Each unit owner has a fractional undivided interest in the common areas and facilities.

Cooperative

In **cooperative** ownership a corporation holds title to the property. Each tenant in the cooperative must pay a maintenance fee to cover the prorated share of the corporation's expenses, which include the mortgage payment, property taxes, insurance and maintenance.

TABLE 1.2 *Types of Ownership*

Characteristic	Severalty	Tenancy in Common	Joint	Tenancy by the Entirety
Number of Owners	One person or legal entity	Two or more	Two or more with right of survivorship	Husband and wife only; law presumes they are one
Title	One title	Each co-owner has separate legal title to his or her undivided interest	One title	One title
Interest	100% ownership	Shares may be unequal; law will interpret them as equal unless stipulated otherwise	Shares must be equal	Each owns 100% of the property
Conveyance	Yes, to whomever the owner stipulates	Yes, without the consent of the other owners	Yes, without the consent of the other owners	When both owners agree
Right to Partition	Not necessary; there are no co-owners	Yes	Yes	No
Status on Death	Passes to heir(s) or devisee(s)	Passes to heir(s) or devisee(s)	Passes to surviving owners	When one spouse dies, the other spouse owns it in severalty
Probate Necessary	Yes, if there is a will	Yes, if there is a will	No	No
Unities	Possession Interest Time Title	Possession	Possession Interest Time Title	Possession Interest Time Title Person
Termination	By sale or death of owner	By sale or death of the owner	When any of the unities are broken	By consent of the parties; death of either party; or on divorce/common ownership

A co-op owner has the tax benefits of his or her share of the mortgage interest and property taxes paid on the property. A cooperative interest can be sold, but the new lessee must meet the qualifications of the co-op before the stock and lease can be transferred.

If one owner fails to pay his or her maintenance fee to the cooperative, then the other co-op owners are responsible for the payment. If the mortgage payment is not made by the cooperative, the entire building can be foreclosed on.

A co-op tenant may be evicted for nonpayment of the monthly fee or for not following the rules and regulations.

FIGURE 1.8 *Condominium Ownership*

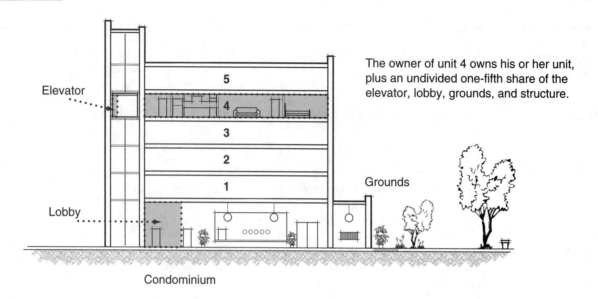

The owner of unit 4 owns his or her unit, plus an undivided one-fifth share of the elevator, lobby, grounds, and structure.

> The purchasers of the cooperative receive shares of stock in the corporation and a **proprietary lease** that grants occupancy of a specific unit in the building.

Time-Shares

A time-share is also known as *interval ownership* because the buyer of a **time-share estate** receives a deed for the property for a specified time each year.

The buyer of a **time-share use** has the *right to occupy* the property and use the facilities for a certain number of years. The developer retains ownership to the property, and when the specified time (30 years is typical) has expired, all interest reverts to the owner.

Townhouse or Rowhouse

A townhouse or rowhouse is an attached single-family dwelling with two floors. Owners of a townhouse purchase their residential structure and the land underlying the structure. The surrounding land, including sidewalks, open spaces and recreational facilities, is owned in common with other members of the community.

Many townhouse developments are **planned unit developments.** A planned unit development is designed for a high density of dwellings and a maximum use of open space.

METHODS OF LAND DESCRIPTION

Review legal descriptions on page 2.

FIGURE 1.9 *Freehold Estates*

Fee Simple

1. Fee Simple Absolute
   a. The highest form of ownership that the law recognizes.
   b. Ownership is for an indefinite duration.
   c. Ownership is freely transferable.
   d. It is an inheritable estate.
2. Fee Simple Defeasible
   A. Special Limitation with Possibility of Reverter
      a. Title transfers "so long as" the property is used for a particular purpose.
      b. There is automatic reversion to the grantor or the grantor's heirs if the land ceases to be used for that purpose.
      c. The possibility of reverter is the possible future interest the grantor's heir(s) could have if the property ceases to be used for that purpose.
   B. Condition Subsequent with Right of Reentry
      a. Title is transferred "on the condition that" there is an activity that the grantee must not perform.
      b. The grantors must take legal steps to get the property back.
      c. The right of reentry is the possible future interest of the grantor.

Life Estates

1. Conventional Life Estate
   A. Ordinary with Remainder or Reversion
      a. Set up by a grantor.
      b. Life tenant has full use and enjoyment of property for his or her life.
      c. Property reverts to grantor on the death of the life tenant (reversion).
      d. Property is transferred to the remainderman or a party other than the grantor.
   B. Life Estate Pur Autre Vie with Remainder or Reversion
      a. Set up by grantor but based on the life of a third party. A conveys title to B, based on the life of C.
      b. Should B predecease C, B's heirs would have a life estate interest in the property as long as C is alive.
      c. Property reverts to A (grantor) on the death of the life tenant.
      d. Property may transfer to D, a remainderman.
2. Legal Life Estates
   a. Set up by law.
   b. Dower
      A wife's interests in her husband's property.
   c. Curtesy
      A husband's interests in his wife's property.
   d. Homestead
      Set up to protect the elderly and the handicapped from certain creditors.

INTERESTS IN REAL PROPERTY

An **estate in land** refers to a party's legal interests or rights to a property. To be an estate, an interest must be possessory or may become possessory in the future; the ownership is measured in terms of duration. An interest in land may not be an estate. For example, an easement is an interest in land, but it is not an estate because it does not allow for possession of the property.

Estates in land can be freehold or nonfreehold. **Freehold estates** include fee simple estates and life estates. (See Figure 1.9). A freehold estate is considered to exist for an uncertain duration. For example, if you own property, how long do you intend to own it? For the right amount of money, would you sell it today?

Nonfreehold estates include **leasehold estates,** which are usually based on calendar time. A lease with a definite duration is an *estate for years.* A leasehold estate also can be for an uncertain duration, such as a *tenancy at will.* Leasehold estates are discussed on page 70.

PLANNING AND ZONING

Municipalities and counties develop a **master plan** or comprehensive plan, to guide the long-term physical development of the area. **Zoning ordinances** are local laws that implement the comprehensive plan and regulate the land use and structures. A zoning board of appeals is established to hear complaints about the effects of zoning.

The following terms are terms associated with zoning:

- **Land use** is regulated by dividing the land into residential, commercial, industrial and agricultural use districts.
- A **buffer zone** separates two different use districts. For example, a park could be planned between a residential district and a commercial district.
- **Bulk zoning** controls density or the ratio of land area to structure area. Bulk zoning is used to avoid overcrowding.
- **Aesthetic zoning** requires that new buildings conform to certain types of architectural styles.
- **Incentive zoning** requires that the street floors of office buildings be used for retail space.
- **Nonconforming property** is property in an area that was zoned for one use but for which the zoning has now changed. For example, when zoning changes the land use from residential to commercial, a residential owner usually is allowed to continue using the property as a residence until the property is sold or destroyed.
- A **variance** may be granted in cases where the zoning creates an unnecessary hardship on the owner, but the variance must not be detrimental to zoning. Variances may be granted for setback lines, height restrictions and the like.
- When a special-purpose property that benefits the public, such as a hospital, library or museum, is approved for construction, a **conditional-use permit** is granted.
- **Spot zoning** is a change of zoning for a particular spot or lot and is generally not permitted.

Nature of Real Property—Key Point Review

1. Public controls include the inherent right of the state to regulate land use for the health, safety and welfare of the public. Such controls include land-use planning, zoning ordinances, subdivision regulations, building codes and environmental protection legislation.

2. Private restrictions are placed on real estate by the developer to control and maintain the desirable quality and character of a subdivision or property. One neighbor can enforce a deed restriction through court action.

3. Real estate is the land and all attachments to the land. Real property is real estate plus the bundle of legal rights that are inherent in its ownership, including air, surface and sub-surface rights.

4. Personal property includes movable items not attached to the real estate. Real property can become personal property by severance from the land.

5. *Fructus naturales*, or fruits of nature, that do not require annual cultivation are considered real property. Crops that require annual planting are known as *emblements* and are considered personal property.

Nature of Real Property—Key Point Review (Continued)

6. A fixture is personal property that has become affixed to the land or improvements so that the law construes it to be a part of the real estate. A trade fixture is personal property owned by a tenant, is attached to rented space and is used in conducting a business. Trade fixtures generally become the property of the landlord if they have not been removed prior to the expiration of the lease. The tenant must leave the property in good repair when trade fixtures are removed.

7. Riparian rights are granted to owners of land along a river, stream or lake. Land adjoining navigable rivers is usually owned to the water's edge; land adjoining nonnavigable streams and lakes is owned to the center of the stream or lake.

8. Littoral rights are granted to owners of land that borders on large, navigable lakes, seas and oceans. Ownership is to the mean high-water mark.

9. An owner is entitled to all increases in land that result from accretion, the deposit of soil by water's action. These deposits are called *alluvion* or *alluvium*. When water recedes, the new land is acquired by reliction. Avulsion is the sudden loss of land, while erosion is the gradual wearing away of land.

10. The courts use four tests to determine the status of property: (1) intention, (2) method of annexation, (3) adaptation to real estate and (4) agreement

11. Ownership in severalty means the title to real estate is presently owned by one party, an individual, a corporation or a government body.

12. Co-ownership or concurrent ownership means title to real estate is presently owned by two or more parties.

13. The basic characteristics of tenancy in common ownership are each tenant holds an undivided fractional interest; the interests may be unequal; there is unity of possession; each co-owner can sell, convey, mortgage or transfer his or her interest without the consent of the other owners; and it is an inheritable estate.

14. Joint tenancy is a concurrent form of ownership characterized by right of survivorship. There must be unities of time, interest and possession for joint tenancy to be created. Each joint tenant has the right to sell, mortgage or lease an interest without the consent of the other owners.

15. If one joint tenant sold his/her property, the new owner would be a tenant in common with the other joint tenants. For example: David, Carrie and Joyce are joint tenants and Joyce sells her share to John. David and Carrie are still joint tenants, and John is a tenant in common with them.

16. When co-tenants cannot voluntarily agree to the termination of their co-ownership, a suit for partition can be filed in which the court dissolves the relationship.

17. Tenancy by the entirety is recognized in some states and allows a legal husband and wife to each have an equal, undivided interest in the property that is characterized by survivorship.

Nature of Real Property—Key Point Review (Continued)

18. A trust is established to manage a property for the owner. The three parties in a trust agreement are the trustor, the trustee and the beneficiary.

19. Community property states regard any property acquired during the marriage as obtained by mutual effort. When one spouse dies, the surviving spouse automatically owns one-half of the community property. Separate property, owned, inherited or received as a gift by either spouse before or during marriage, can be sold or mortgaged without the signature or permission of the nonowning spouse.

20. A partnership is an association of two or more persons who establish a business for profit as co-owners. General partners are personally liable for business losses and obligations and are responsible for the operation of the business. Limited partners are liable for business losses only to the extent of their investment and do not participate in the operation of the business.

21. To create a condominium community, the developer must record a declaration of condominium. The master deed allows the land to be converted to condominium use. The bylaws govern the operation of the homeowners' association.

22. A party purchasing a residential condominium unit owns airspace in a unit and is a tenant in common with other members in the community in the land and its improvements. A limited common area is owned by all but is limited to the use of the owner of the condo.

23. Each condo owner is required to pay a fee to the homeowners' association to cover maintenance, insurance and reserve funds for future improvements. If the fee is not paid, a lien can be placed on the property and the property could be sold at foreclosure.

24. In a cooperative, a corporation owns the property in severalty. Owners purchase shares of stock in the company and receive a proprietary lease. The stock and lease are considered personal property. A maintenance fee includes each unit owner's share of the corporations' expenses.

25. Should a co-op owner default on a payment, the other shareholders are expected to pay. A co-op owner who defaults or breaches the restrictions of the lease agreement may be evicted. If the co-op defaults on a payment to the lender, the lender can foreclose on the entire property.

26. Time-sharing allows for an interval ownership or use by multiple purchasers of the property. When a time-share estate is conveyed, the owner holds a deed to the property. When a time-share use is conveyed, the buyer has the right to occupy and use the property for a stipulated time. At the end of a certain number of years, the right to use ends.

27. An estate in land refers to a party's legal interests or rights to a property. To be an estate, an interest must be possessory or may become possessory in the future. Ownership is measured in terms of duration. An easement is not an estate in land because it does not allow for the possession of the property.

28. Freehold estates include fee estates and life estates. A freehold estate is considered to exist for an uncertain duration. Nonfreehold estates include leasehold estates.

29. In fee simple absolute ownership, a possessory interest is freely transferable, is of indefinite duration, and is an inheritable estate.

Nature of Real Property—Key Point Review (Continued)

30. When a defeasible title with a deed condition is transferred by special limitation with the possibility of reverter, a fee simple defeasible estate is created. The grantee has ownership interests "so long as" the property is used for that particular purpose. The possibility of reverter is the possible future interest of the grantor or the grantor's heirs.

31. When a defeasible title is transferred by condition subsequent, it is transferred "on the condition that," which means there is an action or activity that the grantee must not perform. This deed condition is binding on the future owners of the property. The possible future interest of the grantor or the heirs is called a *right of reentry*.

32. A conventional life estate is a freehold estate that is created by the grantor, is not inheritable and is limited in the duration to the life of its owner(s).

33. The person receiving the life estate, the *life tenant*, has full enjoyment of the ownership as long as he or she is alive. On the death of the life tenant, the property reverts either to the grantor or to a remainderman, a party other than the grantor. The grantor's future interest is called a *reversionary interest*. The future interest of the remainderman is a *remainder interest*.

34. A life estate based on the life of a third party is called a *life estate pur autre vie.*

35. The life tenant has the right to sell, mortgage or lease the property, but not to allow the property to go to waste. Should the life tenant injure the property, the grantor or remainderman could seek injunctive relief or sue for damages. Any lease or deed becomes void upon the death of the life tenant.

36. A life estate that is created by law is a legal life estate. Dower is the legal life estate interest that a wife has in real estate owned by her husband. Curtesy is a legal life estate interest that a husband has in real estate owned by his wife. A homestead is a legal life estate that will protect the family from certain creditors.

37. Municipalities and counties develop a master plan to guide long-term physical development. Zoning ordinances implement the master plan and regulate land use and structures. Zoning powers are given to the local government by state enabling acts.

38. Land use is regulated by dividing the land into residential, commercial, industrial and agricultural use districts. A buffer zone separates two different use districts.

39. Bulk zoning controls density or the ratio of land area to structure area. Aesthetic zoning requires that new buildings conform to certain types of architectural styles. Incentive zoning requires that the street floors of office buildings be used for retail space.

40. When zoning changes, zoning boards must make decisions on nonconforming properties. An owner may be allowed to continue a nonconforming use of a property until the property is sold or destroyed.

41. A variance may be granted if the zoning creates an unnecessary hardship on the owner and the variance is not detrimental to zoning.

42. When a special-purpose property is to be approved, a conditional-use permit is granted for the public benefit.

Content Outline—Services Provided in the Agency Relationship with the Seller

I. Listing Property

    E. Services Provided in the Agency Relationship with the Seller

        1. Net proceeds estimation
        2. Listing agreements, documents provided to the seller
        3. Safeguarding property
        4. Property marketing

NET PROCEEDS ESTIMATION

When listing a property a seller may ask what the net proceeds of the sale will be after the commission and expenses are paid. To learn how to compute the seller's net, see Brokerage Math Review, Chapter 7.

LISTING AGREEMENTS AND OTHER DOCUMENTS PROVIDED TO THE SELLER

A **listing agreement** is a personal service contract securing the employment of a brokerage firm to find a ready, willing and able buyer. Most states require that this agreement be in writing to be enforceable, but in some states oral listings are legal. The typical listing contracts are exclusive-right-to-sell, exclusive-agency, open listings and net listing. (See Figure 1.10.)

Other documents involved in listing the property may include lead based paint, property, and agency dislcosures. The sellers must be provided a copy of any documents they have signed and the length of time a broker is required to keep copies of documents is determined by state law.

FIGURE 1.10 *Types of Listing Agreements*

---

1. ***Exclusive-right-to-sell listing***—One broker lists the property and other brokers have the right to sell the property, if there is a cobrokerage arrangement. The listing broker is paid no matter who sells the property.
2. ***Exclusive-agency listing***—One broker lists the property and the seller retains the right to sell the property. Other brokers may sell the property through a cobrokerage arrangement. If the seller sells the property without the services of a broker, a commission is not due.
3. ***Open listing***—In this agreement, the seller enters into listing agreements with any number of brokerage firms and retains the right to sell the property. The broker that sells the property is paid the commission, but if the seller sells the property, no commission is due any broker.
4. ***Net listing***—This listing does not contain a specified sales price or commission. Net listings are illegal in most states.

Listing agreements normally include the:

a. type of listing;
b. broker's authority and responsibilities;
c. names of all parties to the contract;
d. brokerage firm;
e. listing price;
f. real and personal property descriptions;
g. term or length of time of the agreement;
h. commission;
i. termination provisions;
j. broker protection clause;
k. warranties by the owner;
l. nondiscrimination wording;
m. antitrust wording;
n. authorizations for subagency, use of lockbox, for sale signs, etc.;
o. other provisions as provided by state law;
p. signatures of the parties; and
q. unusual deed conditions on restrictions.

Listings may be **terminated** by:

a. expiration;
b. fulfillment of the contract;
c. mutual consent or a rescission;
d. abandonment by either party;
e. death of the broker or seller;
f. destruction of the premises; and
g. eminent domain.

If the seller terminates the agency agreement without cause, the seller may be liable for the expenses incurred by the broker. The seller may refuse to sell the property even if the full list price is offered. However, the broker would be due a commission under this circumstance.

SAFEGUARDING PROPERTY

The listing agent has duties to safeguard the property. This includes proper management of keys, caring for the property if the owner is out of town for extended periods of time and removing all valuables prior to showing.

PROPERTY MARKETING, KEEPING THE SELLER INFORMED

The two factors to consider in marketing the property are the seller's responsibility and the broker's responsibility. Many brokerage firms have videos or checklists for sellers that include tips on how to make their property more marketable, thus selling faster. The information could include marketing tips for the exterior and interior of the property, such as landscaping, manicured lawn, painting, repair of roof, cleaning or replacing carpet, cleaning closets and renting furniture (if the property is vacant).

Considerations in marketing the property include the frequency and media such as Internet, newspaper, flyers, multiple listing service and open houses that the broker will use in advertising the property. Other considerations include For Sale signs placed in the yard, informing the seller of comments from prospective buyers and other licensees or agents who have seen the property. Agents should be in contact with the seller weekly, even when there is no activity on the property.

Services Provided in the Agency Relationship with the Seller—Key Point Review

1. A listing agreement is a personal service contract securing the employment of the brokerage firm to find a ready, willing and able buyer. Most states require that the listing agreement be in writing to be enforceable.

2. In an exclusive-right-to-sell listing, one broker is hired to list and sell the property. If the seller gives that broker permission to work with cooperating brokers, then other brokers have the right to sell the property. If the property is sold while the listing is in effect, the seller must pay the commission, even if the property is sold by the seller.

3. In an exclusive-agency listing, the seller retains the right to sell the property and authorizes one broker to list the property. If the seller gives the broker permission to place the property in the MLS, other brokers may sell the property. The seller is obligated to pay the commission to the broker only if the broker or cooperating broker was the procuring cause of the sale.

4. In an open listing, the seller can enter into listing agreements with any number of brokerage firms and also retain the right to sell the property himself or herself. The seller is obligated to pay only the broker that secured a qualified buyer.

5. A net listing stipulates that the seller will receive a specified amount of money and anything over that amount is the broker's commission. Net listings are illegal in most states.

6. The agent has responsibilities to safeguard the property, including proper care of the keys and informing the owner as to the care of the vacant property.

7. Agents should inform the sellers on methods of improving the marketability of their property.

8. The agent should keep the seller informed of any activity that occurs with the property.

9. A party should immediately receive a copy of any document she or he has just signed.

10. A broker should keep copies of all records pertaining to the property. State laws determine the length of time the documents are to be kept.

Questions

1. All of the following are true about condominiums EXCEPT
   A. a declaration must be filed before any units may be sold.
   B. each unit owner has a fractional undivided interest in the common areas and facilities.
   C. each owner usually receives a separate tax statement.
   D. each owner has a proprietary lease with the association covering the unit.

2. Horace owns a lot and, in writing, gives his neighbor, Martha, the right to use his driveway to reach Martha's garage. What is Martha's interest or right called?
   A. Lease
   B. Easement
   C. Encroachment
   D. Prescriptive right

3. Victor receives possession of property under a deed that states that he shall own the property so long as the present building standing on the property is not torn down. The type of estate Victor holds is which of the following?
   A. Life estate
   B. Nondestructible estate
   C. Fee simple estate
   D. Special limitation with possibility of reverter

4. The owner of property located along the banks of a stream or river MOST LIKELY has water rights known as
   A. littoral rights.
   B. reliction rights.
   C. riparian rights.
   D. avulsions.

5. How many acres are in a description reading "The NW¼ of the SE¼ and the S½ of the SW¼ of the NE¼ of Section 4"?
   A. 40 acres
   B. 50 acres
   C. 60 acres
   D. 80 acres

6. Which of the following BEST describes a legal life estate?
   A. Homestead estate
   B. Estate conveyed by one party to a second party for the second party's life
   C. Estate created by will
   D. Estate conveyed to a second party subject to a condition

7. Recently, an ordinance was passed stating that no sign placed on a building may extend more than three feet above the highest point of the roof. Thomas wants to place a revolving sign nine feet high on the roof of his store. In order to legally do this, Thomas must get a(n)
   A. residual.
   B. variance.
   C. nonconforming use permit.
   D. aerial clearance.

8. All of the following are false regarding a property that is held by tenancy by the entirety EXCEPT
   A. the cotenants must be husband and wife.
   B. the property in question must be Torrens property.
   C. on the death of a cotenant, the decedent's interest passes to his or her heirs.
   D. in the event of a dispute, the property must be partitioned.

9. All of the following are false regarding a community property state EXCEPT
   A. the property that a person accumulated prior to marriage is called *separate property*.
   B. the property that a person received as a gift during marriage is known as *community property*.
   C. all property owned by a married person is called *community property*.
   D. the property paid for by the earnings of one spouse during marriage is known as *separate property*.

10. The cost approach would MOST LIKELY be used to appraise a
    A. single family home.
    B. twenty unit apartment building.
    C. condominium
    D. house of worship.

11. Broker Carl obtained an exclusive agency listing from Rochelle Green. The broker would not be entitled to a commission if

    A. Carl sold the property himself.
    B. the property were sold through another broker.
    C. the property were sold through the multiple-listing service.
    D. the seller sold the property to a neighbor across the street who had her property listed with another broker.

12. Agent Jayne stood on the back deck of the house she had just listed and saw the fence representing the property boundary line. On the other side of the fence was a park that bordered a small shopping mall.

    The park is MOST LIKELY a(n)

    A. buffer zone.
    B. variance.
    C. set back.
    D. aesthetic zone.

13. Which of the following is NOT associated with fee simple absolute ownership?

    A. It is an inheritable estate.
    B. The estate is freely transferable.
    C. It is the highest ownership recognized by law.
    D. The right of reentry can only be acquired by an heir.

14. Depreciation is said to be incurable if it:

    A. is economically feasible to correct.
    B. affects only the land, but not the improvements.
    C. affects only the improvements, but not the land.
    D. is not economically feasible to correct.

15. Suzie just purchased a condominium. Which of the following statements is MOST LIKELY true regarding her ownership?

    A. Suzie owns her air space in severalty and holds a tenancy in common ownership in the common areas.
    B. Suzie owns her condo in a fee simple defeasible estate and holds a joint tenancy ownership in the common areas.
    C. Suzie's ownership is in the air space and subsurface space only.
    D. Suzie's ownership is held as a conventional life estate.

16. When a developer subdivides a tract of land for a subdivision, he must record which of the following in the county court house where the property is located?

    A. Plat map
    B. Listing contract
    C. Sales contract
    D. Benchmarks

17. A house with outdated plumbing is suffering from

    A. functional obsolescence.
    B. curable physical deterioration.
    C. incurable physical deterioration.
    D. external depreciation.

18. Joseph built a building that has six stories. Several years later, an ordinance was passed banning any building six stories or higher in the area. Joseph is allowed to continue using his building. This is an example of a

    A. nonconforming use.
    B. situation in which the building would have to be demolished.
    C. conditional use.
    D. variance.

19. A real estate listing contract is created when it has been signed by which of the following parties?

    A. Buyer
    B. Buyer and seller
    C. Seller
    D. Broker and seller

20. Robert and Dorothy, no longer needing their large house, decide to sell the house and move into a cooperative apartment building. Under the cooperative form of ownership, Robert and Dorothy will

    A. become stockholders in a corporation.
    B. never lose their apartment if they pay their share of the cooperative's taxes.
    C. take out a new mortgage on their unit.
    D. receive a 20-year lease for their unit.

21. The buyers took possession of the property 30 days after closing. The 300 gallon aquarium that had been attached to the family room wall was missing. The wall had not been repaired. Under these circumstances is the aquarium real property?
    A. No, because all aquariums, no matter how large are personal property.
    B. No, because it was movable.
    C. Yes, because the sellers took it with them.
    D. Yes, because the method of annexation caused damage.

22. When a buyer records a deed to a property, the buyer is giving
    A. actual notice.
    B. notary notice.
    C. constructive notice.
    D. agency notice.

23. The MAJOR DIFFERENCE between a latent defect and a patent defect is that a
    A. latent defect is found by inspection, while a patent defect is a hidden defect.
    B. latent defect must be disclosed in a listing contract, while a patent defect is found in a property disclosure statement.
    C. latent defect is a hidden defect, while a patent defect is found by inspection.
    D. latent defect need not be disclosed, but all patent defects must be disclosed.

24. Which of the following is NOT an example of a legal description?
    A. Geodetic survey
    B. Lot-and-block
    C. Metes-and-bounds
    D. Torrens survey

25. A conventional life tenant has the right to
    A. devise the life estate.
    B. commit waste to the property.
    C. sell, mortgage or lease the life estate.
    D. refuse to pay property taxes.

26. Mr. Homeowner has given a company the right to erect a billboard on his property. Mr. Homeowner has MOST LIKELY given a(n)
    A. implied easement.
    B. easement appurtenant.
    C. prescriptive easement.
    D. gross easement.

27. Sam, Pam and Jerome are joint tenants. Sam sells his interest to Joyce. How is the ownership now held?
    A. Pam, Jerome and Joyce are joint tenants.
    B. Pam, Jerome and Joyce are tenants in common.
    C. Pam and Jerome are joint tenants and Joyce is a tenant in common with them.
    D. Pam and Joyce are joint tenants and Jerome is a tenant in common with them.

28. John, Paul and David decided to enter into a partnership. John is the general partner. This means
    A. his liability is limited to the money he has invested.
    B. all three are personally liable.
    C. Paul and David are personally liable.
    D. John is personally liable.

29. A seller would like to retain the right to sell his property while listing it with only one real estate brokerage firm. The seller should execute a(n)
    A. exclusive right-to-sell listing.
    B. open listing.
    C. net listing.
    D. exclusive listing.

30. When personal property that is used in a business is attached to real estate by the tenant, the personal property would MOST LIKELY
    A. belong to the landlord until the lease expires.
    B. belong to the tenant if removed before the lease expires.
    C. automatically become real property.
    D. stay with the property under any circumstances.

31. Jackie, Karen and Laura own property as joint tenants. Laura dies and her property interest will be
    A. inherited by her heirs if she had a will.
    B. devised to her heirs if she died intestate.
    C. bequeathed to Jackie and Karen in her will.
    D. automatically conveyed to Jackie and Karen.

32. Carrie is buying a single family home for investment purposes. The appraiser will MOST LIKELY use which methods to appraise the property?
    A. Income and cost
    B. GRM and GIM
    C. Sales comparison and income
    D. Market approach and GRM

33. Which of the following would NOT be an encumbrance to property?
    A. fence that is four feet across the boundary line
    B. A foreclosure suit
    C. A utility easement
    D. A license

34. All of the following would affect the value of a property EXCEPT
    A. title insurance.
    B. situs.
    C. zoning.
    D. location.

35. Linda and Brad just got married and purchased their first home. They MOST LIKELY own the property as:
    A. tenants in common.
    B. severalty.
    C. joint tenancy.
    D. tenancy by the entirety.

36. Which form of ownership does not allow the right of partition?
    A. Severalty
    B. Tenancy in common
    C. Joint tenancy
    D. Tenancy by the entirety

37. A broker would NOT have to prove that he was the procuring cause of the sale in which of the following listing agreements?
    A. An exclusive-agency listing
    B. An all-inclusive listing
    C. An open listing
    D. An exclusive-right-to-sell listing

38. All of the following are true regarding an exclusive-right-to-sell listing EXCEPT
    A. an exclusive-right-to-sell listing usually contains provisions for cobrokerage.
    B. the contract may be terminated without liability.
    C. the seller can withdraw the contract at any time without liability.
    D. if the seller sells the property, a commission is still due.

39. Which of the following is necessary to create an estate in land?
    A. A valid deed must be conveyed to create an estate in land.
    B. A certificate of title must be issued to create an estate in land.
    C. A certificate of occupancy must be issued to create an estate in land.
    D. An interest must be possessory or may become possessory in the future to create an estate in land.

40. Yvonne gave a life estate to Mindy based on the life of Jayne and named Jodi as the remainder. This legal arrangement is BEST described as a
    A. life estate.
    B. estate for years.
    C. legal life estate.
    D. life estate pur autre vie.

41. An appraiser who takes into consideration the reproduction cost of a building and then considers depreciation is MOST LIKELY using the
    A. cost approach.
    B. market approach.
    C. income approach.
    D. gross rent multiplier approach.

42. When making adjustments in the comparison of properties under the market approach, which of the following is MOST true?
    A. If the subject is inferior, no adjustment is made in the comparable.
    B. If the comparable is inferior, an adjustment is made by subtracting from the comparable.
    C. If the comparable is superior, an adjustment is made by subtracting from the comparable.
    D. If the subject is superior, no adjustment is made in the comparable.

43. If a vacant city lot is to be listed, what would be the best way to describe the property in a listing contract?
    A. Lot-and-block
    B. Metes-and-bounds
    C. Street address
    D. Monument

44. All of the following are public controls of land use and development EXCEPT
    A. zoning.
    B. building codes.
    C. housing codes.
    D. deed covenants.

45. Which of the following would NOT be associated with life estates?
    A. Reversion
    B. Pur autre vie
    C. Possibility of reverter
    D. Remainder

46. The NW¼ of the SE¼ of the NE¼ and the S½ of the NE¼ contains how many acres of land?
    A. 10
    B. 60
    C. 90
    D. 80

47. What is the major difference between functional obsolescence and deterioration?
    A. Obsolescence occurs when a property appreciates, while deterioration occurs when a property depreciates.
    B. Obsolescence occurs when a property has not been maintained, while deterioration occurs when a property has a poor design.
    C. Obsolescence only occurs in commercial property, while deterioration occurs in residential property.
    D. Obsolescence occurs because of a poor design, while deterioration occurs because of lack of maintenance.

48. All of the following could be used by a real estate agent in helping a seller determine the value of a property EXCEPT
    A. a comparative market analysis.
    B. gross living area.
    C. private mortgage insurance.
    D. an independent appraisal.

49. Which of the following encumbrances would affect the use of a property?
    A. Easement
    B. Mortgage lien
    C. Judgment
    D. Tax lien

50. In appraising a residential property, the appraiser would make a
    A. positive adjustment in the subject property if the subject property had an amenity the comparable did not.
    B. negative adjustment in the subject property if the subject property had an amenity the comparable did not.
    C. positive adjustment in the comparable property if the subject property had an amenity the comparable did not.
    D. negative adjustment in the comparable property if the comparable property did not have an amenity the subject property had.

51. All of the following are freehold estates that are inheritable EXCEPT a
    A. fee simple defeasible estate.
    B. fee simple absolute estate.
    C. special limitation estate.
    D. conventional life estate.

52. All of the following are associated with personal property EXCEPT
    A. chattels.
    B. personalty.
    C. bundle of legal rights.
    D. emblements.

53. A seller listed a property with ABC Realty. The broker for XYZ Realty has the legal right to contact the seller. ABC Realty MOST LIKELY has entered into a(n)
    A. net listing.
    B. open listing.
    C. exclusive listing.
    D. exclusive-right-to-sell listing.

54. When visiting a new subdivision, the buyers asked the agent if there would be commercial development "in their backyard" if they purchased a home on the street they were visiting. The agent assured them the property behind the house was zoned residential. The BEST way for the buyers to confirm the agent's statement is to:
    A. ask the agent's broker.
    B. ask a neighbor.
    C. check the plat map.
    D. check the master plan.

55. A person whose maintenance fee includes her portion of the mortgage payment, property taxes, insurance and maintenance of the property MOST LIKELY owns a
    A. condominium.
    B. single family home.
    C. duplex.
    D. cooperative.

56. Mr. and Mrs. Trapp sign an exclusive-right-to-sell listing that will expire in four months. Three weeks later it is determined they are not being transferred and they no longer want to sell their property. Can the listing be terminated?
    A. No, they signed an exclusive-right-to-sell listing and it cannot be terminated.
    B. No, the listing cannot be terminated because it is for four months.
    C. Yes, the listing can be terminated if the agent agrees.
    D. Yes, the listing can be terminated by mutual consent.

57. Upon the review of a survey the agent found a billboard easement, utility easement and a pipeline easement. These are examples of
    A. appurtenant easements.
    B. prescriptive easements.
    C. gross easements.
    D. easements by necessity.

58. Mr. and Mrs. Muething just purchased ocean-front property. The water rights attached to the property are
    A. accretion rights.
    B. reliction rights.
    C. riparian rights.
    D. littoral rights.

59. Which of the following terms is associated with real estate property taxes?
    A. Caveat emptor
    B. Caveat venditor
    C. Annuit coeptis
    D. Ad valoerm

60. Which of the following would NOT terminate a listing agreement?
    A. Destruction of the premises
    B. Death of the agent
    C. Eminent domain
    D. Expiration

ANSWERS

1. D A co-op owner has a proprietary lease; a condo owner does not.
2. B An easement gives the right to use the land of another.
3. D When a property is transferred "so long as" a condition is met or not met, it is transferred as a special limitation with the possibility of reverter.
4. C Riparian rights are the water rights of a property owner along a river or stream.
5. C $640 \div 4 \div 4 = 40$
$640 \div 2 \div 4 \div 4 = 20$
$40 + 20 = 60$ acres
6. A A homestead or dower creates a legal life estate.
7. B A variance grants relief from the harshness of a zoning ordinance.
8. A Tenancy by the entirety ownership can be held only by a husband and wife.
9. A Separate property is any property that is accumulated prior to marriage.
10. D The cost approach is used to appraise special purpose properties such has houses of worship, museums, hospitals, fire departments, etc.
11. D In an exclusive-agency listing, the seller is not required to pay a commission if the seller sells the property without the assistance of the brokerage firm.
12. A A buffer zone separates two different use districts such as residential and commercial.
13. D The right of reentry is the possible future interest in a conditional subsequent, not fee simple absolute ownership.
14. D Incurable depreciation is not economically feasible to correct.
15. A The owner of a condo owns the air space in severalty, meaning separate from the other condo owners, and is a tenant in common in the common areas.
16. A A plat map must be recorded by the developer.
17. A By definition of functional obsolescence.
18. A By definition of nonconforming use.
19. D The broker and seller are the principals in a listing contract.
20. A When purchasing a cooperative, the owner receives stock in the company (cooperative) and a proprietary lease to the apartment.

21. D If the removal of a fixture will cause damage, it is generally considered real property.
22. C By definition of constructive notice.
23. C By definitions of latent and patent defects.
24. D The Torrens system is a system of land registration, not a legal description.
25. C By definition of conventional life estate.
26. D By definition of gross easement.
27. C A joint tenant does have the right to sell, mortgage or lease the interest in the property without the consent of the other owners. The new owner would be a tenant in common with the other tenants, who still hold a joint tenancy.
28. D John is the general partner and is personally liable.
29. D By definition of exclusive listing.
30. B Personal property of the tenant that becomes attached to the real property is known as a *trade fixture*. It belongs to the tenant and may be removed before the lease expires. If it remains on the property after the expiration of the lease, it belongs to the landlord.
31. D By the definition of joint tenancy. When one tenant dies, the property is automatically conveyed to the surviving joint tenant(s).
32. D The appraiser would use the market approach and the gross rent multiplier (GRM) to determine value.
33. D A license is the privilege to use the property of another. It does not affect the value or use of the property.
34. A The value of property is not affected by an owner's having title insurance.
35. D Tenancy by the entirety is held by a husband and wife.
36. D Tenancy by the entirety does not allow partition.
37. D By definition of exclusive-right-to-sell listing.
38. C The contract could be terminated. However, the seller cannot withdraw at any time without liability.
39. D An estate must be possessory or may become possessory in the future for an estate to exist.
40. D A life estate *pur autre vie* is based on the life of a third party.

41. A By definition of the cost approach to appraising.

42. C When the comparable is superior, an adjustment is made by subtracting from the comparable. When the comparable is inferior, an adjustment is made by adding to the comparable.

43. A A lot-and-block method is the best way to describe this property in a listing contract.

44. D Deed covenants are not public controls; they are private controls placed on real estate.

45. C A possibility of reverter is a possible future interest found in a fee simple defeasible title with a special limitation.

46. C $640 \div 4 \div 4 \div 4 = 10$
$640 \div 4 \div 2 = 80$
$80 + 10 = 90$ acres

47. D By definition of functional obsolescence and deterioration.

48. C Private mortgage insurance would not be used in determining the value of a property.

49. A Generally, an easement affects the use of the property, but not its title.

50. C If the subject property has an amenity that the comparable does not, then the appraiser makes a positive adjustment (adds) to the comparable property.

51. D Conventional life estates are freehold estates that are not inheritable.

52. C The bundle of legal rights are the rights inherent with the ownership of real estate, not personal property.

53. B If a broker has entered into an open listing, other brokers can contact the seller directly without being in violation of the law of agency.

54. D The buyers should check the master plan to determine the zoning for the property.

55. D The maintenance fee of a co-op owner includes their portion of the mortgage payment, property taxes, insurance and maintenance.

56. D The listing can be terminated with the mutual consent of the broker and the sellers.

57. C They are all examples of gross easements that benefit a person or legal entity.

58. D Littoral rights are water rights of owners whose land borders on large, navigable lakes, seas and oceans.

59. D Property taxes are also called *ad valorem* taxes.

60. B Death of the agent would not terminate a listing. Death of the broker or seller would terminate the listing.

2

Selling Property

This chapter covers the following information regarding selling property: contracts and offers, characteristics of real property, agency, advising buyers of outside services and services provided to the buyer.

Content Outline—Contracts and Offers

II. Selling Property

    A. Contracts and Offers

        1. Sales contract forms and provisions

        2. Offers and counteroffers

SALES CONTRACT FORMS AND PROVISIONS

A properly prepared contract legally binds **competent parties** to the terms of the contract. Real estate contracts include listing agreements, offers to purchase, sales contracts, options, binders, mortgages, notes, insurance policies, leases and property management agreements.

To be valid and enforceable, a contract must contain the following essential elements:

- The parties must be *legally competent.* There must be at least two bona fide parties to enter into a contract, and they must be authorized to perform. In most states, a person is considered to be legally competent at the age of 18. Other parties authorized to perform include executors, administrators, anyone operating under court order, a party with the proper power of attorney or if a corporation, the party authorized by the corporation to enter into real estate contracts. The parties also must be mentally competent.

- There must be **offer and acceptance,** also known as *mutual assent* or *meeting of the minds.* An offer must be made by one party (offeror) and accepted without any qualifications or changes by the second party (offeree).

- The contract must be in *proper legal form.* Each state has its own state law, called the *statute of frauds,* that determines which contracts must be in writing. Generally, most real estate contracts must be in writing to be enforceable. Exceptions are some types of listing agreements and management agreements. Leases and listings for less than one year are not required to be in writing in many states.

FIGURE 2.1 *Usual Provisions in a Sales Contract*

- Identification of the seller, buyer and property
- Type of deed being conveyed, with any restrictions
- The price of the property and how the purchaser will pay
- Amount of earnest money and remedies for breach of contract
- Provision for real estate taxes, hazard insurance and rents, etc.
- Date for securing loan, closing, inspection and possession
- Personal property to be left with the real estate
- Personal property the seller intends to remove
- Transfer or payment of any special assessments
- Provision stating time period for acceptance
- Dated signatures of all parties

- The contract must be entered into for a *legal purpose*. A contract to purchase real estate for the purpose of growing marijuana is illegal and would be void.
- There must be *legal* **consideration,** which is a promise made by one party to induce another party to enter into a contract. For example, a party promises to give up smoking and eating sugar for one year in exchange for a vacation. A gift is good consideration, while money or the promise to pay money is a *valuable* consideration. In a sales contract, the consideration is the selling price of the property; therefore, earnest money, or a good-faith deposit, is *not* necessary to create a binding sales contract.
- There must be **reality of consent,** which means the contract was entered into without duress, menace, misrepresentation or fraud. The law protects a person who has been tricked or forced into entering a contract. That is, the contract is voidable by the innocent party, but valid as to the wrongdoer.
- For contracts that are required to be in writing, there must be the *signatures of the parties authorized to perform.* Thus, both the buyer and seller must sign the sales contract for it to be enforceable.

A list of the usual provisions that appear in a real estate contract is shown in Figure 2.1.

Types of Contracts

- **Unilateral contract**—Only one party is obligated to perform in a unilateral contract. Examples: open listings and options.
- **Bilateral contract**—Both parties are obligated to perform in a bilateral contract. Exclusive listings, leases and sales contracts are bilateral contracts.
- **Express contract**—The parties have specifically agreed, either orally or in writing, to enter into a contract. Most real estate contracts are express contracts.
- **Implied contract**—The parties by their actions or conduct enter into a contract. Examples of implied contracts include ordering food in a restaurant, securing the services of a taxi or pumping gasoline into a car at a self-service gas station.
- **Executory contract**—One or both parties have duties to perform in an executory contract. A sales contract is executory because the buyer must financially qualify and the seller must produce a marketable title. Most contracts are executory contracts.
- **Executed contract**—All parties have fulfilled their duties and responsibilities in an executed contract. The sales contract becomes fully executed when the deed is conveyed at the closing and the buyer has paid the purchase price. Please note: The word *execute* means *to sign a document.* This is different from an executed contract.

Status of a Contract

- **Valid**—It meets *all* the essential elements and is an enforceable contract.
- **Void**—It is missing an essential element or is unenforceable by either party.
- **Voidable**—It may be rescinded by one or both parties. Contracts are voidable by the innocent party if entered into
  under duress,
  under undue influence,
  through misrepresentation,
  through fraud,
  with a minor, or
  with an incompetent person.

A contract with a contingency that cannot be met is voidable.

- **Unenforceable**—When neither party can sue the other to force performance, the contract is said to be *unenforceable*. Because a real estate sales contract must be in writing, an oral agreement to purchase a property is unenforceable. A contract not performed within the statutory time period is unenforceable.

Following are other important terms associated with contracts:

- **Time is of the essence**—This clause in a contract that means the contract must be performed within the time limit specified. The party who does not perform on time may be liable for breach of contract.

If a contract does not specify *time is of the essence* or a *date of performance*, then it is required to be performed "within a reasonable time."

- **Assignment**—This is a transfer of rights and/or duties from one contract to another contract or from one person to another person. Most contracts include a clause that either forbids or permits assignment.
- **Novation**—When novation is granted, one contract is substituted for another contract with the intent to discharge the obligation of the original contract. It is a release of liability from the original contract.
- **Ambiguities**—Any ambiguities in a contract are construed against the writer of the contract. Contract terms must be clear and definite.
- **Contingency**—A contingency in a contract requires the completion of a certain act or promise before the contract is binding. A contingency that cannot be completed makes the contract voidable.
- **Equitable title**—In a sales contract, land contract or trust deed, the buyer's interest in the property is called an equitable title interest. Though the legal title is held by another party, the buyer does have an insurable interest in the property.
- **Liquidated damages**—Damages or compensation that will be paid if one party breaches the contract. The earnest money deposit may serve as a liquidated damage clause in a sales contract. Generally, if the buyer defaults and the seller retains the earnest money deposit as liquidated damages, the seller may not sue for any further damages.
- **Right of first refusal**—This term can have two meanings. It can mean the right of a person to have the "first right" to purchase or lease a property, when the owner is ready to sell or lease. It can also be a contingency clause in a sales contract. For example, the seller has accepted an

offer contingent upon the buyer selling their house. If a seller's acceptance contained a right of first refusal, it means the seller can still market his home. If a qualified buyer writes an offer, the seller must give the first buyer the right to buy. If the first buyer cannot buy, then they would release the seller from the contract so he could accept the offer from the "ready, willing and able buyer."

• **Suit for specific performance**—A legal action to enforce the performance of the terms of a contract.
• **Caveat emptor**—Means "let the buyer beware."
• **Caveat venditor**—Means "let the seller beware."

State laws determine the exact terms of a sales contract.

Option Contracts

In the case of an **option** contract, an **optionor** (seller) agrees to keep open an offer to sell or lease real property in return for option money. While the **optionee** (buyer) does not have to buy, the optionor must sell, should the buyer exercise the option. The option money gives the buyer the "right to buy" and may or may not apply toward the purchase price.

Option contracts typically contain the names and addresses of the parties, an identification of the property, the terms of the sale, the sales price, the date the option expires, the method of notice by which the option is to be exercised and provisions for disbursement of the option money if the option is not exercised.

An option contract is assignable, unless the contract states otherwise, and is considered a *unilateral contract* because only the seller is obligated to perform.

Option contracts that have been exercised are *bilateral contracts* because the buyer is then obligated to buy and the seller is obligated to sell. These contracts are still enforceable upon the death of either party.

Lease Option

In a **lease option,** the lessee (tenant) has the right to purchase the property under specified conditions or to renew or extend the lease at its end. The rent or a portion of the rent may be applied to the purchase price.

Land Contract

In a typical **land contract,** the **vendor** (seller) finances the property and retains title to it until the final payment is made or some other condition is met by the **vendee** (buyer). The buyer possesses the property and receives an equitable title.

The vendee agrees to give the vendor a down payment and regular installments of principal and interest for a number of years. Typically, the buyer also pays for property taxes, insurance, repairs and upkeep on the property.

A land contract is also known as a *contract for deed,* an *installment contract, articles of agreement for a warranty deed, bond for title* or *agreement of sale.*

OFFERS AND COUNTEROFFERS

To *offer* means to put forward for acceptance, rejection or consideration. In real estate, an offer demonstrates the intention to enter into a contract. An offer does not become a contract unless it is accepted without changes. The party making the offer is the *offeror,* and the party receiving the offer is the *offeree.*

FIGURE 2.2 *Offers, Counteroffers and Acceptances*

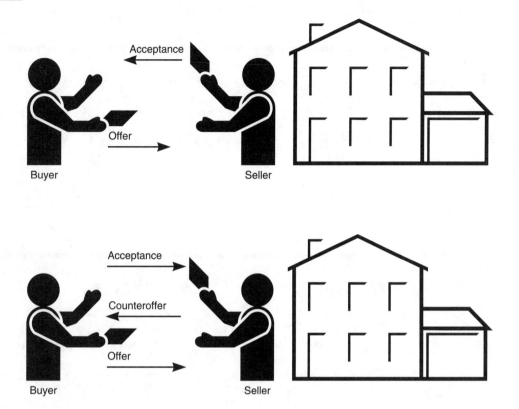

The terms of the offer must be clear and definite and typically will state a time period for acceptance. An offer can be revoked at any time before acceptance. Notice of revocation by the offeree, death of either party, insanity of either party or a counteroffer all terminate an offer.

If any change in terms is made, the offer is void and a **counteroffer** is created. The legal positions of the parties are reversed; that is, the offeror becomes the offeree and the offeree becomes the offeror.

In real estate, all offers are presented to the seller. Until the seller signs the offer there is no legally binding contract. It is also wise to state the time of the acceptance in writing. Some states have passed laws regarding the use of facsimile transmissions in the negotiation of a contract. If this is permitted, a clause stipulating that acceptance is deemed effective when the fax is received should be a part of the contract.

Mailbox Theory

According to the *mailbox theory*, if an offer is made by mail, acceptance occurs and a binding or effective contract is created when the offeree places the accepted contract in the mailbox. The offeror does not have to have received the contract for acceptance to have taken place. In this scenario, the law has been interpreted to mean that the offeror has appointed the post office as his or her agent; therefore, when the contract is placed in the mailbox, acceptance has occurred.

Let's create another scenario. Al mails an offer to Carrie and in the offer gives her four days to accept. On the morning of day two, Al sends another letter to Carrie withdrawing his offer. On the afternoon of day two, Carrie drops an acceptance of Al's offer in the mailbox. What is the status of the contract? Al's offer was deemed accepted the moment Carrie dropped her acceptance in the mailbox. Under the rule, an acceptance does not have to be received by the offeror, it must only be placed in the mailbox. However, a *withdrawal* of the contract *must be received by the offeree before it is considered valid.* Most states do not recognize the mail-box theory.

Because a listing contract is considered an employment contract, if the seller is offered the full list price of the property and does not accept the offer, a commission is still due the broker because the broker was hired to secure a ready, willing and able buyer.

Contracts and Offers—Key Point Review

1. A valid and enforceable contract must contain the following essential elements: legally competent parties, offer and acceptance, proper legal form, legal purpose, consideration, reality of consent, and the signature(s) of the party or parties authorized to perform.

2. Only one party is obligated to perform in a unilateral contract. Open listings and options are unilateral contracts.

3. Both parties are obligated to perform in a bilateral contract. Exclusive listings, leases and sales contracts are bilateral contracts.

4. In an express contract, the parties have specifically agreed, either orally or in writing, to enter into a contract.

5. In an implied contract, the parties by their actions or conduct have entered into a contract.

6. One or both parties have duties to perform in an executory contract.

7. In an executed contract, all parties have fulfilled their obligations.

8. A contract is valid when it meets all the essential elements and is enforceable.

9. A contract is void if it is missing an essential element and is unenforceable by either party, such as a contract entered into by an incompetent party.

10. A contract is voidable if it can be rescinded by one or both parties. Contracts entered into under duress or undue influence, through misrepresentation or fraud, or with a minor or an incompetent person are voidable by the innocent party.

11. A contract is unenforceable if neither party can sue to force performance of the contract.

12. When "time is of the essence" is found in a contract, the contract must be performed within the time limit specified.

Contracts and Offers—Key Point Review (Continued)

13. An assignment is a transfer of rights and/or duties from one contract to another or from one person to another person.

14. Novation means one contract has been substituted for another. It is a release of liability from the original contract.

15. Any ambiguities in a contract will be construed against its writer. To add or delete a provision in a contract, a supplement or addendum should be signed by the parties.

16. A contingency in a contract requires the completion of a certain act or promise before the contract is binding.

17. In a sales contract, land contract or trust deed, the buyer's interest in the property is an equitable title. Legal title is held by another party, and the buyer has an insurable interest in the property.

18. A liquidated damage clause in a contract states that compensation will be paid if one party breaches the contract.

19. Caveat emptor means "let the buyer beware." Caveat venditor means "let the seller beware."

20. An option is an agreement wherein the seller agrees to keep open an offer to sell or lease real property in return for option money, which may or may not apply toward the purchase price.

21. An option contract binds the optionor to sell should the optionee exercise the option.

22. An option contract should contain the names and addresses of the parties, identification of the property, sales price, date of the expiration of the option, method of notice by which the option is to be exercised and provisions for forfeiture of the option money if the option is not exercised; it may contain a clause forbidding assignment.

23. An option contract is a unilateral contract. An option that has been exercised is a bilateral contract.

24. In a land contract, the seller is the vendor and the buyer is the vendee. Typically, the seller retains title to the property until the final payment is made. A land contract is also known as a contract for deed, an installment contract, articles of agreement for a warranty deed, bond for title or agreement of sale.

25. To offer means to put forward for acceptance, rejection or consideration. An offer does not become a contract unless it is accepted without changes.

26. The offeror makes the offer; the offeree receives it.

27. The terms of the offer must be clear and definite and typically will state a period for acceptance. An offer can be revoked at any time before acceptance or terminated by notice of revocation by the offeree, death or insanity of either party, or a counteroffer.

Contracts and Offers—Key Point Review (Continued)

28. If any change is made in an offer, the original offer is void, a counteroffer is created and the legal positions of the parties are reversed.

29. The mailbox theory states that if an offer is made by mail, a contract is created at the time the offeree places the accepted contract in the mailbox. The offeror does not have to receive the acceptance for it to take place.

30. Because a listing contract is considered an employment contract, if a seller is offered the full list price of the property and does not accept the offer, a commission still is due the broker because the broker secured a ready, willing and able buyer.

Content Outline—Characteristics of Real Property

II. Selling Property

    A. Characteristics of Real Property

        1. Rights of ownership
        2. Right of property subdivision
        3. Planning and zoning
        4. Material facts
        5. Physical condition of property
        6. Other required disclosures

RIGHTS OF OWNERSHIP

An *estate* is the bundle of rights associated with real property or the legal interest or rights in the land, but not the physical quantity of the land. At closing, the grantor transfers the bundle of rights to the grantee, allowing the grantee to possess, enjoy, control, exclude and dispose of the property.

RIGHT OF PROPERTY SUBDIVISION

The right of property subdivision can be regulated by the government either on a state or local level. As land becomes scarce in a given location, the regulation of the division of it becomes critical. It is not uncommon even in agricultural areas to minimize the division of land to several acres. There can also be private control of property subdivision through deed conditions.

PLANNING AND ZONING

There are no federal zoning laws. Zoning is a police power conferred on municipal governments by **state enabling acts.** This is why many communities have a zoning and planning board to evaluate current needs, project and plan for future growth in a stable manner.

Zoning allows the use of land for agricultural, residential, commercial, industrial, or special purposes, such as houses of worship and hospitals. Residential zoning include single family and multi-family dwellings. Commercial uses include office buildings, shopping centers, service stations, restaurants, motels and hotels. Industrial or manufacturing is a broad category of zoning that contains subcategories from light to heavy industry. **Performance standards** regulate the air, noise and water pollution allowed by manufacturing facilities.

The federal or state government may, through special legislation, regulate land use in **special study zones.** This would be used to control development in high risk flood prone or geological areas. It could also include scenic easements, coastal management and environmental laws.

MATERIAL FACTS

When listing a property, it is important for an agent to verify zoning, property taxes, building codes, building permits, certificates of occupancy and other land use restrictions that may apply. The local zoning board will have a zoning administrator who will assist the public with such questions.

Any other encumbrances, such as deed restrictions and conditions, regulations of the home-owners' association, special assessments, or any other condition that would burden the use, enjoyment or disposition of the property would need to be disclosed.

PHYSICAL CONDITION OF PROPERTY

Many states require the owner to fill out property disclosure statements. Information is given about the house systems, foundations and structure, roof, land drainage, boundaries, water supply, sewer systems, construction or remodeling, homeowners' association dues, and environmental hazards.

Disclosure of environmental hazards would include

- **urea formaldehyde**—used in building materials, especially insulation; emits gases that can cause respiratory problems, eye and skin irritations
- **asbestos**—used in building materials, especially insulation; microscopic fibers can result in respiratory diseases; harmful only if disturbed or exposed
- **lead-based paint**—elevated levels of lead in the body can cause damage to the brain, kidneys, nervous systems and red blood cells; estimated that one in six children may have dangerously high amounts of lead in his or her body
- **radon gas**—an odorless and tasteless gas that is produced by the natural decay of other radioactive substances; breathing radon gas can cause respiratory problems and lung cancer
- **carbon monoxide**—an odorless and colorless gas that occurs as a byproduct of burning fuels such as wood, oil and natural gas to incomplete combustion; with improper ventilation, carbon monoxide inhibits the blood's ability to transport oxygen, which can cause nausea and even death

FIGURE 2.3 *Environmental Hazards*

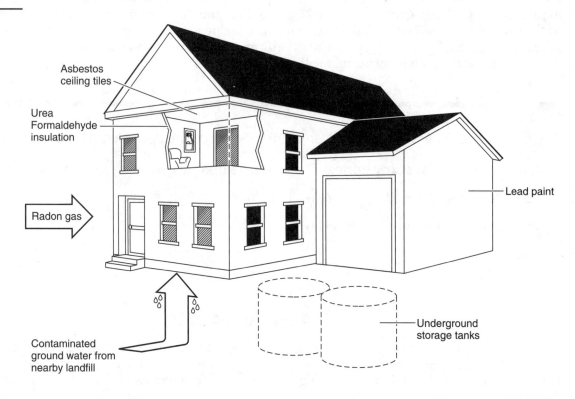

- **underground storage tanks**—commonly found where gas stations, auto repair shops, printing and chemical plants, dry cleaners, etc. for the storage of chemicals; if used to store toxic wastes and the tanks are neglected, they leak hazardous substances into the environment; this can contaminate the soil and groundwater

OTHER REQUIRED DISCLOSURES

By federal law, persons selling or leasing residential housing constructed before 1978 must disclose the presence of known lead-based paint. They must also provide purchasers or tenants with records and reports regarding prior testing for lead-based paint. A lead-based paint disclosure statement must be attached to sales contracts if the residential property was built prior to 1978. A lead hazard pamphlet must be given to all buyers and tenants, and purchases must be given ten days in which to conduct an inspection.

A property may be **stigmatized** if the past history of the property makes it undesirable. This could be a murder, suicide, shooting, illegal drug sales or if the house is "haunted." Few states have laws requiring the disclosure of stigmatized properties; therefore, a broker should seek competent legal counsel when dealing with this type of property.

Characteristics of Real Property—Key Point Review

1. An estate is the bundle of rights associated with real property or the legal interest or rights in the land. These rights include the rights to possess, enjoy, control, exclude and dispose of the property.

2. The right of property subdivision can be regulated by the government or by private controls, such as deed conditions.

3. State enabling acts allow municipal governments to create zoning and planning boards to evaluate current needs, and project for future growth in a stable manner.

4. Special study zones are used to control development in high risk flood prone or geological areas.

5. Agents must disclose material facts that would affect the value of a property such as zoning, property taxes, land use restrictions and special assessments.

6. Many states require that property disclosure statements include the physical condition of the improvements and land, as well as environmental hazards.

7. A property may become stigmatized if an event has occurred on the property that may make it undesirable. Because few states have laws requiring the disclosure of stigmatized properties, brokers should seek competent legal counsel when dealing with such properties.

8. Federal laws requires lead-based paint disclosures on residential property built prior to 1978.

Content Outline—Advising Buyers of Outside Services

II. Selling Property

    A. Advising Buyers of Outside Services

        1. Home protection plans
        2. Insurance
        3. Inspection reports
        4. Surveys

HOME PROTECTION PLANS

It is the buyer's responsibility to conduct an inspection of the property to make sure the housing systems are functioning properly. **Home protection (warranty) plans** are available which provides insurance that covers the repair or replacement of electrical, plumbing, heating, appliances, air-conditioning, and other systems within the home. The policy may be purchased by the agent, seller or buyer. Typical coverage is for one year, but it can be renewed if desired.

INSURANCE

To protect their investment, property owners generally purchase **insurance** to cover the liability of various risks. The three general categories of risk include protection against (1) destruction of the premises, (2) injury to others on the premises and (3) theft of personal property of the homeowner or family members. Most **homeowners' insurance policies** cover all these risks. Policies should be examined carefully to determine the terms of such coverage.

Most homeowners' insurance policies contain a coinsurance clause that requires that the homeowner maintain insurance equal to at least 80 percent of the replacement cost of the dwelling. Please note: this coverage does not include the value of the land. A homeowner may choose to insure 100 percent of the value of the improvements. Lenders generally require insurance that covers the mortgage balance. Be sure to read coinsurance test questions carefully.

INSPECTION REPORTS

Many buyers purchase property contingent on an inspection by an independent third party or property inspector. An inspection report should include an analysis of the structure, electrical and plumbing systems and any problems with water leakage.

Lenders may require a pest control report before agreeing to secure a loan on a property. This report must show that the property is free and clear of any live, visible infestation by wood-destroying organisms.

In the development of property, there must be an adequate and safe water supply, and the disposal of sewage must meet health and safety standards. Property owners who use septic tanks are required to have a *percolation test*, which tests the soil's absorption or drainage capacity. Only if the soil has the ability to absorb and drain water can the land be developed.

Many lenders also require a flood certification and environmental inspection before negotiating a loan on the property. This would determine if the property is in a flood prone area, or if it is a site where any known environmental hazards have been disposed.

SURVEYS

Most lenders require a **survey** before agreeing to negotiate a loan. The purpose of the survey is to determine the exact area of the land being purchased, to identify any existing encroachments and easements and to determine compliance with setback and other zoning requirements. The survey is usually at the buyer's expense, unless a discrepancy is found between the new survey and the original one. Should a discrepancy be found, the seller may be required to remedy the condition and pay for the survey.

The three major types of surveys are the *geodetic* or *government survey*, which measures the shape and size of the earth; the *cadastral survey*, used to determine the boundaries of parcels for defining ownership (used also in the tax assessment process); and the *topographic survey*, used to measure the features of the earth's surface and the location of roads.

Advising Buyers of Outside Services—Key Point Review

1. Home warranty plans are available that provide for insurance that covers the repair or replacement of home systems.

2. Buyers normally buy homeowners' insurance to protect against loss due to destruction of the premises, injury to others and theft of personal property.

3. Most homeowners' insurance policies require the owner to maintain insurance equal to at least 80 percent of the replacement cost of the dwelling.

4. Many buyers have an independent property inspection prior to purchasing a property. Lenders may require a pest inspection, flood certification, and environmental inspection before releasing funds for the loan.

5. Most lenders require a survey to determine the exact area of the land being purchased, to identify any existing encroachments and easements, and to determine compliance with setback and other zoning requirements.

Content Outline—Services Provided to the Buyer

II. Selling Property

A. Services Provided to the Buyer

1. Information to determine prospective buyer's price range and financing
2. Preview and choose property to show buyer
3. Current market conditions
4. Show properties

INFORMATION TO DETERMINE
PROSPECTIVE BUYER'S PRICE RANGE AND FINANCING

Assessing the buyer's price range depends on three basic factors: (1) stable income, (2) net worth and (3) credit history. It seems like a simple process, but it involves more than just the use of mathematical formulas. The four basic steps for securing a loan for the purchase of real estate are

1. applying for the loan,
2. analysis of the borrower and the property,
3. processing the loan application, and
4. closing the loan.

To determine the **stable income** of the borrower, the lender may require pay check stubs, tax returns, W2s, and verification of employment for the past two years. To determine the **net worth,** the borrower's liabilities are subtracted from their assets. Upon authorization, the loan officer will pull the credit report of the borrower/s. The report will include a **credit score** that takes into account the applicant's employment and credit history.

The property must be appraised, and once all the information is secured, the risk of the loan is evaluated by a loan underwriter. If the loan is approved, a title search is ordered. The loan will close if the title is marketable and any other underwriting conditions have been met.

The two ratios that an underwriter analyzes are the mortgage-to-income ratio and the debt service ratio.

To confirm the borrower's **assets,** the lender will require statements from checking, savings, stocks, bonds, retirement accounts, and money market accounts. They will also verify the ownership of real estate, automobiles, household goods, collections, and other cash or property of value.

The borrower must also disclose **liabilities** such as car payments, mortgage or rent payments, credit card debt, student loans, alimony or child support, and any other debts.

---

1. The mortgage-to-income ratio is the ratio of the monthly housing expense to stable monthly income. In many loans, the mortgage expense can be no more than 28 percent of the stable monthly income.
2. The debt service ratio expresses the relationship of the total monthly debt payments to the borrower's income. In many loans, the total debt service expenses should be no more than 36 percent of the borrower's stable monthly income. FHA and VA ratios are generally 29 percent and 41 percent, respectively.

PREVIEW AND CHOOSE PROPERTY TO SHOW BUYER

After qualifying a buyer regarding the price range of property he or she can afford, other needs must be identified to help the buyer select a property. These needs include space, location, schools, etc. Once these needs have been determined, the agent can review the properties currently available that meet the requirements. The proper brokerage firm then is contacted, and an appointment is made to show the property selected by the purchaser.

Many buyers are previewing properties via the Internet. Upon finding a property they want to see, they may "drive by" and then call an agent.

CURRENT MARKET CONDITIONS

An agent needs to be aware of current market conditions affecting the value and sale of real estate, including interest rates, employment levels, vacancy rates, demographics and the absorption rate. It may be best to identify these last two terms.

Demographics is the *statistical study of the population in reference to size, density and distribution in a given area.* A company moving into or out of the area will have an impact on the employment levels, vacancy rates, supply and demand and absorption rate.

The **absorption rate** is an *estimate of how quickly new construction will be sold or occupied each year.* Because an agent cannot be certain exactly how and when demographic factors will affect current market conditions, he or she can never guarantee future profits from or appreciation of real estate.

SHOW PROPERTIES AND NOTE AMENITIES

Because buyers rarely purchase the first home they see, the agent should have some system in place to help the buyer make notes on each property shown. This helps the buyer decide if a property meets his or her needs.

Services Provided to the Buyer—Key Point Review

1. Assessing the buyer's price range depends on three basic factors: (1) stable income, (2) net worth and (3) credit history.

2. A loan underwriter evaluates a loan application to determine the desirability of the loan.

3. The mortgage-to-income ratio is the ratio of the monthly housing expense to stable monthly income.

4. The debt service ratio is the sum of the total monthly debt payments in relationship to the borrower's stable monthly income.

5. An agent must be aware of current market conditions affecting the value and sale of real estate.

Questions

1. Every enforceable contract for the sale of real estate must be in writing and signed by all parties, in accordance with the
   A. Real Estate License Act.
   B. Uniform Commercial Code.
   C. Statute of frauds.
   D. Truth-in-Lending Act.

2. Sandra and Cyril entered into a one-year contract wherein Cyril agreed to provide complete lawn care and snow removal services for Sandra. However, after the first snowstorm of the year, Cyril decided he wanted to move south even though the contract had six months left. Eric wanted to provide the services Cyril had provided, and the parties agreed that Sandra and Eric would enter into a new contract and that the contract between Sandra and Cyril would be canceled. The above is an example of a(n)
   A. assignment.
   B. novation.
   C unenforceable agreement.
   D. rejection.

3. If a prospective buyer has an option to purchase a certain parcel of real estate, the prospective buyer has
   A. paid consideration for the option right.
   B. the obligation to purchase the property at a reduced price.
   C. the right to subject the seller to a new mortgage.
   D. the obligation to pay existing liens.

4. Victor enters into a contract to sell certain land to Sally. During the course of the negotiations, Victor wrongfully represents the nature of the soil, claiming that a basement can be built. This contract is
   A. void.
   B. voidable by Sally because of misrepresentation.
   C. voidable by Victor because of mistake.
   D. voidable by neither because no harm was done.

5. The essential elements of a contract include which of the following?
   A. A notarial seal
   B. Mutual agreement
   C. A three-day cancellation right
   D. Equal bargaining power

6. What characterizes a bilateral contract?
   A. Only one of the parties is bound to act.
   B. Promises have been exchanged by two parties and both are obligated to perform.
   C. A restriction is placed by one party to limit the actual performance by the other party.
   D. A duty is to be performed by one party only.

7. What characterizes an executed contract?
   A. Only one party to the contract has made a promise.
   B. At least one party to the contract may still sue for specific performance.
   C. All of the parties have fully performed their duties.
   D. One of the conditions of the contract has been completed.

8. Charlene and Patricia enter into a contract wherein Charlene agrees to sell her house to Patricia. Charlene thereafter changes her mind and defaults. Patricia then sues Charlene to force her to go through with the contract. This is known as a suit for
   A. specific performance.
   B. damages.
   C. rescission.
   D. forfeiture.

9. To create a contract, the offeree must accept the offer
   A. immediately and cannot be given more than 24 hours to consider the offer.
   B. without changes.
   C. before the close of the tenth business day following the offer.
   D. only with the advice of his or her attorney.

10. When a real estate sales contract has been agreed to, signed by a purchaser and spouse, then given to the seller's broker with an earnest money check to present to the seller,
    A. the transaction constitutes a valid contract in the eyes of the law.
    B. the purchaser can sue the seller for specific performance.
    C. this transaction is considered an offer.
    D. the earnest money will be returned if the buyer defaults.

11. An option is a contract that
    A. sets a time limit to keep an offer open.
    B. is an open-end agreement.
    C. does not set the sale price for the property.
    D. transfers title when it is signed by the seller.

12. An option contract that has been exercised is a(n)
    A. unilateral contract.
    B. bilateral contact.
    C. executory bilateral contract.
    D. executory unilateral contract.

13. After the snowstorm of the century, Warren offers to pay $6 to whoever will shovel his driveway. This is an example of which of the following?
    A. Implied contract
    B. Bilateral contract
    C. License
    D. Unilateral contract

14. Carl made a written offer on Kristen's property. After reviewing the contract with her attorney, Kristen accepted the offer in writing. At this point, what type of title does Carl have to the property?
    A. Legal
    B. Equitable
    C. Indefeasible
    D. Defeasible

15. As a general rule, an oral sales contract involving the sale of real estate
    A. can be enforced through a court action.
    B. can be assigned to a third party.
    C. can be subject to a real estate commission.
    D. is unenforceable.

16. What is the legal procedure or action that may be brought by either the buyer or the seller to enforce the terms of a contract?
    A. An injunction
    B. Suit for specific performance
    C. Lis pendens
    D. An attachment

17. In an option to purchase real estate, the optionee
    A. must purchase the property, but may do so at any time within the option period.
    B. has no obligation to purchase the property.
    C. as a matter of right is limited to a refund of the option consideration if the option is exercised.
    D. is the prospective seller of the property.

18. An individual seeking to be excused from the dictates of a zoning ordinance should request a
    A. building permit.
    B. certificate of alternate usage.
    C. restrictive covenant.
    D. variance.

19. Local zoning ordinances often regulate all of the following EXCEPT the
    A. height of buildings in an area.
    B. density of subdivision.
    C. size of the lots.
    D. price of the property.

20. Zoning ordinances control the use of privately owned land by establishing land-use districts. Which one of the following is not a usual zoning district?
    A. Residential
    B. Commercial
    C. Industrial
    D. Rental

21. The major intent of zoning regulations is to
    A. demonstrate the police power of the state.
    B. ensure the health, safety and welfare of the community.
    C. set limits on the amount and kinds of businesses in a given area.
    D. protect residential neighborhoods from encroachment by business and industry.

22. All of the following are considered a part of the bundle of legal rights associated with real property ownership EXCEPT the right to
    A. possess, enjoy, control and exclude.
    B. sell, lease, devise and improve.
    C. mortgage, mine, drill and bequeath.
    D. trade, exchange, cultivate and explore.

23. John and George have an arrangement in which George has agreed to let John make an offer on his property should he decide to sell. Which of the following BEST describes this arrangement?
    A. Offer and acceptance
    B. Mutual assent
    C. Land contract
    D. Right of first refusal

24. Which of the following is NOT a consideration in a buyer agency agreement?
    A. Description of the property the buyer desires to purchase
    B. Sales associate's compensation
    C. Broker's accountability to the buyer
    D. Disclosure of the dual agency relationship to the seller

25. Which of the following BEST describes a material fact that should be disclosed to buyers who do not have an agent representing them in a transaction?
    A. the seller is getting a divorce.
    B. the seller has AIDS.
    C. the seller owes special assessments on the property.
    D. the seller's spouse died on the property and that's why it's for sale.

26. A seller has set an appointment with an agent to list a property. The agent knows the property is stigmatized. What would be the BEST action for the agent to take?
    A. List the property and ignore the fact that the property is stigmatized.
    B. Secure the listing and advertise the property as stigmatized without the seller's permission.
    C. Disclose the fact that the property is stigmatized only to those buyers the agent thinks would be interested in knowing that the property is stigmatized.
    D. Discuss the matter with the broker and secure legal advice before discussing with the seller listing the property.

27. Which of the following environmental hazards requires a disclosure form to be completed by landlords and sellers of residential property built prior to 1978?
    A. Asbestos
    B. Carbon monoxide
    C. Radon gas
    D. Lead-based paint

28. An underwriter is determining the desirability of a loan. The underwriter is LEAST LIKELY to take into consideration which of the following?
    A. The appraisal
    B. Pest control inspection
    C. Flood certification
    D. Home warranty plan

29. A zoning board is reviewing a request for the building of a factory in the community. In making the decision regarding the location of the factory, the board will MOST LIKELY consider
    A. the taxes to be paid by the employees.
    B. how far the employees will have to drive to work.
    C. the number of managers the factory will need.
    D. the performance standards that regulate air, noise and water pollution.

30. Which of the following would be used to determine if soil has adequate absorption and drainage capacity to meet health and safety standards?
    A. Topography test
    B. Absorption test
    C. Percolation test
    D. Drainage test

31. The dwelling on a property has been valued at $95,000 and the land has been valued at $35,000. Fire destroys the dwelling. The homeowner with a standard insurance policy would MOST LIKELY file a claim for the maximum amount of
    A. $95,000.
    B. $130,000.
    C. $104,000.
    D. $76,000.

32. Which of the following documents would LEAST LIKELY be required by a lender for final approval of a loan?
    A. Pest control report
    B. The listing agreement
    C. Survey
    D. Title search

33. The terms *stable income, net worth* and *credit history* describe three basic factors
    A. in assessing the sale price of the property.
    B. in assessing the buyer's qualifications.
    C. needed to appraise the property.
    D. that prove the seller has a good and marketable title.

34. The process of evaluating the loan to determine desirability of negotiating the loan is called loan
    A. underwriting.
    B. approval.
    C. application.
    D. officer.

35. The monthly principal and interest payment made on a loan is often referred to as the
    A. mortgage-to-income ratio.
    B. debt service.
    C. loan-to-value ratio.
    D. loan-to-income ratio.

36. A seller received an offer by mail from a buyer that gave the seller five days to accept it. On the third day the buyer sent a notice to the seller stating that he was withdrawing his offer. On the third day the seller mailed his acceptance to the buyer and had no knowledge that the buyer wanted to withdraw the offer. Which of the following is true regarding the status of the contract?
    A. The offer is void because a buyer has the right to rescind a contract any time prior to acceptance.
    B. The offer is valid, and an executory sales contract was created when the seller dropped the acceptance in the mailbox.
    C. The offer is valid and an executed sales contract was created when the seller received the offer.
    D. The offer is void because the buyer did not receive notice of acceptance before the withdrawal occurred.

37. *Time is of the essence* in a contract means
    A. that the duties and responsibilities of the contract must be fulfilled on or before a stipulated time indicated in the contract.
    B. that the buyer is obligated to fulfill all duties stipulated in the contract by a certain date, but the seller is not.
    C. that the seller is obligated to fulfill all duties stipulated in the contract by a certain date, but the buyer is not.
    D. that the agent is obligated to fulfill all duties stipulated in the contract by a certain date, but the buyer and seller are not.

38. At closing, a title is transferred to the buyer. Until that event occurs, a contract entered into by a buyer and a seller is
    A. executory.
    B. executed.
    C. void.
    D. unenforceable.

39. In most states, all of the following contracts would need to be in writing to be enforceable EXCEPT
    A. a three-month lease agreement on an apartment.
    B. a contract for the sale of air rights.
    C. the sale of an easement to the airport.
    D. a sales contract for a principal place of residence.

40. Carrie negotiated an option contract with Mindy, wherein Mindy had six months to purchase the property. Month four Mindy found another buyer for the property. If Mindy can transfer her option contract to the new buyer, she can do so because of the right of
    A. novation.
    B. first refusal.
    C. contingency.
    D. assignment.

41. After three extensions of a sales contract, the buyers and sellers finally met at the title company for closing. The primary role of the agent at the closing is to
    A. explain the closing documents to the buyer.
    B. explain the closing documents to the seller.
    C. notarize documents.
    D. verify and receive the broker's fee.

42. Most states require a listing contract to contain which of the following to be valid?
    A. The buyer's name
    B. The lender negotiating the loan
    C. The interest rate the buyer will pay
    D. The expiration date

43. An agent forgot to get her buyer to sign the offer. What is the status of the offer?
    A. Valid
    B. Void
    C. Voidable
    D. Acceptable

44. Which of the following would LEAST LIKELY be found in a sales contract?
    A. The identity of the buyer and a description of the property being purchased
    B. The type of listing contract and its expiration date
    C. The identity of the seller and the type of deed being conveyed, including covenants, conditions and restrictions
    D. Any appurtenances the seller intends to leave with the property

45. A contract entered into based on a misrepresentation is
    A. voidable by the aggrieved party.
    B. void between the parties.
    C. voidable by either party.
    D. valid enforceable contract.

46. In a land contract, which of the following would MOST LIKELY happen?
    A. The vendor finances the property and makes installment payments.
    B. The vendee receives possession and the vendor retains an equitable title.
    C. The vendor pays the property taxes, insurance, repairs and upkeep on the property until the final payment is made.
    D. The vendor retains the title to the property until the final payment is made.

47. Which of the following BEST describes the term option?
    A. Unilateral contract
    B. Bilateral contract
    C. Redeemable contract
    D. Executory redeemable contract

48. A seller listed a property for $100,000. The buyer made an offer for the full list price and gave the seller three days to accept. Two days later the seller had not yet accepted. Regarding this situation, which of the following is true?
    A. The buyer cannot withdraw an offer for the full list price.
    B. The seller must accept the offer because it is for the full list price.
    C. The seller may reject the offer, but the commission is due the broker.
    D. The buyer must wait the entire three days before the offer can be withdrawn.

49. What do the terms *offer and acceptance, mutual assent* and *meeting of the minds* have in common?
    A. They all mean there is an unqualified acceptance of an offer, which is an essential element of a contract.
    B. They all mean there is a qualified acceptance of an offer, which is an essential element of a contract.
    C. They all affect only contracts for the transfer of easement rights in a lease agreement.
    D. They all affect only contracts for the transfer of personal property at a foreclosure sale.

50. A husband in the military is currently stationed in Germany. He and his wife decide to sell their house in the States so she can join him. To provide a good and marketable title to the buyer, the wife should
    A. secure a specific, durable power of attorney from her husband and sell the property.
    B. sign her husband's name to all documents after showing her marriage certificate.
    C. let her husband's twin brother sign any necessary documents for him.
    D. sign all documents for him because she is his wife.

51. Certain documents must be in writing because of which of the following laws?
    A. Statute of frauds
    B. Statute of evidence rules
    C. Statute of laches
    D. Statute of limitations

52. A contract has written contingencies. The status of this contract is
    A. voidable.
    B. void.
    C. executed.
    D. fraudulent.

53. In a conventional loan, the usual debt to service ratio is
    A. 28 percent.
    B. 29 percent.
    C. 36 percent.
    D. 41 percent.

54. A buyer is going to attend a foreclosure sale. When discussing his possible purchase with a friend, his friend advised "caveat emptor." This means
    A. "let the seller beware."
    B. "let the bank beware."
    C. "let the neighbors beware."
    D. "let the buyer beware."

55. When purchasing a commercial property, the buyer placed $10,000 in an escrow account, and the offer stipulated the seller was to place $10,000 in an escrow account. If either party breached the contract, the aggrieved party was to receive the $20,000. This is BEST described as a(n)
    A. equitable damage clause.
    B. subordination clause.
    C. earnest money clause.
    D. liquidated damage clause.

56. A developer entered into an agreement with a prospective buyer wherein the buyer will pay rent for one year. The buyer also has the right to purchase the property within the year, but is not obligated to do so. The developer and buyer have MOST LIKELY entered into a
    A. lease purchase contract.
    B. lease option contract.
    C. periodic tenancy contract.
    D. tenancy at will contract.

57. In a lease purchase contract, the primary consideration is the
    A. purchase price.
    B. monthly lease payment.
    C. term of the lease.
    D. broker's commission.

58. All of the following would render an offer voidable EXCEPT the contract that is
    A. missing an essential element.
    B. entered into under duress.
    C. entered into with misrepresentation.
    D. entered into through fraud.

59. The buyer's offer stipulated that the closing must take place by April 15. This clause is known as
    A. the settlement clause.
    B. time is of the essence.
    C. a contingency clause.
    D. transfer clause.

60. The word *estate* can be BEST defined as the:
    A. physical size of the land as described in a survey.
    B. history of all the owners of the property.
    C. land and all attachments to the land.
    D. bundle of legal rights and interests in the land.

ANSWERS

1. C Contracts for the sale of real estate must be in writing to be enforceable according to the statute of frauds.

2. B Novation is the substitution of a new party or contract for an existing one.

3. A In an option contract, the buyer must pay money or consideration for the option right.

4. B Victor, the seller, gave invalid information to the buyer, Sally. A contract entered into under misrepresentation is voidable by Sally, the aggrieved party.

5. B One of the essential elements of a contract includes mutual agreement between the parties.

6. B By definition of a bilateral contract.

7. C An executed contract exists when all parties have fully performed their duties.

8. A By definition of specific performance.

9. B An offer must be accepted without changes.

10. C The buyer has signed the contract, but the seller has not; therefore, only an offer exists.

11. A By definition of option contract.

12. C When the buyer informs the seller that he or she is going to purchase the property, the option is exercised and an executory bilateral contract exists.

13. D Because only one party, Warren, is obligated to perform, a unilateral contract exists.

14. B Equitable title is the buyer's interest in the property when the legal title is held by another party.

15. D Real estate contracts must be in writing. An oral real estate contract is unenforceable by either party.

16. B By definition of specific performance.

17. B The optionee (buyer) has no obligation to purchase the property. He or she has purchased an option to the property, and is not entitled to a refund of the option money if he or she does not.

18. D By definition of variance.

19. D Zoning does not regulate the price of the property.

20. D Rental is not a land-use district. The land-use districts are agricultural, residential, commercial, industrial and special-purpose properties.

21. B The major intent of zoning is to ensure the health, safety and welfare of the public.

22. C The bundle of legal rights does not include the right to bequeath, which is to leave personal property in a will.

23. D A right of first refusal gives a person the first right to buy or lease a property.

24. B The broker's commission would be in the agreement, but not the agent's.

25. C This is a material fact which should be disclosed to the buyer.

26. D If a property is stigmatized, it should be discussed with the broker and the attorney before the listing.

27. D The federal government requires the disclosure of lead-based paint in residential properties built prior to 1978.

28. D The underwriter would least likely be concerned about the home warranty plan.

29. D Performance standards would be a major consideration in the location of the factory.

30. C By definition of a percolation test.

31. D A standard insurance policy covers 80 percent of the value of the dwelling.

32. B A copy of the listing agreement is not required for loan approval.

33. B Assessing the buyer's qualifications depends on stable income, net worth and credit history.

34. A By definition of loan underwriting.

35. B By definition of debt service.

36. B Under the mailbox theory, an offer is accepted when a contract is dropped in the mailbox by the offeree. A withdrawal by the offeror must be received by the offeror before it is valid.

37. A By the definition of time is of the essence.

38. A It is an executory contract because there are still obligations to be performed.

39. A In most states, leases for less than one year do not have to be in writing.

40. D An assignment is the transfer of rights and duties from one person to another person.

41. D The primary purpose of the agent at the closing is to collect the broker's check.

42. D The expiration date of the listing is generally required by law.

43. B The offer is missing an essential element or the signature of the offeror and is void.

44. B The type of listing contract would least likely be found in a sales contract.

45. A A contract entered into with misrepresentation is voidable by the aggrieved party.

46. D The vendor will most likely retain the title to the property until the final payment is made.

47. A An option is a unilateral contract because only the seller must perform.

48. C An offer can be withdrawn at any time before acceptance. A seller does not have to accept the full list price for the property, but the commission is still due.

49. A By definition of offer and acceptance, mutual assent and meeting of the minds.

50. A When one spouse cannot be present to sign documents, that spouse should create a power of attorney so documents can be properly transferred.

51. A By definition of statute of frauds.

52. A A contract with contingencies is voidable.

53. C In a conventional loan the debt to service ratio is normally 36 percent.

54. D Caveat emptor means let the buyer beware.

55. D A liquidated damage clause is compensation agreed upon in advance if one party breaches the contract.

56. B In a lease option, the buyer leases the property and has the option of purchasing it.

57. A The primary consideration in the lease purchase is the sales price.

58. A If an offer is missing an essential element, it is void. (Not voidable)

59. B *Time is of the essence* means the contract must be performed within the time limit specified.

60. D By definition of estate.

Property Management

This chapter covers the following information regarding property management: services to land-lords and services to tenants. Property management covers both residential real estate and commercial properties. Residential real estate includes single-family homes and multifamily residences, while commercial properties include office and retail properties. Each of these categories has even more detailed classifications. *The topics bracketed by bullet points (•) appear on the broker exam only.*

Content Outline—Contracts and Offers

III. Property Management

    A. Services to Landlords

        1. Marketing property
        2. Evaluating rental market
        3. Obtaining tenants
        4. Screening applicants
        5. Tenant complaints and conflicts among tenants
        6. Income, expenses and rate of return for property
        7. Fees, security deposits and rent collection
        8. Negotiating property management agreements
        9. Environmental and safety hazards
      10. • Operating budgets •
      11. • Trust accounts •
      12. • Owners' financial statements •

MARKETING PROPERTY

A property manager can choose from a range of advertising media to reach a target audience. This could include a sign on the property identifying the management firm and the person to call for further information; newspaper advertising, regional magazines and trade journals, radio, television, direct mail and brochures.

EVALUATING RENTAL MARKET

A market is created when two or more people meet for the purpose of selling or leasing a commodity. These transactions occur at a national, regional or local level. A property manager must be able to evaluate market trends or supply and demand cycles to determine the rent that may be charged.

This would include supply and demand, local economic conditions, as well as a neighborhood market analysis.

Regional Market Analysis

A regional market analysis should include demographic and economic information in the area where the property is located. This information includes population statistics, income and employment data, a description of transportation facilities and supply and demand trends.

Neighborhood Market Analysis

Property managers rely on a neighborhood market analysis because much of their business may be generated at a local level. The major areas in the neighborhood market analysis are boundaries and land usage, transportation and utilities, economy, supply and demand and neighborhood amenities and facilities.

Once the regional and neighborhood market surveys are complete, the property manager analyzes the data to determine the special features of his or her property and how it fits the needs of potential tenants.

OBTAINING TENANTS

The best method of renting property is to secure referrals from satisfied tenants. Many times an owner will pay cash or rental incentives (concessions) to current tenants for such referrals. Press releases sent to local newspapers and brokers may gain free publicity for the property when leasing new or large developments. The interest also provides a new media for advertising and obtaining tenants.

SCREENING APPLICANTS

One of the first areas of qualification of potential tenants must be in meeting a tenant's needs as far as space requirements are concerned. The needs would be totally different for a residential tenant than for a commercial tenant.

Tenant Considerations

- Motives for moving
- When the current lease expires
- Parking and transportation needs
- Any special needs of the tenant
- Projected budget for the new space

In negotiating a commercial lease the property manager must be sure that the person being interviewed has the authority to negotiate contracts for the company. This can be accomplished by asking for a copy of the articles of incorporation or partnership agreement.

Each prospective tenant should be required to fill out a lease application. For residential tenants, credit references, personal references and rental history must be secured and checked by the property manager. For commercial property, a profit and loss statement of the company should demonstrate that the company is financially sound. All federal laws such as fair housing and the Americans with Disabilities Act must be obeyed when screening applicants.

TENANT COMPLAINTS AND CONFLICTS AMONG TENANTS

A property manager establishes communication with a prospective tenant during the initial interviewing process. This communication continues and is strengthened during the screening and the negotiation of the lease. Complaints that constitute an emergency would be handled immediately, while other complaints should be resolved in compliance with the lease.

Tenants must know that they cannot use their space in such a way as to infringe on the rights of others and that noncompliance with building rules, violations of the law or any activities that disrupt other tenants are grounds for eviction.

INCOME, EXPENSES AND RATE OF RETURN FOR PROPERTY

In developing a management plan for the owner, a property manager must include an operating budget for the property. The optimum rents for the property must be determined by the manager and adjustments made to reflect the specific advantages and disadvantages of the property.

Next, the manager computes the gross rental income of the property. The gross income of an apartment complex may be based on the room count of the space, whereas commercial properties may be computed by the square footage of the space. Projected vacancy rates and rent losses are subtracted from the gross rent, and the manager then adds income from other sources to arrive at the anticipated income of the property for the year.

Expenses such as real estate taxes, salaries, utilities, supplies, maintenance, repairs, insurance, administrative costs, management fees and reserve funds are deducted to compute the net operating income before debt service. The debt service is subtracted to determine the before-tax cash flow of the property.

In summary, the basic formula used by property managers is

$$
\begin{array}{l}
\text{Potential gross income} \\
-\ \text{Vacancy and rent loss} \\
+\ \text{Additional income} \\
\hline
\text{Total anticipated revenue} \\
-\ \text{Expenses} \\
\hline
\text{Net operating income before debt} \\
\text{service} \\
-\ \text{Debt service} \\
\hline
\text{Before-tax cash flow} \\
-\ \text{Taxes} \\
\hline
\text{After-tax cash flow}
\end{array}
$$

The return on investment (ROI) is one way to measure the profitability of a property. The ROI is the ratio of the property's after-tax cash flow (ATCF) to the money invested (**equity** [E]) in the property. The formula for computing the return on investment is

$$
\text{ROI} \ = \ \frac{\text{ATCF}}{\text{E}} \ \times \ 100\%
$$

The ROI also may be computed on a before-tax basis.

A property with a $10,000 ATCF in which the owner has $100,000 invested would have an ROI of 10 percent. When this formula is used to analyze the owner's investment, it is called a *cash-on-cash investment.*

FEES, SECURITY DEPOSITS AND RENT COLLECTION

Fees

The owner and the property manager negotiate the relationship between them. This relationship can be employer-employee, principal-agent or trustor-trustee. A written management agreement between the parties stipulates whether payment is to be on a flat-fee basis or percentage of the gross income. Whichever relationship or method of payment is negotiated, the property manager still has a fiduciary relationship with the owner.

The property manager must also be aware of state laws regarding the limitation on the fee charged for rent application, credit reports, security deposits and late payment penalties that can be charged.

SECURITY DEPOSITS

Property managers must be aware of state laws regulating **security deposits.** These laws could include identifying the deposit in the lease, the bank and account number where the security deposit is located, the limit of the deposit to be collected, the interest that must be paid and the procedure for the return and deduction of the deposit.

Rent

Rent is paid in advance, usually on the first of the month, and the property manager must know state and local laws regarding eviction procedures as they relate to rent. The lease agreement should specify the day the rent is due, the grace period and the late fee and when eviction procedures will begin. If a lease agreement does not specify the due date, then rent is due at the end of the leasing period.

Rent control is a regulation by the state or local government agencies restricting the amount of rent landlords can charge their tenants. The primary purpose of rent control was to remedy high rents caused by the imbalance between supply and demand in housing.

NEGOTIATING PROPERTY MANAGEMENT AGREEMENTS

A written management agreement is negotiated between the owner and the person or firm that will manage the property. States may have specific laws regarding such agreements, but generally the following must be included to establish the scope of the agent's authority:

- Identification of the parties
- Legal description of the property

FIGURE 3.1 *Maintenance*

Preventive maintenance—preserves the physical building and eliminates costly problems before major repairs become necessary

Corrective maintenance—fulfills the owner's responsibilities to the tenant by keeping the building's equipment, utilities and amenities functioning properly

Routine maintenance—includes routine housekeeping, such as maintenance of the common areas and grounds, and maintaining the physical cleanliness of the building itself

New construction maintenance—occurs to meet the needs of a tenant, and could be something as simple as installing new carpeting or as complex as upgrading or remodeling the property to meet the tenant's needs

---

- Statement of owner's purpose
- Duties and responsibilities of the manager
- Responsibilities of the owner
- Rate and schedule of compensation
- Accounting and report requirements
- Starting date, termination date and provisions for renewal options
- Amount and method of determining the minimum security deposit to be collected from the tenants for each unit managed
- Procedure for returning or retaining the security deposit
- Provision setting forth the conditions under which the manager is authorized to pay expenses of the property being managed
- Signatures of the parties

ENVIRONMENTAL AND SAFETY HAZARDS

Property managers must have a working knowledge of hazardous substances and wastes and the laws regulating owners. A hazardous *waste* is a byproduct of a manufactured item, while a hazardous *substance* may include everyday items such as household cleaning products and paint. The Environmental Protection Agency (EPA) was established to centralize the federal government's environmental responsibilities.

The hazardous substances that a property manager most likely will come in contact with are asbestos, radon, contents of underground storage tanks, urea formaldehyde, polychlorinated biphenyls (PCBs) and lead paint.

• OPERATING BUDGETS •

An operating budget is based on the anticipated revenues and expenses. When the property manager develops the budget, it must reflect the owner's long-term goals. The budget will allocate money for continuous, fixed expenses such as employees' salaries, property taxes, and insurance. It will also establish a cash reserve fund for variable expenses such as repairs and supplies.

· TRUST ACCOUNTS ·

Property managers are required to maintain escrow or trust accounts in which security deposits are placed. Laws vary by state, but usually these accounts must be separate from business and personal accounts. The tenants are usually informed of the bank and the account number where their security deposits are located. State laws also regulate the disbursement of security deposits.

· OWNERS' FINANCIAL STATEMENTS ·

A property manager sends the owner a monthly report of income and expenses. Quarterly, semiannual or annual profit and loss statements are compiled from these monthly reports. From this, the owner can analyze how the property was managed, decide what changes should be made and make projections for the next year.

Only the interest portion of each mortgage payment should be deducted as an expense on the profit and loss statement, whereas on the monthly reports the entire debt service is used.

The following is an example of a profit and loss statement:

Profit and Loss Statement
Period: January 1, XXXX to December 31, XXXX

Receipts	$198,948.43
Operating Expenses	– 74,343.89
Operating Income	$124,604.54
Total Mortgage Payment	– 54,567.89
Mortgage Loan Principal Add-Back	+ 6,493.20
Net Profit	$ 76,529.85

The profit and loss statement may be compared with the operating budget that was prepared for the year. Such a comparison can measure the performance of the property manager and determine the changes that will need to be made in the future.

Services to Landlords—Key Point Review

1. The property manager can advertise in newspapers, regional magazines, trade journals, radio, television, direct mail and brochures.

2. The objectives of a property manager are to generate the highest net operating income while maintaining the property.

3. In screening an applicant, one of the first areas of qualification must be in meeting the space requirements of a prospective tenant.

4. Tenants should be aware that they cannot use their space in such a way as to infringe on the rights of others in the building or the community.

5. The property manager will develop an operating budget. The manager must determine the optimum rents for the property and make adjustments to reflect its advantages and disadvantages.

Services to Landlords—Key Point Review (Continued)

6. The return on investment (ROI) is the ratio of the property's net income after taxes (ATCF), to the money invested (equity) in the property. The ROI also may be computed on a before-tax basis.

7. A property owner must file the proper federal and state income tax reports with the appropriate government agencies.

8. Owners are responsible for keeping the property habitable and for complying with local building and housing codes.

9. Preventive maintenance preserves the physical building and eliminates costly problems before major repairs become necessary.

10. Corrective maintenance includes keeping the building's equipment, utilities and amenities functioning properly.

11. Routine maintenance includes maintenance of the common areas and grounds, and the physical cleanliness of the building.

12. New construction maintenance occurs to meet the needs of the tenant, such as installing new carpeting or remodeling the property.

13. The relationship between the property manager and the owner can be an employer-employee, principal-agent, or trustor-trustee. A written management agreement should stipulate if the compensation will be paid on a flat-fee basis or as a percentage-of-the-gross income.

14. Property managers must be aware of state laws regulating security deposits.

15. The property manager's rights and responsibilities should be specified in the property management agreement.

16. A property manager sends the owner a monthly report of income and expenses. Periodical profit and loss statements are compiled from these monthly reports to enable the owner to analyze how the property was managed, decide what changes should be made and make projections for the year.

17. Only the interest portion of each mortgage payment should be deducted as an expense on the profit and loss statement.

18. Comparing the profit and loss statement with the operating budget prepared for the year measures the performance of the property manager and determines the changes that need to be made.

19. Property managers must have a working knowledge of hazardous substances and wastes and the laws regulating owners. A hazardous waste is a byproduct of a manufactured item; a hazardous substance may include everyday items such as household cleaning products.

Services to Landlords—Key Point Review (Continued)

20. Asbestos or asbestos-containing material formerly was used in the manufacture of flame-proof building materials and for heat insulation.

21. Radon is an invisible, odorless and tasteless radioactive gas produced by the natural decay of radioactive substances.

22. Underground storage tanks are commonly found on sites where petroleum products have been or are being used. Underground storage tanks may leak toxic products, which can contaminate groundwater.

23. Urea formaldehyde, used in building materials, reacts to high temperatures and emits a poisonous gas when burned.

24. Property managers should investigate transformers and electrical equipment to determine the leakage of Polychlorinated Biphenyls (PCBs). If necessary they must secure the services of local electrical utility experts to remove the PCBs.

25. The property manager must be aware of federal, state and local laws regarding lead paint in rental properties.

26. The property manager has a fiduciary relationship with the owner. The primary goals of a property manager are to generate for the owner the highest net operating income while maintaining the property.

Content Outline—Services to Tenants

III. Property Management

    B. Services to Tenants

        1. Lease agreements used in property management
        2. Rental and lease agreements
        3. Material facts
        4. Showing property to prospective tenants
        5. Occupancy terms
        6. Proration of rents and leases

LEASE AGREEMENTS USED IN PROPERTY MANAGEMENT

A **lease** is an agreement that transfers exclusive possession and use of real estate from the landlord/owner/lessor to the tenant/lessee. This lease agreement can be oral or written. The owner has a **reversionary right** to retake the property on the expiration of the terms of the lease. Figure 3.3 lists the various types of leases used in property management.

FIGURE 3.2 Types of Leases—Nonfreehold Estates

Estate for Years or Tenancy for Years
- A lease with a definite time period or specified beginning and ending dates.
- No notice is needed to terminate the estate.
- A tenant who remains in possession after expiration is considered a holdover.

Estate from Period to Period/Periodic Tenancy
- A lease with an indefinite time period that automatically renews until proper notice to terminate is given.

Estate at Will or Tenancy at Will
- A lease that gives the tenant the right to possess the property with the consent of the landlord for an uncertain time period. The lease can be terminated at any time by the landlord or the tenant giving proper notice to the other party.
- Death of either party also terminates the lease.

Estate at Sufferance or Tenancy at Sufferance
- A tenancy created when a tenant remains in possession of the property without the consent of the landlord after the lease expires.
- If the landlord gives permission to a tenant to remain on the property after the expiration of a lease, the tenant may be treated as a holdover, and a tenancy at will or periodic tenancy may be created.

RENTAL AND LEASE AGREEMENTS

The lessor's interest is called a **leased fee interest,** and the lessee's interest is called a **leasehold interest.** By an implied covenant of quiet enjoyment, the lessor guarantees that the lessee has exclusive possession and the landlord will not interfere with the tenant's possession or use of the property.

Owners are responsible for keeping the property habitable and for complying with local building and housing codes. These responsibilities include the upkeep of common areas and of electrical, heating and plumbing systems; trash removal; maintenance of elevators; and any other services promised in the lease.

The provisions of a valid lease are essentially the same as for any valid contract. A valid lease *must* have

- offer and acceptance,
- consideration,
- capacity to contract,
- legal objectives, and
- a description of the premises.

Other provisions include the use of the premises, term of the lease, safekeeping and return of the security deposit, improvements to the property, maintenance of the premises, condemnation clause, compliance clause (which party is responsible for complying with any new local, state or federal regulations), insurance clause, noncompliance clause, renewals and increases, expansion options, and responsibilities of the landlord and the tenant.

Assignment

Leases can be assigned or subleased unless there is a clause in the lease forbidding it. (See Figure 3.3.) A tenant who transfers *all* the leasehold interests *assigns* the lease. For example, the lessor executes a 20-year commercial lease with the lessee. Ten years into the lease, the business is sold. The new owner of the business (assignee) will be assigned all the leasehold interests. The previous owner of the business may not be released of liability for making the rental payments.

FIGURE 3.3 *Assignment versus Subletting*

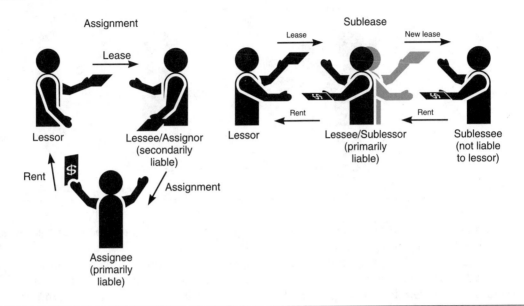

However, the landlord does expect payment from the new tenant (assignee), and will pursue the previous tenant (assignor) as a last resort.

Sublease

A sublease is created when a tenant transfers less than all the leasehold interests by subleasing them to a new tenant. In this arrangement, there are two landlord-tenant relationships. For example, the lessor enters into a one-year lease on an apartment with a lessee. Six months into the lease, the tenant is transferred and decides to sublease the apartment. The original lease agreement between the lessor and lessee remains, with a landlord-tenant relationship; a landlord-tenant relationship also is created between the lessee and the sublessee.

The lessor expects a rent check from the lessee, and the lessee (sublessor) expects a rent check from the sublessee. The sublessor can charge more rent and retain the profit. The sublessor's interest is called a *sandwich lease*.

Other types of leases are:

- **lease option**—The tenant has the option to purchase the property at a specified price within a certain time. A portion of the monthly rental payment may be credited toward the purchase price.
- **lease purchase**—The tenant agrees to purchase the property at a specified price within a certain period, which is usually the end of the lease.
- **gross, or straight, lease**—The tenant pays a fixed rental amount, and the owner pays all other ownership expenses for the property. The owner usually pays property taxes, insurance and maintenance, while the tenant pays for the utilities.
- **net lease**—The tenant agrees to pay ownership expenses, usually utilities, property taxes and special assessments. In a net-net lease the tenant pays for insurance as well. In a net-net-net lease, the tenant also pays for some agreed-on items of repair and maintenance. Thus, the terms *net, double net* and *triple net* can be used to describe the lease, depending on the ownership expenses the tenant agrees to pay.
- **percentage lease** (used for retail space)—The tenant agrees to pay a fixed base rental fee plus a percentage of the gross income in excess of a predetermined minimum amount of sales. The

---

FIGURE 3.4 *Sale-Leaseback*

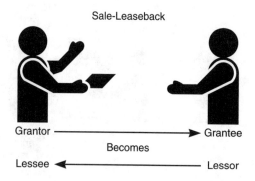

Sale-Leaseback

Grantor ——————————————→ Grantee

Becomes

Lessee ←—————————————— Lessor

---

percentage lease also can be computed from the first dollar of sales. See Chapter 7 to learn how to compute the rent paid in a percentage lease.

- **sale-leaseback**—The grantor sells the property to the grantee, and then leases it back. (See Figure 3.4.) For example, a buyer wants to purchase a unit being used as a model in a new condominium development. The developer had intended to use the unit as a model for the next six months. The developer and buyer enter into a sale-leaseback. The developer/owner/grantor sells the property to the buyer/grantee. When the sales transaction is complete, the grantee becomes the lessor and leases the property to the previous owner, the developer, who becomes the lessee. The developer has the property to use as a model for the next six months and the buyer has the condo she wants.

- **graduated lease**—The graduated lease is used to attract tenants to a property that is difficult to rent. It allows for a periodic step-up of rent payments. For example, tenants enter into a five-year lease in which they agree to pay $400 a month for the first two years, $450 for the next two years and $500 for the final year.

- **index lease**—The rent is tied to an index outside the control of both the landlord and the tenant. Index leases contain an **escalation clause** that allows the lease payment to change based on the index used, for example, the consumer price index. Index leases are more common in times of inflation, when the property manager does *not* want to enter into long-term fixed rentals that would cause the value of the property to decrease.

Termination of Leases

Leases may be terminated by the expiration of the term of the lease, proper notice as defined in the lease, surrender and acceptance, abandonment, merger, or destruction or condemnation of the property.

Death of the lessor or lessee does not terminate a lease. Should the property be sold, the grantee takes the title subject to all existing leases and cannot make any changes until each lease expires, unless the leases indicate otherwise.

Eviction Proceedings

Eviction procedures will vary by state, but the proper procedure must be followed by the property manager. A tenant is usually evicted or ejected because of nonpayment of rent, unlawful use of the premises or noncompliance with health and safety codes.

Actual eviction is when the landlord files a suit for possession because the tenant has breached the lease. **Constructive eviction** is when the landlord breaches the lease and the tenant must leave the premises because they have become uninhabitable.

MATERIAL FACTS

Even though the property manager has a fiduciary relationship with the owner, the manager must disclose to the tenant material facts that would affect the lease.

SHOWING PROPERTY TO PROSPECTIVE TENANTS

When the spatial needs have been determined and the prospective tenant has been qualified, the property manager should show property that best meets the needs of the prospective tenant. While showing the property, the manager describes the benefits of the space, building and neighborhood as they meet the tenant's needs. The manager should show the prospective tenant a range of space that would meet his or her needs (but be careful not to show too much space and complicate the decision-making process). Objections must be handled with diplomacy.

OCCUPANCY TERMS

The occupancy terms to be negotiated include concessions, rent schedules, rebates, length of the leasing period, tenant alterations, expansion options, noncompeting tenant restrictions and the defraying of moving expenses. The property manager must negotiate these terms to meet the needs of both the owner and the tenant.

Once the lease agreement has been negotiated, the landlord must give exclusive possession of the property to the tenant. The **covenant of quiet enjoyment** means the landlord must honor the tenants' right of possession and may not enter the property without the tenant's permission unless it is an emergency, to provide services or make repairs, or other unusual circumstances.

The **warranty of habitability** requires the landlord to keep the property in good condition. This would include maintenance of the common areas and equipment, providing utilities and being in compliance with state and local codes.

The tenant is obligated to use appliances in a safe manner and to keep the property in good repair.

PRORATION OF RENTS AND LEASES

On the sale of the property, the current owner is required to prorate the rent collected to the new owner of the property. See Chapter 7 for calculating the proration of rent.

Services to Tenants—Key Point Review

1. A lease gives the tenant the right to exclusive occupancy of the property and is considered personal property.

2. An estate for years, or a tenancy for years, has a definite time period—for years, months or days—and no notice is needed to terminate. When the ending date arrives, the tenant is to vacate the premises and surrender the property.

3. An estate from period to period, or periodic tenancy, has an indefinite time period; it automatically renews until proper notice is given. This tenancy can be month to month, week to week or year to year.

4. An estate at will gives the tenant the right to possess the property with the consent of the landlord for an uncertain period. The lease can be terminated at any time either by the landlord or the tenant giving proper notice or by death of either party.

5. An estate at sufferance is created when, without the consent of the landlord, a tenant remains in possession of the property after the lease expires. If the landlord gives permission to a tenant to remain on the property, a holdover tenancy may be created.

6. A lease agreement can be oral or written. The owners' right to retake the property after the expiration of the lease is a reversionary right. Oral leases are unenforceable.

7. The lessor's interest is called a *leased fee interest,* and the lessee's interest is called a *leasehold interest.*

8. By an implied covenant of quiet enjoyment, the lessor guarantees that the lessee has exclusive possession and the landlord will not interfere with the tenant's possession or use of the property.

9. The essentials of a valid lease are essentially the same as those of a valid contract. Other terms include the use of the premises; term of the lease; provisions for the management of the security deposit; provisions for making improvements to and maintaining the premises; condemnation, compliance, insurance, noncompliance clauses; renewals and increases; and responsibilities of the landlord and the tenant.

10. A tenant is usually evicted because of nonpayment of rent, unlawful use of the premises or noncompliance with health and safety codes. Filing a suit for possession is known as actual eviction.

11. When the landlord breaches the lease agreement, the tenant may sue for constructive eviction, but the tenant must first leave the premises.

Services to Tenants—Key Point Review

12. A tenant who transfers all the leasehold interests assigns the lease, creating a new landlord-tenant relationship between the lessor and the assignee. The lessor now expects payment from the assignee.

13. A sublease is created when a tenant transfers less than all the leasehold interests to a new tenant. In this arrangement, there are two landlord-tenant relationships: the original lease agreement between the lessor and lessee, and a landlord-tenant relationship between the lessee and the sublessee. The lessee can charge more rent and keep the profit. The lease between the sublessor and the sublessee is called a *sandwich lease.*

14. In a lease option, the tenant has the option to purchase a property at a specified price within a certain period. A portion of the monthly rental payment may be credited toward the purchase price.

15. In a lease purchase, the tenant agrees to purchase the property at a specified price within a certain period, usually the end of the lease.

16. In a gross, or straight, lease the tenant pays a fixed rental amount and the owner pays all other ownership expenses for the property. The tenant normally pays for utilities.

17. The tenant who enters into a net lease agrees to pay ownership expenses such as property taxes, insurance and maintenance.

18. In a percentage lease, a commercial tenant agrees to pay a fixed base rental fee plus a percentage of the gross income in excess of a predetermined minimum amount of sales.

19. In a sale-leaseback, the grantor sells the property to the grantee and then leases it back.

20. A graduated lease allows for a periodic step-up of rent payments and may be used to attract tenants to a property that is difficult to rent.

21. In times of inflation, the property manager may negotiate an index lease, wherein the rent is tied to an index outside the control of either the landlord or the tenant. Index leases contain an escalation clause that allows the lease payment to change based on the index.

22. Leases may be terminated by the expiration of the term of the lease, proper notice as defined in the lease, surrender and acceptance, abandonment, merger, or destruction or condemnation of the property. The death of the lessor or lessee does not terminate a lease.

23. Should the property be sold, the grantee takes the title subject to all existing leases and cannot make any changes until each lease expires.

24. The occupancy terms include concessions, rent schedules, rebates, length of the leasing period, tenant alterations, expansion options, noncompeting tenant restrictions and the defraying of moving expenses. The property manager must negotiate these terms to meet the needs of both the owner and the tenant.

Questions

1. In assuming responsibility for the maintenance of a property, the manager is expected to do which of the following?

   A. Directly or indirectly supervise the routine cleaning and repair work of the building

   B. Execute an inverse severance contract

   C. Review all housing disclosure reports

   D. Approve all exchange agreements

2. A property manager works for the BEST interest of

   A. the tenants.

   B. the owner.

   C. the banker.

   D. government authorities.

3. A management agreement usually covers which of the following items?

   A. Authorization of payment of expenses

   B. Estoppel certificates

   C. Joint and several liability

   D. Waiver of subrogation

4. Cheryl leases a retail space to conduct her bookstore business and installs built-in bookcases. The built-in bookcases will become the property of the landlord

   A. automatically because they are considered permanent fixtures.

   B. on the expiration of the lease, if they are still attached to the property.

   C. only if removal will cause damage to the property.

   D. automatically on the expiration of the lease.

5. The landlord of tenant Carl has sold his building to the state so that an expressway can be built. Carl's lease expires, but the landlord is letting him remain until some unknown time when the building will be torn down. Carl continues to pay the same rent as was prescribed in his lease. What is Carl's tenancy called?

   A. Tenancy by the entireties

   B. Month-to-month tenancy

   C. Tenancy at sufferance

   D. Tenancy at will

6. The manager of a commercial building carries out many duties in connection with its operation and maintenance. The manager is usually the agent of the

   A. lessor of the building.

   B. lessee in the building.

   C. lessor and lessee.

   D. trustee.

7. Hobart entered into a five year lease agreement. The premises have become too small for Hobart's business. Marcia is interested in possessing the premises for three years, and paying Hobart directly. Which of the following agreements would Hobart and Marcia execute to effect Marcia's wishes?

   A. Assignment

   B. Novation

   C. Sublease

   D. Tenancy at sufferance

8. A property manager normally is charged with all of the following duties EXCEPT

   A. renting space to tenants.

   B. preparing a budget.

   C. developing a management plan.

   D. repairing a tenant's fixture.

9. Brenda is a tenant under an estate for years lease agreement. Under such an estate

   A. the term of the lease must be for at least one year.

   B. the lease will have a definite beginning and ending.

   C. a 30-day notice is required to terminate the lease.

   D. the lease is classified as a freehold estate.

10. A tenant and a property manager just executed a lease that begins on April 15, 2001, and ends on April 15, 2003. This lease is BEST described as a(n)

   A. estate for years.

   B. tenancy at will.

   C. periodic tenancy.

   D. estate from year to year.

11. Which of the following is the MOST IMPOR-
TANT record kept by the property manager?
    A. Accounting report of income and expenses
    B. Tenants' complaints
    C. Property manager's personal expense
       account
    D. Utilities paid by the property manager

12. The tenant has agreed to pay a fixed monthly
rent, a portion of the property taxes and maintenance on a 1,200-square-foot retail space in
a mall. This lease is BEST described as a
    A. percentage lease.
    B. gross lease.
    C. net lease.
    D. retail lease.

13. George leased a property to a college student.
The lease was to expire on May 15. On May
16, George visited the property and discovered that the student was still residing in the
apartment and hadn't even started packing.
The student offered George a check for the
next month's rent. Which of the following
BEST describes this situation?
    A. The tenant is a trespasser and George may
       physically remove him from the property
       without any notice.
    B. The lease agreement is converted to an
       estate for years unless George refuses the
       check.
    C. An estate at sufferance is created if George
       refuses to accept the check.
    D. A tenancy by the entireties is created if
       George accepts the check.

14. Which of the following would a property
manager LEAST LIKELY do?
    A. Screen and qualify tenants
    B. Place security deposits in the proper
       escrow account
    C. Accept a rebate from a service provider
    D. Negotiate a lease and present it to the
       owner for approval

15. Regarding a sublease, all of the following are
true EXCEPT the
    A. sublessor's interest is called a *sandwich
       lease.*
    B. lessee has a leased fee interest and the
       lessor has a leasehold interest in the
       property.
    C. sublessor may charge a higher rent to the
       sublessee and make a profit on the lease.
    D. lessor expects the agreed-upon rental
       payment from the sublessor.

16. Regarding an assignment, all of the following
are false EXCEPT
    A. the lease between the assignor and the
       assignee is called a *transfer lease.*
    B. when the lease has been assigned, the
       lessee then expects payment from the
       assignee.
    C. the assignor transferred all the leasehold
       interests in the lease.
    D. when the lease has been assigned, there is a
       new landlord-tenant relationship between
       the lessor and the assignor.

17. Which of the following is the BEST method
for attracting tenants to a property?
    A. Cooperating with brokers in the area
    B. Developing an advertising campaign
    C. Having press releases published in the
       local newspapers to create publicity
    D. Securing referrals from satisfied tenants

18. Harry has entered into a property management agreement with Sterling Properties, Inc.
Harry's agreement MOST LIKELY stipulates
that he will be paid a percentage of
    A. last year's net income.
    B. this year's potential income.
    C. this year's gross income.
    D. last year's gross income.

19. Which of the following criteria is the MOST
IMPORTANT for a property manager to use
to qualify and screen a potential tenant?
    A. The space requirements, financial history
       and projected moving date
    B. Having lunch with the owner of the
       potential tenant's company
    C. Any special needs of the potential tenant
    D. The parking needs of the potential tenant

20. A percentage lease would MOST LIKELY be negotiated in all of the following spaces EXCEPT a(n)

    A. duplex.
    B. apparel shop.
    C. gasoline station.
    D. convenient mart.

21. Which of the following is LEAST LIKELY to terminate a lease agreement?

    A. The property is taken by eminent domain.
    B. The life tenant who had leased the property dies.
    C. The lessor sells the property.
    D. The lessee buys the land from the lessor.

22. A time-share lease is MOST LIKELY a

    A. freehold tenancy at will.
    B. freehold tenancy at sufferance.
    C. nonfreehold periodic tenancy.
    D. nonfreehold estate for years.

23. Which of the following would LEAST LIKELY be necessary for a one-year lease to be enforceable?

    A. Notarization and recording of the lease
    B. Signature of the party authorized to perform
    C. Sufficient property description
    D. Consideration and term of the lease

24. The mayor rented an entertainment hall from April 30 to May 3. What type of leasehold estate does she have?

    A. Estate at sufferance
    B. Estate from year to year
    C. Estate at will
    D. Estate for years

25. What is the BEST way for a property manager to minimize problems with a tenant?

    A. To talk with the tenant about his or her conduct
    B. To tell the tenant to ask the other tenants how to behave
    C. To discuss and give a copy of the rules and regulations to the tenant
    D. To say nothing until there is a problem

26. A lease will MOST LIKELY be considered a(n)

    A. unilateral contract.
    B. bilateral contract.
    C. voidable contract.
    D. exculpatory contract.

27. The responsibilities of upkeep of the common areas, cleanliness of the buildings and maintenance of the grounds BEST describes

    A. routine maintenance.
    B. preventive maintenance.
    C. corrective maintenance.
    D. new construction maintenance.

28. The primary goals of a property manager are to

    A. generate the highest net operating income for the owner while maintaining the investment.
    B. generate the highest gross income for the owner while maintaining the investment.
    C. negotiate the lowest rent possible for the lessee while providing as many amenities as possible.
    D. negotiate the highest rent possible for the lessor while providing as many amenities as possible.

29. Who is accountable for keeping the property habitable and for complying with local building and housing codes?

    A. Lessee
    B. Lessor
    C. Buyer
    D. Agent

30. A net lease usually includes payment by the lessee for all of the following EXCEPT

    A. property taxes.
    B. debt service.
    C. insurance.
    D. maintenance.

31. A lease agreement stipulates that the landlord is responsible for paying the water bill. The tenant came home one afternoon and discovered the water had been turned off. If the tenant chooses to leave the premises, this would be called

    A. constructive eviction.
    B. actual eviction.
    C. landlord eviction.
    D. tenant eviction.

32. The landlord's interests and rights in leased property are known as a

    A. leasehold interest.
    B. leased fee interest.
    C. leased indefeasible interest.
    D. leased defeasible interest.

33. In a lease agreement, the landlord guarantees that the lessee has exclusive possession of the property and that the landlord will not interfere with the tenant's possession or use of the property. This is known as the covenant of
    A. seisen.
    B. possession and use.
    C. warranty forever.
    D. quiet enjoyment.

34. In a sale-leaseback, the grantor becomes the
    A. lessor.
    B. lessee.
    C. new owner.
    D. landlord.

35. Which of the following would NOT be in a property management agreement?
    A. The duties and responsibilities of the manager and the owner
    B. The conditions under which the manager is authorized to pay expenses of the property being managed
    C. Starting date, termination date and provisions for renewal options
    D. The amount and method of determining the good-faith deposit to be collected from the tenants for each unit managed

36. Which of the following is a responsibility of the property manager to the tenants that does NOT violate his or her responsibility to the owner?
    A. Development of an operating budget
    B. Supervision of routine maintenance of the property
    C. Filing of proper federal and state income tax reports
    D. Accounting for security deposits

37. All of the following would MOST LIKELY be negotiated between the owner and the property manager in the management agreement EXCEPT the
    A. name of a tenant who just signed a 20-year lease with the owner.
    B. duties and responsibilities of the manager.
    C. beginning and termination dates of the contract and provisions for renewal.
    D. rate and schedule of compensation.

38. A property manager must take which of the following into consideration to determine the net operating income a property produces?
    A. Debt service
    B. IRS taxes
    C. After-tax cash flow
    D. Vacancy and rent loss

39. To compute the return on investment, a property manager must
    A. divide the before-tax cash flow by the after-cash tax flow.
    B. multiply the before-tax cash flow by the after-cash tax flow.
    C. divide the after-tax cash flow by the equity and multiply by 100 percent.
    D. multiply the after-tax cash flow by the equity and divide by 100 percent.

40. An agent has become a manager of a property that is difficult to lease. Which of the following leases would she MOST LIKELY use to secure a contract with a prospective tenant?
    A. Percentage lease
    B. Graduated lease
    C. Sublease
    D. Gross lease

41. The primary purpose of a profit and loss statement is to analyze
    A. how the property was managed, what changes should be made and projections for the new year.
    B. if the property manager did a good job of following the operating budget.
    C. the ratio of the operating expenses to the operating income.
    D. the ratio of the rate of return to the debt service.

42. On a profit and loss statement, all of the following are entered EXCEPT
    A. mortgage loan principal add-back.
    B. receipts.
    C. operating expenses.
    D. property manager's compensation.

43. What do asbestos, radon and urea formaldehyde all have in common?
    A. They are classified as environmental hazards, and a property manager must be aware of the identification and effect of them.
    B. They are all classified as hazardous substances.
    C. They are all produced as a result of the natural decay of radioactive substances.
    D. They are classified as environmental hazards, but a property manager need not be concerned about the effect of any such substances.

44. All of the following are grounds for actual eviction EXCEPT
    A. nonpayment of rent.
    B. unlawful use of the premises.
    C. the lessor's breach of the lease.
    D. the tenant's noncompliance with health and safety codes.

45. An operating budget allowed $2,500 for the property manager to buy new carpet. The property manager can negotiate a contract with a carpet company
    A. to purchase carpet for the property, as well as his or her personal residence, all billed to the owner.
    B. to purchase carpet for the property and accept a rebate from the carpet company.
    C. if given that authorization in her or his employment contract.
    D. only after securing sealed bids from at least three companies.

46. KMK Law Firm just agreed to lease a space in downtown Cincinnati for the next 20 years. Which of the following terms BEST describes KMK's interest in the property?
    A. Tenant's interest
    B. Reversionary interest
    C. Leasehold interest
    D. Leased fee interest

47. Mr. Meade just offered to purchase an occupied fourplex. Should his offer be accepted, which of the following is true regarding the current leases?
    A. The leases will be void.
    B. The leases will be unaffected.
    C. The lessee can cancel the leases.
    D. The lessor can raise the rent.

48. Which of the following would NOT be a factor in the development of a marketing plan by the property manager?
    A. Supply and demand
    B. Local economic conditions
    C. Location of the property
    D. Availability of good maintenance employees

49. The ABC Company agreed to lease a space for ten years. Five years later, ABC sold its company to XYZ. If the lease contains no provision regarding an assignment, ABC may
    A. assign the leasehold interest to XYZ.
    B. not assign the leasehold interest to XYZ under any circumstances.
    C. assign the leasehold interest to XYZ on the approval of its attorney.
    D. not assign the leasehold interest, but they may sublease the space to XYZ.

50. Which of the following is an environmental hazard associated with leakage near electrical equipment?
    A. Urea formaldehyde
    B. Radon
    C. Polychlorinated biphenyls (PCBs)
    D. Asbestos

51. All of the following occupancy terms are negotiated between a property manager and a prospective tenant EXCEPT
    A. expansion options.
    B. length of the leasing period.
    C. tenant alterations.
    D. the owner's profit.

52. The duties and responsibilities of a property manager would be LEAST LIKELY to include which of the following?
    A. Investing profits generated by the property for the owner
    B. Supervising the remodeling of the property
    C. Showing the property to prospective tenants
    D. Collecting the rent from current tenants

53. Sandy has shown a prospective tenant an available apartment. Which of the following would NOT be a consideration in qualifying the potential tenant?
    A. Credit history
    B. Race
    C. Space requirements
    D. Personal references

54. Which of the following does NOT normally terminate a lease?
    A. Death of the lessor
    B. Nonpayment of rent
    C. Constructive eviction by the lessee
    D. Condemnation of the property

55. A property manager is developing an operating budget. Which of the following is LEAST LIKELY to be considered an operating expense?
    A. Utility bills
    B. Debt service
    C. Maintenance expenses
    D. Management fees

56. Julie owns a four-plex. She lives in one unit and has an apartment available for rent. She would like for the new tenant to be a non-smoker. Can she advertise for a non-smoking tenant?
    A. Yes, because smokers are not protected by Federal Fair Housing laws
    B. Yes, because the four-plex is owner occupied
    C. No, because it would be discriminatory advertising
    D. No, because only the owner of a duplex can discriminate because of smoking

57. Brian just negotiated a property management agreement with Meade and Associates. The property management agreement
    A. is a personal service contract which terminates upon the death of either party.
    B. creates a special agency relationship.
    C. need not be in writing in most states.
    D. creates a universal agency relationship.

58. Rob is the owner of a 20-unit apartment building. He has just accepted an offer on his property. At closing, the security deposits will be
    A. returned to the tenants by Rob.
    B. prorated between Rob and the new owner.
    C. kept in Rob's name until each tenant leaves.
    D transferred to the new owner.

59. An automatic renewal clause would MOST LIKELY be found in which of the following leases?
    A. Tenancy for years
    B. Periodic tenancy
    C. Estate at will
    D. Estate at sufferance

60. Melanie pays a fixed rental amount and the owner pays all other ownership expenses for the property. The lease agreement they have negotiated is MOST LIKELY a(n)
    A. index lease.
    B. percentage lease.
    C. net lease.
    D. gross lease.

ANSWERS

1. A Being responsible for maintenance is one of the property manager's duties.
2. B The property manager's fiduciary responsibility is to the owner.
3. A The authorization of the payment of the expenses would be a part of the agreement.
4. B The tenant has the right to take trade fixtures before the lease expires, but is expected to leave the property in good repair.
5. D A tenancy at will is a lease in which a person holds or occupies real estate for an uncertain duration, with the permission of the owner.
6. A The lessor is the owner and the property manager is an agent of the owner.
7. C Because less than all the leasehold interest is being conveyed, the parties negotiate a sublease.
8. D The property manager is not responsible for the repair of a tenant's fixture.
9. B An estate for years has a definite duration and no termination is required.
10. A By definition of an estate for years.
11. A An accounting report of income and expenses is used to develop all other reports the manager must provide the owner, including the profit and loss statement.
12. C By the definition of a net lease, the tenant agrees to pay ownership expenses.
13. C The tenant is in possession of the property after the expiration of the lease. George has not accepted the check; therefore, an estate at sufferance is created.
14. C A property manager may not accept a rebate from a service provider, unless the manager had the consent of the owner to do so.
15. B In any lease, the lessor's interest is a leased fee interest and the lessee's interest is a leasehold interest.
16. C In an assignment, all of the leasehold interest is transferred to the assignee.
17. D All the answers provide methods that a property manager can use to attract tenants. However, securing referrals from satisfied tenants is the best method.
18. C Property managers are typically paid a percentage of the gross income.
19. A When qualifying a potential tenant, a property manager must consider many factors. The space requirement, financial history and projected moving date are the most important criteria.
20. A A percentage lease is used in the rental of commercial properties, not a duplex.
21. C When the lessor sells the property, the buyer must abide by the existing lease.
22. D Leases are nonfreehold estates. A time-share lease has a definite duration, making it an estate for years.
23. A Normally, a lease does not have to be notarized and recorded to be enforceable, though most states do have this requirement for long-term leases.
24. D The mayor entered into an estate for years with a definite beginning and ending.
25. C The property manager should discuss and give a copy of the rules and regulations to the tenant to minimize any problems.
26. B A lease is considered to be a bilateral contract wherein both parties are obligated to perform.
27. A By definition of routine maintenance.
28. A The primary goals of a property manager are to generate the highest net operating income on the property while maintaining the owner's investment.
29. B The lessor/owner is responsible for keeping the property habitable and for complying with local building and housing codes. These duties may be delegated to the property manager.
30. B The debt service is not normally paid by the tenant in a net lease.
31. A Constructive eviction is when the landlord does not fulfill his obligations and the tenant leaves the premises.
32. B The landlord's interest is a leased fee (ownership) interest, while the tenant's interest is a leasehold interest.
33. D By definition of covenant of quiet enjoyment as it pertains to leases. The covenant of quiet enjoyment in a deed guarantees that the grantee will have the property free from interference from third parties.

34. B The grantor or seller of the property becomes the lessee or new tenant at the end of the transaction.

35. D A property manager does not collect a good-faith deposit, which is another term for escrow deposit. The manager would collect a security deposit from the tenant.

36. D The security deposit belongs to the tenant, not the owner. Therefore, the primary accountability for the security deposit is to the tenant, but it does not violate the fiduciary relationship with the owner.

37. A The name of a tenant would not be found in the written property management agreement between the owner and the property manager.

38. D Potential gross income
    – Vacancy and rent losses
    + Additional income
    Total anticipated revenue
    - Expenses
    Net operating income before debt service

39. C The return on investment formula is: after-tax cash flow ÷ equity × 100%.

40. B A graduated lease is used to attract tenants to properties that are difficult to lease.

41. A The purpose of a profit and loss statement is to analyze how the property was managed, what changes should be made and projections for the new year.

42. D The property manager's compensation is not entered on a profit and loss statement.

43. A Asbestos, radon and urea formaldehyde are all environmental hazards of which a property manager must be aware.

44. C Actual eviction occurs when the tenant has breached the lease.

45. C The property manager can act only within the scope and authority of the employment contract negotiated with the owner.

46. C KMK is a tenant, and the tenant's interest is best described as a leasehold interest.

47. B When the property is sold, the current leases remain binding and effective.

48. D The marketing plan does not consider the hiring of maintenance employees.

49. A Unless a lease forbids assignment and subleasing, the tenant may do so.

50. C PCBs can be found in electrical equipment.

51. D The owner's profit is not a term negotiated with a tenant.

52. A The property manager does not invest the owner's profit.

53. B The race of a potential tenant is not a consideration of the property manager when negotiating a lease.

54. A The death of the lessor does not affect the lease in any way.

55. B The debt service is not an operating expense.

56. A Smokers are not a protected class under Federal Fair Housing.

57. A A property management agreement is a personal service contract that would create an general agency relationship.

58. D The security deposits would be transferred to the new owner.

59. B A periodic tenancy would have an automatic renewal clause.

60. D In a gross lease the tenant pays a fixed rent, and the owner pays all ownership expenses.

4

Settlement/Transfer of Ownership

This chapter covers the following information regarding settlement and the transfer of ownership: tax issues, titles, settlement procedures, characteristics of real property and additional services. *The topics bracketed by bullet points (•) appear on the broker exam only.*

Content Outline—Tax Issues

IV. Settlement/Transfer of Ownership

    A. Tax Issues

        1. Real property taxation

        2. Tax terminology

REAL PROPERTY TAXES

Real property taxes are **ad valorem taxes.** *Ad valorem* is Latin, meaning "according to valuation." Property taxes are computed on the assessed valuation of each property. To review the formulas for computing property taxes, see page 174.

REAL PROPERTY TAXES

Note that while property taxes are a tax deduction, special assessments are *not* deductible!

Special assessments are improvements that are made to the property such as sidewalks, water lines, etc.

TAX TERMINOLOGY

An agent should keep informed of the rapid changes occurring in the industry. Real estate is complicated, and the agent needs to know when to advise a buyer to seek legal and professional counsel regarding tax consequences, investment strategies, environmental risks and so on when purchasing or leasing property.

For example, a new change in tax law is that first time home buyers may make penalty-free withdrawals from their tax-deferred individual retirements funds (IRAs) for a down payment. The limit of the withdrawal is $10,000.

Homeowners' Interest Tax Deductions

The federal government encourages home ownership by providing income tax advantages such as tax deductions, deferments and exclusions to buyers of homes. These tax benefits are different for a property used as a principal place of residence than for property purchased for investment purposes. In general, homeowners may deduct the following from their gross income to reduce their taxable income:

- Mortgage interest payments on first and second homes that meet the definition of "qualified residence interest"
- Real estate property taxes, but not interest paid on overdue taxes
- Certain loan discount points
- Certain loan origination fees
- Loan prepayment penalties
- Casualty losses to the real estate not covered by insurance

Capital Gains

The Taxpayers Relief Act of 1997 established the exclusion of capital gains on the sale of the principal residence. **Married** homeowners who file **jointly** may exclude up to **$500,000** from capital gains tax for profits on the sale of a principal residence. **Single filers** may exclude **up to $250,000** from capital gains tax for profits on the sale of a principal residence.

Homeowners whose gain exceeds the maximum for exclusion must pay tax on the amount over the exclusion. The exclusion can be taken more than once. However, the home must have been used as a principal residence for two of the preceding five years. The rule does not apply to second homes or vacation property.

Capital gains computations are covered in Chapter 7, the math review chapter.

Income Tax Implications for Real Estate Investments

In the past, real estate investments were advantageous because tax laws allowed investors to use losses generated by these investments to shelter incomes from other sources. Present-day tax benefits include tax deductions for depreciation, the deferment of capital gains when property is exchanged and deductions of losses from real estate investments. A buyer of investment property should seek professional tax advice to keep abreast of the changing laws in this area.

A capital gain is considered a short-term gain if the asset is owned for 12 months or less. It is considered long-term if the asset is owned for more than 12 months. The **maximum tax rate** on long-term capital gains is **10 percent** for taxpayers in the **15 percent tax bracket** and **20 percent for all others.**

A capital gain is the taxable profit that is realized from the sale or exchange of an asset. New capital gains laws became effective May 7, 1997.

The following is an example of how the capital gain is computed on investment property:

Selling Price:			$125,000
Less:			
	7% Commission	$8,750	
	Closing costs	+800	
		$9,550	− 9,550
Net Sales Price			$115,450
Basis:			
	Original cost	$60,000	
	Improvements	+5,000	
		$65,000	
Less:			
	Depreciation	−12,000	
Adjusted basis		$53,000	
			− 53,000
Total capital gain			$62,450

Exchanges

Under **Internal Revenue Code Section 1031,** if an investor exchanges property instead of selling it, payment of the capital gain may be deferred. The property must be of *like kind;* that is, real estate for real estate of equal value. Sometimes additional money or personal property is given to make up the difference between the value of the exchanged property. This money or personal property is known as a *boot,* and capital gains must be paid immediately on the boot.

Depreciation

Depreciation, or *cost recovery,* is a form of tax deduction. It allows an investor to recover the cost of an income-producing property used in a trade or business. The cost of the property may be depreciated or deducted over an arbitrary period. *Land cannot be depreciated; only the improvements on it can be depreciated.* Only the straight-line method of depreciation, meaning *depreciation taken periodically in equal amounts,* is used now.

For example, the cost attributable to an improvement is divided by the number of years of its economic life or remaining useful life. If a building cost $100,000 and has a remaining useful life of 30 years, then the rate of depreciation is $3,333 ($100,000 divided by 30).

Investors may be able to deduct other losses from their real estate investments. Because these laws are complicated, investors should obtain professional advice.

Syndicate

A **syndicate** is formed when two or more people unite and pool their resources to own, develop and/or operate an investment. A syndication may take the form of a Real Estate Investment Trust (REIT), general partnership, limited partnership, corporation, tenancy in common or joint tenancy.

Real Estate Investment Trust

The main advantage of a REIT is that investors can avoid double taxation when certain requirements are met. The trust does not have to pay corporate income tax as long as 95 percent of its income is distributed to its shareholders, 75 percent of the trust's income comes from real estate and certain other qualifications are met.

SECURITY

A security originates when a party joins with others in the expectation of making a profit from the efforts of others. Any pooling of money that attracts investors and meets the definition of a public offering may be federally regulated by the Securities and Exchange Commission (SEC) or by state **blue-sky laws.**

Tax Issues—Key Point Review

1. Real estate property taxes also are known as *ad valorem* taxes.

2. Homeowners may deduct the interest payments made on loans for first and second homes that meet the necessary qualifications, certain loan origination fees and loan discount points, loan prepayment penalties and real estate property taxes.

3. A capital gain is the profit realized from the sale or exchange of an asset.

4. Married homeowners who file jointly may exclude up to $500,000 from capital gains tax for profits on the sale of a principal residence. Single filers may exclude up to $250,000 from capital gains tax for profits on the sale of a principal residence. If the capital gain exceeds the exclusion, capital gains tax must be paid on the excess amount.

5. The exclusion can be taken more than once. The home must have been used as a principal place of residence for two of the preceding five years.

6. Depreciation, or cost recovery, is a form of tax deduction. It allows an investor to recover the cost of an income-producing property used in a trade or business.

Tax Issues—Key Point Review (Continued)

7. The cost of the improvements may be depreciated or deducted over an arbitrary period of time. Land cannot be depreciated.

8. The Internal Revenue Code Section 1031 allows investors to trade like-kind property. If no boot, which is cash or equivalent, is involved in the trade, it is a tax-free exchange. If boot is involved, tax must be paid on the boot.

9. A syndicate is formed when two or more people unite and pool their resources to own, develop and/or operate an investment.

10. The main advantage of a real estate investment trust (REIT) is that investors can avoid double taxation when certain requirements are met.

11. A security is created when a party joins with others in the expectation of making a profit from the efforts of others. Securities sold interstate are regulated by the Securities and Exchange Commission. Securities sold intrastate (within state lines) are regulated by blue-sky laws.

Content Outline—Titles

IV. Settlement/Transfer of Ownership

B. Titles

1. Title search
2. Title insurance
3. Title problems
4. Legal procedures
5. Liens
6. Legal proceedings against property

TITLE SEARCH

A deed transfers the title from the grantor to the grantee. The **title** is found within the deed and is used to show ownership of land. This means that the title represents facts that, if proven to be true, will enable a person to recover or retain ownership of a parcel of real estate. A title search is conducted on the property to assure both buyer and lender that the seller can deliver a marketable title at the closing. The title search is carried out by a lawyer, abstractor or title insurance company that prepares a **chain of title,** which is a successive series of title transfers, as well as the abstract of title.

An **abstract (of title)** is a condensed legal history of all transactions affecting the property. The legal history includes all conveyances, wills, records of judicial proceedings, recorded liens and encumbrances affecting the property and their current status. The abstractor searches public records at the courthouse and then summarizes the information in chronological order. An abstractor is liable for mistakes in his or her search of the public records. The abstractor is *not* liable for forgery, missing heirs or encroachments not found in the search.

Marketable Title

A **marketable title** or *merchantable title* is one that is free from reasonable objections, that is, one that will not place the buyer in a position of legal liability or threaten the buyer's right to quiet enjoyment of the property. If the buyer accepts a deed that has a problem with the title, the buyer's only recourse is to sue the seller based on the covenants found within the deed, if there are any.

Easements, restrictions, violations of zoning ordinances, lis pendens notices, mortgages, liens, federal tax liens, property tax liens and encroachments could render a title unmarketable, though slight encroachments may not do so. An unmarketable title does not prevent the property from being transferred by deed. The buyer may accept the property with certain defects that may limit or restrict ownership. However, a lender may refuse to negotiate a loan if the title is unmarketable.

TITLE INSURANCE

Title insurance indemnifies (protects) the policyholder against losses that arise from defects in the title that occurred before the policy was issued and that were not found in the title search. The title insurance company will defend any claim made against the policyholder. For example, if a buyer purchases title insurance and there was an undiscovered defect in the title that antedated the buyer's ownership, the buyer would probably be protected.

Title insurance *does not cover* all title defects. For example, prior defects and liens found in the title search, defects known to the buyer and any changes in land use brought about by zoning.

Standard coverage includes protection against losses arising from forged documents, missing heirs, incompetent grantors, incorrect marital statements, improperly delivered deeds and defects found in public records. Extended coverage also can be purchased that indemnifies the insured against loss from situations not disclosed by public records, such as some mechanics' liens, tax liens, unrecorded rights of persons in possession and encroachments.

Owner's Policy

An owner's title policy is issued for the benefit of the owner or the owner's heirs. If the owner is a corporation, its successors by dissolution, merger or consolidation are included.

Mortgagee's Policy

A mortgagee's (lender's) policy covers the loan balance and decreases as the balance is reduced. The premium is a one-time premium, and coverage continues until the property is conveyed to a new owner.

TITLE PROBLEMS

Title problems occur when there is a hidden mistake in a prior deed, will, mortgage or other document that may give someone else a valid legal claim against a property. These hidden defects include

- *incorrect information,* such as a wrong name, in a deed, mortgage or other documents of public record, that would affect the title;
- *a lien or claim against the property or seller* that could become the new owner's responsibility after the sale, such as unpaid mortgages, taxes, sewer and water assessments, or bills owed to workers or other creditors; it would also include attachments;
- *claims to ownership,* including a claim to a marital interest by the spouse of a former owner or by a child of former owners who was not mentioned in his or her parents' wills; and
- *the transfer of an invalid deed,* such as transfer by a previous seller who did not actually own the property, or by a previous owner who was not mentally or legally competent.

LEGAL PROCEDURES

Should there be a claim against a title, the title insurance company negotiates with the other party to settle the claim, defends the title in court (if necessary), satisfies any covered claim for which it is responsible and pays for the costs incurred in defending the title. Adverse possession, foreclosure, bankruptcy and judgments are examples of legal procedures discussed in this book that would affect a title. When a person dies testate (with a will), the property will be devised or transferred to the devisee. When a person dies intestate, the laws of descent and distribution in the state where the property is located will determine who receives the property.

A cloud on title is any claim that creates a defect of title or casts doubt on the title's validity. An example is when a mortgage has been paid in full but the mortgage **release** or **satisfaction** document has not been recorded to verify the payoff.

Suit To Quiet Title

A **suit to quiet title** is a court action intended to establish or settle the question of ownership of or interest in a particular property. This could include a range of claims, such as the release of abandoned easements, dower or curtesy rights, adverse possession claims, foreclosures, bankruptcy and judgments.

When a title insurance company makes a payment to settle a claim, the company requires that the policyholder **subrogate** rights to the claim. This means the policyholder will allow the title insurance company to represent him or her in proceedings against the third party or claimant.

LIENS

A **lien** is created when a debt is established by two parties and the **lienor** (lender) is given, by agreement, a claim to the property of the **lienee** (borrower) as security for a debt. For a lien to be established, it must be recorded in public records.

Terms Related To Liens

- **General lien**—claim against all property of the lienee, both real and personal property
- **Specific lien**—claim against a particular property only
- **Voluntary lien**—established intentionally by the lienee
- **Involuntary lien**—created by law without any action on the part of the owner (voluntary or involuntary liens may be statutory or equitable)
- **Statutory lien**—created by law, such as a judgment
- **Equitable lien**—created by the court based on "fairness," such as the payment of the balance on a delinquent charge account
- **Property taxes**—specific, involuntary liens placed on the owner's property

- **Special assessments**—levied for improvements made to property, special assessments are specific and statutory but may be either voluntary or involuntary liens
- **Mortgage lien (deed of trust)**—voluntary lien securing the loan for the lender until the debt is paid in full
- **Mechanic's lien**—placed on property by a party who performed labor or furnished material to improve the property
- **IRS tax lien**—general, statutory, involuntary lien on all real and personal property owned by a debtor

The **priority** of liens is generally as follows:

- If not current, real estate taxes and special assessments are paid first.
- The debtor in the first, or senior, lien position is next.
- The debtors in junior lien positions (second, third, and so on) are paid in the order of recording.
- Mechanics' liens generally become effective on the day the work began, the day the materials were delivered, the date the work was completed, the date the contract was signed or the work was ordered, or the date the lien was recorded.
- An IRS lien becomes effective from the date of filing or recording. It does not supersede previously recorded liens.

LEGAL PROCEEDINGS AGAINST PROPERTY

- **Judgment**—court decision on the respective rights and claims of the parties in a suit; a general, involuntary, equitable lien on both real and personal property of the debtor that normally covers only the property in the county where the judgment is rendered
- **Lis pendens notice**—recorded to give constructive notice that an action affecting the property has been filed in court, meaning that a lawsuit has been filed, but a judgment has not been decreed; warns of a future lien on the property and renders a property unmarketable
- **Writ of attachment**—creditor asks the court to retain custody of the property while a court suit is being decided, thus preventing the debtor from transferring unsecured real estate before a judgment is rendered; ensures that the property will be available to satisfy the judgment
- **Writ of execution**—a court order authorizing an officer of the court, such as a sheriff, to sell the property of a defendant to satisfy a judgment

Methods of Recording

Recording a document at a public office gives constructive notice (or legal notice) of a party's interest in a property. This means that a party such as a potential buyer is responsible for learning about the property because the facts are readily available.

Types of Notice

Constructive notice—Legal notice created by recording documents such as deeds, mortgages, and long-term leases in the county where the property is located. *Physical possession* of the property also gives constructive notice of the rights of the parties that are in possession.

Actual notice—A party knows or has *actual knowledge* of the fact. When a party has actual notice of a third party's prior rights to a property and still accepts an interest in the property, that party accepts the deed subject to the third party's prior rights. For example, a person who accepts a deed with a judgment lien on the property becomes responsible for the judgment.

Torrens system—A method of legal registration of land where title does not transfer and encumbrances are not effective against the property until the proper documents are registered at the Torrens office. In some states, this means that the title cannot be lost through adverse possession.

Titles—Key Point Review

1. A deed transfers the title from the grantor to the grantee. The title is found within the deed and is used to show ownership of land.

2. A title search is conducted to assure the buyer and the lender that the seller can deliver a marketable title that would neither place the buyer in a position of legal liability nor threaten the buyer's right to quiet enjoyment of the property.

3. Easements, restrictions, violations of zoning ordinances, lis pendens notices, mortgages, liens, federal tax liens, property tax liens and encroachments could render a title unmarketable. Slight encroachments may not render a title unmarketable.

4. Title insurance protects the policyholder against losses that arise from defects in the title that occurred before the policy was issued. Prior defects and liens found in the title search, defects known to the buyer and changes in zoning are not covered in a title policy. Standard coverage includes protection against forged documents, missing heirs, incompetent grantors, incorrect marital statements, improperly delivered deeds and defects found in public records.

5. An owner's (mortgagor's) title policy is issued for the benefit of the owner or the heirs of the owner. A lender's (mortgagee's) title policy covers the loan balance and decreases as the balance is reduced.

6. A cloud on title is any claim that creates a defect of title or casts doubt on the title's validity.

7. When a title insurance company makes a payment to settle a claim, the company requires that a policyholder subrogate any rights to the claim. Subrogation allows the title insurance company to represent the policyholder.

8. A title search is carried out by a lawyer, abstractor or title insurance company. It is a condensed legal history of all transactions affecting the property.

9. A lien is created when a debt is established by two parties and the lienor (mortgagee) is given, by agreement, a claim to the property of the lienee (mortgagor) as security for a debt.

10. A general lien is a claim against all property of the lienee. A specific lien is a claim against only a particular property.

11. A voluntary lien is established intentionally by the lienee. An involuntary lien is placed on the property without any action on the part of the owner.

12. A voluntary or involuntary lien may be statutory or equitable. A statutory lien is created by law, such as a judgment. An equitable lien is created by the court based on "fairness."

13. Property taxes are specific, involuntary liens.

14. Special assessments are levied for the improvements made to property and are specific and statutory but may either be voluntary or involuntary liens.

15. A mortgage lien or deed of trust is a voluntary lien on real estate that secures the loan for the lender until the debt is paid in full.

Titles—Key Point Review (Continued)

16. A mechanic's lien is placed on the property by a party who performed labor or furnished material to improve the property. Generally, a mechanic's lien becomes effective on the day the work began or the materials were delivered.

17. A judgment is a decision by the court on the respective rights and claims of the parties in a suit. It is a general, involuntary, equitable lien on real and personal property in the county where the judgment is rendered.

18. A creditor seeks a writ of attachment so the court will retain custody of the property while a suit is being decided, preventing the debtor from transferring unsecured real estate before a judgment is rendered.

19. A lis pendens notice gives constructive notice that an action affecting the property has been filed in court and that a future lien may be placed on the property. A lis pendens notice renders a property unmarketable.

20. An IRS tax lien is a general, statutory, involuntary lien on all real and personal property owned by the citizen who owes taxes. It becomes effective from the date of filing or recording, but does not supersede previously recorded liens.

21. The priority of liens is generally as follows: real estate taxes and special assessments; a first, or senior, lien; junior liens in the order of recording.

22. Under the Torrens system of land registration, the title does not transfer and encumbrances are not effective against the property until the proper documents are registered at the Torrens office.

Content Outline—Settlement Procedures

IV. Settlement/Transfer of Ownership

    C. Settlement Procedures

        1. Purposes and procedures of settlement
        2. Real Estate Settlement Procedures Act
        3. Closing statements
        4. Obligations of settlement agent
        5. Calculations regarding proration/prepayment
        6. Warranties associated with deeds
        7. Settlement statement (HUD Form 1)
        8. Other settlement documents
        9. Transfer tax
       10. Negotiations leading to a sales agreement

PURPOSES AND PROCEDURES OF SETTLEMENT

A real estate settlement, or closing, takes place to consummate or finalize a real estate transaction. The transfer of the property can take place in a formal face-to-face closing or by closing in escrow, depending on local trade and custom of the area.

Upon closing, the buyer makes a final inspection to ensure a marketable title and to receive the property as promised in the sales contract. The seller receives the funds promised by the buyer in the sales contract. Both parties receive a copy of the settlement or closing statement, which they inspect to ensure that all monies have been accounted for properly. Each party may have an attorney present at the closing.

A face-to-face closing is a formal meeting of all parties involved. By local custom, a settlement agent presides over the closing. A closing in **escrow** means that a disinterested third party is authorized to act as an escrow agent for the buyer and the seller and to handle all closing activities. The closing may be conducted by an attorney, a real estate agent, a settlement agent of the title company or an agent of the escrow company.

REAL ESTATE SETTLEMENT PROCEDURES ACT

The **Real Estate Settlement Procedures Act (RESPA)** is a federal act that requires that the buyer and seller in a real estate transaction have knowledge of all settlement costs.

RESPA requires the disclosure of closing costs on federally related mortgage loans and first and second liens for the purchase or refinancing of one- to four-family dwellings.

RESPA requires the disclosure of closing costs on federally related mortgage loans, and first and second liens for the purchase or refinancing of one- to four-family dwellings.

RESPA requires that lenders and settlement agents make certain disclosures at the time of the loan application and at the closing of the loan. These include the following:

- The booklet *Settlement Costs and You* must be given to a prospective borrower within three business days from the time that person receives or prepares a loan application.
- Within three business days of application, the lender must provide the borrower with a good-faith estimate of the settlement costs the borrower will likely incur.
- The Uniform Settlement Statement (HUD Form 1) must be used to itemize all charges related to the transaction.
- The lender is prohibited from receiving any kickbacks or other referral fees from service providers.

Lenders cannot charge a fee for the preparation of the settlement statement. The settlement statement must be made available to the borrower for inspection one day prior to closing and the buyer and seller must receive a copy of the settlement statement at the closing.

RESPA does not apply to a land contract; a purchase-money mortgage, wherein the seller is solely financing the property; or a transaction where the buyer is assuming the seller's existing loan and the lender charges less than $50 for the assumption.

FIGURE 4.1 *Types of Deeds*

General Warranty Deed
- Best type of deed for the buyer to receive.
- Contains the covenants of seisin, against encumbrances, of quiet enjoyment, further assurance and of warranty forever.
- Grantor will defend the title against himself or herself as well as against all who previously held title.

Special Warranty Deed
- Has three warranties.
- Warranty that the grantor received title.
- Warranty that property was unencumbered by grantor.
- Warranty that the grantor will defend the title for his or her period of ownership only.

Bargain and Sale Deed
- Includes no express warranties.
- Implies that the grantor holds title and possession.

Quitclaim Deed
- Contains no express or implied covenants or warranties.
- Conveys whatever interests the grantor has, if any.
- Used to convey less than a fee simple estate, to correct an error in a deed or release an interest.

Deed in Trust
- Used like a management agreement.
- Conveys title from trustor to trustee.
- Trustee manages the property for the beneficiary.

CLOSING STATEMENTS

See Chapter 7 on page 167.

OBLIGATIONS OF SETTLEMENT AGENT

The settlement agent conducts the closing and calculates the official settlement statement. The agent's responsibilities include reviewing and preparing all documents necessary for the transaction to close, and they may include the filing of Form 1099-S with the IRS. A settlement agent could be a closing agent from the title company, an attorney, a lender or a real estate agent.

CALCULATIONS REGARDING PRORATION/PREPAYMENT

See Chapter 7 on page 179.

WARRANTIES ASSOCIATED WITH DEEDS

A **deed** is the written instrument that transfers the title from the grantor/seller to the grantee/buyer. Many different types of deeds can be used to convey the title, and the distinguishing characteristics of deeds are the covenants or promises made by the grantor. (See Figure 4.1.) State laws may have their own requirements for a deed.

Essential Elements of a Valid Deed

- The name of the **grantor** or party with the legal authority to transfer the property
- A **grantee** identified with reasonable certainty (a deed cannot be transferred to a deceased person or to a corporation that does not exist)
- **Consideration,** although it may not be the actual selling price
- A **granting clause** or words of conveyance
- An optional **habendum clause,** which defines ownership
- **Restrictions** or limitations placed on the conveyance of the property
- An accurate **legal description**
- The **signature of the grantor**
- **Delivery** and acceptance of the deed by the grantee

Acknowledgment

In most states, a deed must be acknowledged and attested to be recorded. The primary purpose of **acknowledgment** is to verify that the person who signed the written document did so voluntarily and of his or her own free will. The secondary purpose of acknowledgment is to verify the identity of the signer. *Attestation* is the act of witnessing a person's signing of a document.

A general warranty deed contains five covenants or promises made by the grantor. They are the:

- covenant of seisin—promises the grantor owns the property and has the right to convey
- covenant against encumbrances—promises that there are no encumbrances other than those stated in the deed
- covenant of quiet enjoyment—promises that the grantor has a superior title and no one will object to the conveyance
- covenant of further assurances—promises that the grantor will correct any title defects found in the future
- covenant of warranty forever—promises that the grantor will defend the title in disputes brought by third parties

Inter Vivos and Testamentary Trusts

A trust may be inter vivos or testamentary. **Inter vivos** means to set up a trust during one's life, and **testamentary** means that the trust is established by will.

Reconveyance Deed

A **deed of reconveyance** is used in a deed in trust or a deed of trust to reconvey the title to the trustor. (See Figure 4.2.) There are federal, state and security regulations that govern trust agreements.

Administrator's, executor's, sheriff's and guardian's deeds are examples of deeds executed *pursuant to court order.* Property transferred by court order must meet the requirements of the state where it is located. For example, when a person who resides in one state dies intestate and also owns property in another state, the laws in the state where the property is located determine who receives the property.

SETTLEMENT STATEMENT (HUD FORM 1)

See pages 181–182 for a copy of a settlement statement.

FIGURE 4.2 *Trust Deeds*

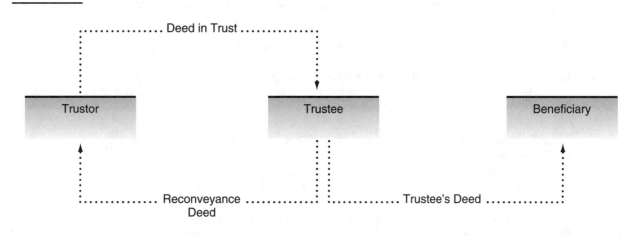

OTHER SETTLEMENT DOCUMENTS

- A **mortgage** is a pledge of property to the lender for security for the payment of the debt.
- A **note** is the evidence of the debt and states the terms of repayment.
- An **affidavit** of the seller is a document in which the seller affirms that from the time the sales contract was accepted until the date of closing, he or she has done nothing to burden the title that would not be revealed in the title search.
- A **bill of sale** is used to show the transfer of personal property.
- **Payoff statement** indicates the payoff of the seller's existing note/s.
- An **insurance policy** is required by buyer to show payment of homeowners' insurance.
- **Other** documents the lender may require.

TRANSFER TAX

Most states impose a transfer tax, which is normally paid by the seller or lessor when the property is conveyed by a deed, contract for deed, lease, sublease or assignment. The transfer tax may be paid by the *purchase of tax stamps or payment of a transfer fee.*

NEGOTIATIONS LEADING TO A SALES AGREEMENT

Buyers normally don't buy the first property they visit, so when they find a house and decide to make an offer, the critical process of negotiating begins. Most buyers believe the seller is willing to take less than the list price. Most sellers believe the buyer will pay more than their first offer if they really want the house. Personal items may also be a part of the offer.

Agency law determines that proper disclosures be made depending if the agent is representing the buyer, seller or both parties in the transaction. It is the agent's responsibility to follow state laws regarding contracts, agency disclosure, lead-based paint disclosure, etc. Other information on agency relationships and responsibilities are discussed in different parts of this book.

Settlement Procedures—Key Point Review

1. A real estate settlement or closing takes place to consummate or finalize a real estate transaction. It could be a face-to-face closing or a closing in escrow.

2. The Real Estate Settlement Procedures Act requires that the parties in a real estate transaction have knowledge of all settlement costs. Disclosures must be made on loans that are financed by a federally related mortgage.

3. RESPA applies to first and second liens for the purchase or refinancing of one- to four- family dwellings. RESPA does not apply to a land contract; a purchase-money mortgage wherein the seller is solely financing the property; or a transaction where the buyer assumes the seller's existing loan and the lender charges less than $50 for the assumption.

4. RESPA requires that within three business days after applicants receive a loan application, they must receive a copy of *Settlement Costs and You,* and a good-faith estimate of the settlement costs the borrower will likely incur; that the Uniform Settlement Statement (HUD Form 1) be used to itemize all charges related to the transaction; and that the lender must not receive any kickbacks or other referral fees from service providers.

5. Lenders cannot charge a fee for the preparation of the settlement statement. The settlement statement must be made available to the borrower for inspection one day prior to closing, with copies to the buyer and seller at the closing.

6. When a contract is rescinded, it is canceled, terminated or annulled and the parties are returned to their legal positions before they entered into the contract.

7. A deed is the written instrument that transfers the title from the grantor to the grantee. The essential elements of a valid deed are: the name of the grantor who has the legal capacity to transfer the property; a grantee who is identified with reasonable certainty; consideration, although it need not be the actual consideration; words of conveyance or a granting clause; an optional habendum clause that defines the extent of ownership taken by the grantee; a designation of any limitations placed on the conveyance of the property; an accurate legal description; the signature of the grantor; and delivery and acceptance of the deed.

8. In most states, a deed must be acknowledged and attested to be recorded. The primary purpose of acknowledgment is to verify that the person who signed the written document has done so voluntarily. The secondary purpose is to verify the identity of the signer.

9. A general warranty deed is the best type of deed for the buyer to receive because it provides the most covenants and binds the seller to those covenants back to the origins of the property.

10. The usual covenants found in a general warranty deed are the covenant of seisin, which promises that the grantor owns the property and has the right to convey title; the covenant against encumbrances, which promises that the property is free from liens and encumbrances except those stated in the deed; the covenant of quiet enjoyment, which promises that the grantor has a superior title to the property; the covenant of further assurance, which promises that the grantor will obtain and deliver any instrument needed to make the title good; and the covenant of warranty forever, which promises that the grantor will compensate the grantee for any loss sustained if the title fails in the future.

Settlement Procedures—Key Point Review (Continued)

11. With a special warranty deed, the grantor promises that the title was not encumbered during the period in which the grantor held the title. Liabilities are limited to the grantor's period of ownership.

12. A bargain and sale deed makes no express promises or warranties against encumbrances. This deed implies that the owner holds title and has possession of the property. The grantee would have limited legal recourse if a title defect were to appear later.

13. A quitclaim deed provides the buyer with the least protection because it provides no promises or warranties. This deed makes no assurances that the seller has any interest in the property. The grantee has no legal recourse against the grantor should a title defect be found in the future.

14. Quitclaim deeds are used to convey title, to release interests in real estate or to correct an error found in a deed.

15. A reconveyance deed is used in a deed in trust or a deed of trust to reconvey the title to the trustor.

16. Administrator's, executor's, sheriff's and guardian's deeds are examples of deeds executed pursuant to court order.

17. Most states have imposed a transfer tax, which is normally paid by the seller.

Content Outline—Characteristics of Real Property

IV. Settlement/Transfer of Ownership

   D. Characteristics of Real Property

      1. Ways of holding and conveying title
      2. Rights of home ownership
      3. Rights of others related to property
      4. Nature and types of common interest ownership
      5. Eminent domain proceedings

WAYS OF HOLDING AND CONVEYING TITLE

See pages 19–22 for review.

RIGHTS OF HOME OWNERSHIP

See page 23 for review.

RIGHTS OF OTHERS RELATED TO PROPERTY

The individual's right to the ownership of property is subject to certain powers by the federal, state and/or local governments. These powers include police power, eminent domain, taxation and escheat.

Government Powers

- **Police power**—The right of the government to regulate for the purpose of promoting the health, safety and welfare of the public (i.e. zoning, building codes and subdivision regulations).
- **Eminent domain**—The right of a government, a quasi-government body or a public company to take property for public use. Just compensation must be paid to the owner. The government exercises its right to take the property by the process of **condemnation.**
- **Taxation**—The right of the government to charge a property owner a fee to raise funds to meet the public needs.
- **Escheat**—When a property owner dies **intestate,** that is, leaves **no will and no heirs** can be found, the property reverts (escheats) to the state or the county.

Private Powers

The individual's right to the ownership of property is also subject to certain private powers or interests of other individuals, including the rights acquired by adverse possession, encroachments, license and the rights of adjoining owners.

Adverse Possession

If a party uses someone else's property for a statutory period and that use is open, notorious, hostile and continuous, the party may acquire title to the property through **adverse possession.** The rights of the party in possession are **squatter's rights.**

To acquire a title through adverse possession, the squatter must file a **suit to quiet title** after the statutory period has been met in the state where the property is located. Periods of ownership by different squatters can be combined, enabling a party who has not been in possession for the entire time to establish a claim. This is known as **tacking.** Adverse possession is an involuntary alienation or conveyance of property. When a squatter receives a title through an adverse possession claim, it is called a *title by prescription.*

An **encroachment** is an unauthorized intrusion of an improvement onto the real property of another. This could be an intrusion into the air, surface or sub-surface space of the property's boundary lines or building setback lines. A survey is the best way for a buyer to determine if there are any encroachments on a property.

License

A **license** is a personal, revocable and nonassignable right to use the land of another and is void on the death of either party or the sale of the property.

Lateral and Subjacent Support

A property owner has an incidental right to the lateral support provided by the adjoining neighbors' property and the right to the **subjacent support** the earth receives from its underlying strata. That is, a property owner cannot excavate or mine his or her land in such a way that it will cause a neighbor's land to collapse or sink.

NATURE AND TYPES OF COMMON INTEREST OWNERSHIP

Ownership that allows for a sharing of interests with other co-owners of real property includes condominiums, cooperatives, time-shares and townhouses. Such ownership provides the benefits of home ownership with a sharing of amenities and expenses.

Eminent Domain Proceedings

See page 100 for review.

Characteristics of Real Property—Key Point Review

1. The right of the government to take property for public use and pay just compensation to the owner is called *eminent domain*. The government exercises this right by the process of condemnation.

2. *Taxation* is the right of the government to charge the owner of real estate a fee to raise funds to meet public needs.

3. When a property owner dies intestate and the government can find no heirs, the property escheats to the state or county.

4. A party who uses someone else's property for a statutory period, if that use is open, notorious, hostile and continuous, may acquire title to the property by adverse possession. The rights of the party in possession are called *squatter's rights*.

5. Periods of ownership by different squatters can be combined, which is known as *tacking*.

6. To acquire a title through adverse possession, the claimant must file a suit to quiet title. Such a title is called a *title by prescription*.

7. An *encroachment* is an unauthorized intrusion onto the real property of another. A survey is the best way for a buyer to determine if there are any encroachments.

8. A license is a personal, revocable, nonassignable right to use the land of another for a specific purpose. It is void on the death of either party or the sale of the property.

Questions

1. When land is to be condemned or taken under the power of eminent domain, which of the following must apply?
   A. The taking must be for a public purpose.
   B. Statutory dedication must be executed.
   C. Adverse possession claim must be taken.
   D. Constructive notice must be given.

2. What do the police powers of governmental authority include?
   A. Foreclosure
   B. Defeasance
   C. Building codes and zoning regulations
   D. Alienation

3. The Real Estate Settlement Procedures Act requires
   A. that closing of a real estate transaction be held within 90 days of the execution of the purchase agreement.
   B. that disclosure be made of all closing costs prior to the closing.
   C. the seller's approval of the buyer's statement.
   D. a qualified buyer.

4. Henry sold a parcel of real estate to Marlin and gave Marlin a quitclaim deed. On receipt of the deed Marlin may be certain that
   A. Henry owned the property.
   B. there are no encumbrances against the property.
   C. Marlin now owns the property subject to certain claims of Henry.
   D. all of Henry's interests in the property as of the date of the deed belong to Marlin.

5. Normally, title to property passes when a deed is delivered. Which of the following is an EXCEPTION to the general rule?
   A. Title to abstract property is transferred when the deed is recorded.
   B. Title to Torrens property is transferred when the certificate is registered.
   C. Title to abstract trust property is transferred on the death of the beneficiary.
   D. Title to Torrens property is transferred when the deed is delivered to the agent.

6. Which of the following is TRUE regarding a deed and title?
   A. A deed can be prepared only by an attorney, while a title can be prepared by an attorney or an owner.
   B. A deed is valid only if it is recorded, and a title does not have to be recorded to show ownership.
   C. The purpose of a deed is to transfer title from the grantee to the grantor.
   D. The purpose of a deed is to convey title from the grantor to the grantee.

7. Boris sells certain property to David and gives David a special warranty deed. Which of the following is TRUE?
   A. Boris is making additional warranties beyond those given in a warranty deed.
   B. Boris's property is Torrens property.
   C. Boris is warranting that no encumbrances have ever been placed against the property that have not been satisfied or released.
   D. Boris's warranties are limited to the time he held the property.

8. Sandra and Neva bought a store building and took title as joint tenants with right of survivorship. Neva died testate. Sandra now owns the store
   A. as a joint tenant with rights of survivorship.
   B. in severalty.
   C. in absolute ownership under the law of descent.
   D. subject to the terms of Neva's will.

9. Samantha sold her house to Buddy. Buddy, however, did not record the deed. Under these circumstances
   A. the transfer of property between Samantha and Buddy is ineffective.
   B. Buddy's interest is not fully protected against third parties.
   C. the deed is invalid after 90 days.
   D. the deed is invalid after six months.

10. For a deed to be valid, the
    A. grantor must be legally competent.
    B. signature of the grantor must be witnessed.
    C. documents must pass through the hands of an escrow agent.
    D. grantee must sign the deed.

11. A quitclaim deed
    A. carries no covenant or warranty.
    B. may not transfer the seller's title.
    C. carries full warranty.
    D. provides a limited warranty.

12. Condominium owners
    A. hold common elements as tenants in common.
    B. hold common elements as joint tenants.
    C. hold individual elements only.
    D. hold limited common elements.

13. Which of the following BEST describes a capital gain?
    A. The taxable profit that is realized from the sale of a capital asset.
    B. A capital gain is the difference between the sale price and the original investment.
    C. The taxable profit that investors must pay when as asset is sold.
    D. A capital gain is the difference between the sale price and the selling expeses.

14. Roger is selling limited partnerships in a real estate venture. The offering is being made within state lines and all purchasers are residents of the state. The offering is MOST LIKELY regulated by
    A. the Securities and Exchange Commission.
    B. the real estate commission.
    C. blue-sky laws.
    D. white-sky laws.

15. A defect or cloud on the title to property may be cured by
    A. obtaining quitclaim deeds from all other interested parties.
    B. bringing an action to register title.
    C. paying cash for the property at the closing.
    D. bringing an action to repudiate title.

16. Sally is in the process of purchasing Jack's house. To protect its interest, her mortgagee decides to take out title insurance. The title insurance policy
    A. may act as the instrument of transfer.
    B. indemnifies the holder against some, but not all, of the possible defects in title.
    C. protects Sally from all defects in the title.
    D. protects Jack from a lawsuit.

17. Under the condominium form of ownership, the interest of the owner in the unit he or she possesses is normally a
    A. life estate.
    B. fee simple interest.
    C. proprietory leasehold interest.
    D. reciprocal proprietary easement interest.

18. Deed restrictions are a means whereby
    A. local zoning laws are enforced.
    B. the planning commission's work is made effective.
    C. villages and cities can control construction details.
    D. the seller can limit or control the buyer's use.

19. Normally, a deed is considered valid even if
    A. signed by an authorized attorney-in-fact rather than the seller.
    B. the grantor was an illegal alien.
    C. the deed was signed by a minor and not the guardian of the minor.
    D. the grantor did not deliver the deed.

20. George sold his house to Sylvia. In the deed used in the transaction, George guaranteed that the property was not encumbered during the time he held title except as noted in the deed. The type of deed George gave to Sylvia is a
    A. general warranty deed.
    B. quitclaim deed.
    C. special warranty deed.
    D. limited quitclaim deed.

21. Which of the following is NOT usually prorated between buyer and seller at the closing?
    A. Recording charges
    B. Property taxes
    C. Rents
    D. Utility bills

22. Tom has a claim affecting the title to Bill's property. Bill has no mortgages against the property and has been trying to sell it. Tom is concerned about the possibility of a bona fide purchaser buying it before he obtains a judgment. To protect himself during the course of the court action, Tom should

    A. publish a notice in a newspaper.
    B. seek an attachment.
    C. bring a quick summary proceeding.
    D. notify Bill that any attempt to sell the property will be considered fraud.

23. Which of the following transfers is an involuntary alienation of property?

    A. Quitclaim
    B. Inheritance
    C. Eminent domain
    D. Gift

24. All of the following are required by RESPA EXCEPT

    A. lenders must provide borrowers with a good-faith estimate of loan closing costs.
    B. a uniform settlement sheet must be used at closings.
    C. the borrower must be given five days to back out of the loan transaction after receiving the required settlement information.
    D. no kickbacks may be given to any party in connection with the loan transaction.

25. How may title to real estate be transferred?

    A. Descent and distribution
    B. Involuntary alienation
    C. Delivery of the deed
    D. All of the above

26. All of the following are intended to convey legal title to real estate EXCEPT a(n)

    A. warranty deed.
    B. deed of trust.
    C. trustee's deed.
    D. equitable title.

27. The words "to have and to hold" in a deed define the ownership that is being transferred. This phrase is known as the

    A. granting clause.
    B. habendum clause.
    C. alienation clause.
    D. distributor clause.

28. The deed MOST LIKELY to be used to correct errors in a deed is a

    A. quitclaim deed.
    B. warranty deed.
    C. bargain and sale deed.
    D. grant deed.

29. For a deed to be recorded, it must be acknowledged. The primary purpose of acknowledgment is to

    A. convey title to the grantee.
    B. ensure the identity of the grantee.
    C. verify that the deed was signed without duress.
    D. guarantee a marketable title.

30. All of the following are true regarding RESPA EXCEPT that it

    A. requires the disclosure of all closing costs.
    B. covers one- to four-family dwellings.
    C. sets the interest rate that the lender can charge.
    D. regulates the amount the lender can collect from the borrower to place in escrow.

31. Which of the following statements is TRUE regarding title insurance?

    A. Title insurance is paid monthly and is included in the mortgage payment.
    B. Title insurance covers losses due to a defect in the title, but it does not pay for the cost of defending the title.
    C. There are two title polices that may be purchased. The owner's policy covers the owner, while the mortgagee's policy covers the lender.
    D. Title insurance normally does not cover defects caused by forgery.

32. Which of the following is FALSE regarding ad valorem taxes?

    A. Ad valorem is another term for property taxes.
    B. Unpaid ad valorem taxes could create a general lien on the property.
    C. Ad valorem taxes are tax deductible.
    D. Unpaid ad valorem taxes could create a specific lien on the property.

33. What is the major difference between a general lien and a specific lien?
    A. A general lien may be filed only on personal property, while a specific lien is filed on real estate.
    B. A general lien may be filed by a corporation, while a specific lien may be filed by a specific individual.
    C. A general lien may be filed by an attorney, while a specific lien can be filed by anyone.
    D. A general lien may be filed against real and personal property, while a specific lien may be filed against only a specific property.

34. In 1969 a person moved into an abandoned log cabin. Over the years he repaired the property and paid the property taxes. In 1999 another man appears with a deed to the property. Both claim to own the property. To settle this matter, there needs to be a
    A. suit to settle ownership interests.
    B. suit to settle the will.
    C. suit to quiet the title.
    D. suit for adverse possession.

35. When a property is abandoned, it may revert to the county or state by the process of
    A. escheat.
    B. eminent domain.
    C. testate.
    D. intestate.

36. Middleton decided he could make more money from his tree farm by dividing it into small parcels and selling them. Subsequently, Middleton entered into a series of purchase agreements, in connection with which he agreed to continue to operate the property and distribute proceeds from its income to the buyers. Under the circumstances, Middleton has sold
    A. real estate, because the object of the sale was land.
    B. securities, because the buyers were investors relying on Middleton's activities to generate a profit from the premises.
    C. real estate, because the property was subdivided before the sales took place.
    D. securities, because the object of the purchase was trees; the underlying land was merely incidental to the sale.

37. Steward entered into an agreement to sell his house to the Manders. The closing is scheduled to take place April 15. In January, Steward paid the taxes for the entire year, although the Manders are assuming responsibility for taxes attributable to the period following the closing. At the closing, on the settlement statement, the adjustment made for property taxes appears as a
    A. debit to the buyer and a credit to the seller.
    B. credit to the buyer and a debit to the seller.
    C. credit to the buyer.
    D. debit to the seller.

38. Harry and Edith entered into an agreement to sell their house. Some time ago, a special assessment was levied against their property for sidewalk and street improvements in front of their house. Under the agreement with the purchaser, the buyers will not assume the special assessment. If the assessment has not been paid off prior to the closing, the amount remaining due will appear as a
    A. credit to the buyer.
    B. debit to the seller.
    C. credit to the seller and a debit to the buyer.
    D. debit to the seller and a credit to the buyer.

39. Expenses involved in the closing of a real estate transaction are shown on the settlement as a
    A. debit to either the buyer or the seller.
    B. credit to either the buyer or the seller.
    C. debit to both the buyer and the seller.
    D. credit to both the buyer and the seller.

40. RESPA requirements apply to any residential real estate transaction
    A. in a state that has adopted RESPA.
    B. involving a federally related mortgage loan.
    C. involving any mortgage financing less than $100,000.
    D. involving any sale price less than $100,000.

41. A purchaser of property can be guaranteed of receiving good title to the property if at the closing she or he receives a
    A. general warranty deed.
    B. quitclaim deed.
    C. contract for deed.
    D. none of the above.

42. Broker Bonnie represented the seller in a transaction. Her client informed her that he did not want the deed to recite the actual consideration paid for the house. After seeking legal advice, Bonnie
    A. must inform her client that only the actual price of the real estate may appear on the deed.
    B. may show a price on the deed other than the actual price, provided it does not vary by more than 10 percent of the purchase price.
    C. may advise her client that he may show consideration of $10 on the deed if permitted by state law and advise him to seek legal counsel to answer any other questions.
    D. should inform the seller that either the full price should be stated or all references to consideration should be removed from the deed.

43. In the sale of a time-share
    A. the selling broker must be a licensed security broker.
    B. each of the owners of the unit has the right to occupy it for a specific period each year.
    C. the seller is the vendee.
    D. the selling agent must be an employee of the developer.

44. Which of the following is NOT an example of constructive notice?
    A. Recording a deed at the court house
    B. A legal notice in the newspaper
    C. An unrecorded lien
    D. Possession of the property

45. Which of the following federal tax rules BEST applies to a homeowner who sells a home?
    A. The homeowner may defer the payment of capital gains tax if another home is purchased within two years that is equal to or greater than the adjusted sales price of the old residence.
    B. The homeowner may exclude the payment of capital gains tax if he or she has lived in the home two out of the last five years and the exclusion does not exceed the government allowance.
    C. The homeowner can depreciate the improvements on the property as long as the depreciation does not exceed $125,000.
    D. The homeowner must pay capital gains tax within nine months of the sale of the property.

46. Which of the following is TRUE regarding an abstract of title?
    A. It can be developed only by an attorney.
    B. It contains the names of missing heirs.
    C. It contains information taken from public records.
    D. It is necessary before a property can be listed.

47. Jayne decided to buy investment property. She negotiated a first and second mortgage on a property at the same time. What is the major difference between these loans?
    A. The second mortgage would have a higher rate of interest than the first mortgage.
    B. The second mortgage would have a lower rate of interest than the first mortgage.
    C. The second mortgage would be for a shorter term than the first mortgage.
    D. The second mortgage would be in a junior lien position, while the first mortgage would be in a senior lien position.

48. An owner's title insurance policy normally covers all of the following EXCEPT
    A. missing heirs.
    B. incorrect marital status.
    C. zoning restrictions.
    D. forgery.

49. RESPA regulates all of the following transactions EXCEPT a(n)
    A. FHA-insured mortgage.
    B. contract for deed.
    C. VA-guaranteed mortgage.
    D. conventional mortgage sold to Fannie Mae.

50. The process an airport would use to take property for public use while paying the owner just compensation is
    A. eminent domain.
    B. escheat.
    C. adverse possession.
    D. condemnation.

51. At a closing, Howard received a deed in which the grantor implied possession and ownership of the property. Howard MOST LIKELY received a
    A. general warranty deed.
    B. bargain and sale deed.
    C. special warranty deed.
    D. grantee's deed.

52. Lis pendens is BEST described by which of the following?
    A. A notice filed when the property is foreclosed
    B. Constructive notice that a property owner is in litigation that could result in a future lien on the property
    C. Actual notice that a judgment has been secured against a property owner
    D. A notice that allows the court to maintain custody of a property until it is sold in bankruptcy

53. Lucas wishes to take title to a property with a deed that BEST protects his interest. Lucas wishes a(n)
    A. fee simple interest conveyed by a quitclaim deed.
    B. estate for years interest conveyed by a bargain and sale deed.
    C. fee simple interest conveyed by a warranty deed.
    D. periodic estate interest conveyed by a grant deed.

54. Sandy signs a deed conveying her property to her friend Steve. She tells no one, and places the deed in her safe-deposit box. Several months later she dies intestate and the deed is found. Who receives the property?
    A. Steve, because the deed has been signed by Sandy
    B. Sandy's heirs, as determined by the laws of descent and distribution
    C. Another friend Sandy told could have the property three days before her death
    D. The state, because she died intestate

55. All of the following documents would MOST LIKELY be recorded EXCEPT
    A. general warranty deed.
    B. mortgage.
    C. mortgage release.
    D. sales contract.

56. Joe just purchased his first investment property. His accountant has advised him that all of the following would be a tax deduction EXCEPT
    A. mortgage interest paid on the loan.
    B. principal paid on the loan.
    C. property taxes.
    D. discount points paid on the loan.

57. Mr. and Mrs. Redford paid $250,000 when they purchased their primary residence in 1986. In 2001 they sold the property for $500,000. In regard to capital gains they
    A. can exclude up to $500,000 if they file joint tax returns.
    B. have a once in a lifetime exclusion of $250,000 each.
    C. can only exclude $500,000 of capital gains once in their lifetime.
    D. can only take the exclusion if they are over the age of 55.

58. Sterling owns a 20-unit apartment building and has depreciated the building as much as she can. David also owns a 20-unit apartment building and has depreciated the building as much as he can. An accountant would probably advise them to
    A. sell the properties individually with a brokerage firm that charges a five percent commission.
    B. do nothing.
    C. leave the property to their favorite charity in their wills.
    D. have the properties appraised, then exchange properties to start the depreciation again.

59. Gary, Tom, and Angie have decided to pool their resources for investment purposes. This process is
    A. called syndication.
    B. suit for performance.
    C. a limited partnership.
    D. illegal in most states.

60. Which of the following would not be associated with an adverse possession claim?
    A. Title by prescription
    B. Suit to quiet the title
    C. Squatter's rights
    D. A license

ANSWERS

1. A   The government has the right to take private property through eminent domain, but the taking must be for the public benefit and just compensation must be paid.

2. C   Police powers are the right of the government to regulate for health, safety and welfare of the public. Building codes and zoning regulations are examples of police power.

3. B   According to RESPA, a buyer must receive a good-faith estimate within three days of application, have the right to review the settlement sheet one day prior to closing, and receive a copy of the settlement sheet at the closing.

4. D   A quitclaim deed makes no warranties. It transfers whatever interest the giver has, if any.

5. B   All documents must be registered at the Torrens office to be official.

6. D   A deed conveys the title from the grantor to the grantee.

7. D   By definition of special warranty deed.

8. B   The surviving joint tenant owns the property in severalty.

9. B   When the grantee does not record the deed, his interests are not protected against third parties.

10. A   The grantor must be legally competent when he or she signs the deed. The signature must be acknowledged and attested if it is to be recorded.

11. A   By definition of a quitclaim deed.

12. A   In a condominium, ownership of the airspace is held in severalty and ownership of the common areas is held as a tenant in common.

13. A   By definition of capital gains.

14. C   Securities sold intrastate are regulated by blue-sky laws.

15. A   Quitclaim deeds signed by the parties that have an interest in the property are the best way to perfect a title.

16. B   Indemnification is an agreement to reimburse someone for a loss. The holder of title insurance is indemnified against some, but not all, possible defects.

17. B   The owner's interest in the unit is normally a fee ownerhip interest, held in severalty, meaning separate from other owners.

18. D   By the definition of a deed restriction .

19. A   A deed must be transferred by a competent party. The attorney-in-fact is considered a competent party.

20. C   By definition of special warranty deed.

21. A   The recording fee is an expense of the buyer and is not prorated.

22. B   By definition of attachment.

23. C   Alienation in real estate means conveyance. Eminent domain is involuntary alienation of real estate.

24. C   RESPA does not offer the buyer a five-day right of rescission in a sale contract.

25. D   All are ways a title may transfer.

26. D   An equitable title is an insurable title, but it does not transfer legal title.

27. B   By definition of habendum clause.

28. A   A quitclaim deed most likely would be used to correct an error in a deed.

29. C   The primary purpose of acknowledgment is to verify that the document was executed without duress. The secondary purpose is to ensure the identity of the party signing the document.

30. C   RESPA does not set interest rates.

31. C   The owner's policy covers the owner, while the lenders' policy covers the lender and decreases as the mortgage balance is reduced.

32. B   Unpaid property taxes create a specific lien on the property, not a general lien.

33. D   By the definition of general and specific liens.

34. C   In an adverse possession claim, there needs to be a suit to quiet the title to determine who is the rightful owner of the property.

35. A   When a person dies without a will and there are no heirs, the property is considered abandoned and reverts to the state by escheat.

36. B   By the definition of an investment contract, which is a type of security.

37. A   The taxes were paid in advance for the entire year; therefore, they are a debit to the buyer and a credit to the seller.

38. B   The buyers will not assume the assessment; therefore, the entry will be a debit to the seller.

39. A   Expenses could be a debit to either the buyer or the seller on a settlement sheet.

40. B RESPA regulates federally related mortgage loans.
41. D Nothing can provide a 100 percent guarantee of clear title.
42. C The actual consideration need not be stated in a deed unless state law requires it.
43. B By definition of time-sharing.
44. C An unrecorded lien would not give constructive notice.
45. B By the new laws regarding exclusion of capital gains.
46. C An abstract of title is a history or digest of information taken from public records.
47. D A lien position is established by the order of recording at the courthouse.
48. C Zoning changes or zoning regulations are not covered under title insurance.
49. B A contract for deed is a land contract and the transaction is financed by the owner. RESPA does not regulate such transactions.
50. D The right of the government to take the land is eminent domain. The process is condemnation.

51. B By definition of bargain and sell deed.
52. B By definition of lis pendens.
53. C A fee simple absolute ownership conveyed by a general warranty deed would best protect the grantee's interest.
54. B The deed was not delivered during the lifetime of the grantor; therefore, the property transfers to Sandy's heirs by the laws of descent and distribution in the state where the property is located.
55. D The sales contract is not recorded at the courthouse.
56. B The principal paid on the loan is not a tax deduction.
57. A Married homeowners who file jointly may exclude up to $500,000 in capital gains.
58. D They should trade properties and start the depreciation again.
59. A By the definition of syndicate.
60. D A license is the personal privilege to be on the land of another and would not be associated with adverse possession.

5

Financing

This chapter covers the following information regarding financing: sources of financing, types of loans, terms and conditions, and common clauses and terms in mortgage instruments.

Content Outline—Sources of Financing

V. Financing

    A. Sources of Financing

        1. Institutional
        2. Seller financing
        3. Assumption of existing financing
        4. Other sources of financing

INSTITUTIONAL

The **primary mortgage market** and the **secondary mortgage market** are sources of funds for financing. Primary mortgage market lenders originate or make loans directly to borrowers, while the secondary mortgage market buys mortgages from primary market lenders.

Primary Mortgage Market

Savings and loans

- specialize in long-term, single-family home loans.
- may offer conventional, FHA or VA mortgages.

Mutual savings banks

- are located primarily in the northeastern United States.
- are state chartered, owned by their depositors and originate FHA or VA loans.

Commercial banks

- Have historically specialized in short-term loans (such as home improvement loans, mobile-home loans and commercial loans).

- Have become more active in the negotiation of long-term residential loans.

Insurance companies

- specialize in large-scale, long-term loans that finance commercial and industrial properties.
- may require an equity kicker or participation financing in the loans they negotiate.

Mortgage bankers

- originate loans and package mortgages, selling them to investors and continuing to service them after they are sold.

Mortgage brokers

- do not originate loans.
- bring borrowers and lenders together and are paid a percentage of the money borrowed.

Credit Unions

- are a source of funds for their members.

Pension funds

- work through mortgage bankers and mortgage brokers in real estate financing.

Rural Economic and Community Development

- is a federal agency under the Department of Agriculture that negotiates loans to people in rural areas.
- negotiates loans for the purchase of property, to operate farms or to purchase farm equipment. The interest paid on the loan is determined by the income of the borrower.
- originates loans either through a private lender or directly by the agency.

Federal Reserve

The Federal Reserve (the Fed) was established to stabilize the economy by controlling the money supply and credit available in the country. It does this by creating money, regulating reserve requirements and setting the discount rate of interest.

- An oversupply of money creates inflation; an undersupply can cause a recession.
- When the reserve requirements are increased, the money supply shrinks, thus increasing interest rates.
- If the reserve requirements are decreased, the money supply grows, thus decreasing interest rates.
- The discount rate of interest is the rate the Fed charges for loans to its member banks, and it can move money into or out of commercial banks by buying or selling government bonds.

Real estate borrowers compete with other businesses for money. When the money supply is limited, interest rates are high and qualifying buyers can be difficult. When money is plentiful, interest rates are low and qualifying buyers is much easier.

SELLER FINANCING
Land Contracts

In a **land contract** the seller/vendor agrees to finance the sale of the property. Typically, the buyer/vendee makes a down payment and monthly payments until the balance is paid in full. The seller normally retains title to the property until the final payment. Should the buyer default, the seller can evict the buyer and retain all money paid. Many states now have laws that give a defaulted buyer more legal protection, and the seller must foreclose on the property to reclaim it.

Be aware that there is no mortgage involved in a land contract. A mortgage is a *pledge of property to a lender as security for the payment of a debt*, but the land contract is itself the security instrument.

The buyer's interest in a land contract is an equitable interest or equitable title. An **equitable title** represents the buyer's interest in the property when the legal title is held by another party. It also is an insurable interest, meaning the buyer can secure insurance on the property. Most land contracts stipulate that the buyer secure insurance, pay property taxes and maintain the property.

Purchase-Money Mortgage

A **purchase-money mortgage** (PMM) is a creative financing technique that developed when interest rates were high. Usually the seller agrees to finance a portion or all of the purchase price, as opposed to the land contract, where the amount financed is always the entire amount, less the buyer's down payment. A PMM is also known as a *take-back mortgage.*

Here is an example of a purchase money mortgage as it is used in today's market. A buyer has a 5 percent down payment, excellent credit, job stability and savings. If the seller would agree to loan the borrower 15 percent of the sale price, then the lender would view the borrower as having a 20 percent down payment and would not require private mortgage insurance. This is known as an 80/15/5 loan. (There is also an 80/10/10 loan.)

At the closing, the seller pays of the existing mortgage and "takes back" a mortgage on the property just sold. To secure the loan, the seller establishes a junior lien on the property and receives payments from the buyer until the loan is paid in full. This would occur with the approval of the lender negotiating the 80 percent loan.

ASSUMPTION OF EXISTING FINANCING

FHA-insured and VA-guaranteed loans are assumable loans. For FHA-insured loans originated after December 1, 1986, and VA-guaranteed loans originated after March 1, 1988, the buyer must meet approval. A third party can buy the property subject to the mortgage or assume the mortgage.

Subject to the Mortgage

When a property is taken "subject to" the mortgage, the original borrower, or obligor, remains liable for the debt, even if the third party, or buyer, defaults. If a default occurs, the buyer loses the property and the original borrower can reclaim it by buying the property, or by buying the mortgage from the lender and foreclosing.

Assumption of the Mortgage

When a third party "assumes" the mortgage, the third party becomes liable for the debt. Should the new buyer default, the buyer is primarily liable for the debt, and the original borrower is secondarily liable.

A **novation** is a substitution of one contract for another. If the lender grants novation in the assumption of an existing mortgage, the original borrower is released from liability.

OTHER SOURCES OF FINANCING

See page 111–112 for review.

Sources of Financing—Key Point Review

1. The primary mortgage market includes savings and loan associations, mutual savings banks, commercial banks, insurance companies, mortgage bankers, mortgage brokers, credit unions, pension funds and the Rural Economic and Community Development agency, formerly the Farmers Home Administration.

2. Savings and loans are an important source of funds for single-family home loans.

3. Commercial banks have specialized in short-term loans, but they are becoming more active in the negotiation of long-term residential loans.

4. Insurance companies specialize in large-scale, long-term loans that finance commercial and industrial properties. They may require an equity kicker or participation financing, meaning they become a partner with the borrower.

5. Mortgage bankers originate loans with money from insurance companies, pension funds or individuals. They package and sell mortgages and continue to service a loan after it is sold.

6. Credit unions are a source of funds for their members.

7. The Rural Economic and Community Development agency negotiates loans to people in rural areas for the purchase of property, to operate farms and to purchase farm equipment. These loans can be originated through a private lender or directly from the agency.

8. In a purchase-money mortgage, the seller agrees to finance all or a portion of the purchase price. At the closing, the seller pays off the existing mortgage and "takes back" a mortgage on the property sold. Purchase-money mortgages usually create a junior lien on the property.

9. When a property is taken subject to the mortgage, the original borrower or obligor remains liable for the debt. When a third party assumes the mortgage, the third party becomes primarily liable for the debt, and the original borrower is secondarily liable.

10. The Federal Reserve stabilizes the economy by controlling the money supply and credit available in the country. It does this in three ways. (1) It creates money: An oversupply of money creates inflation, while an undersupply can cause a recession. (2) It regulates reserve requirements for depository institutions: increasing reserve requirements shrinks the money supply and increases interest rates; decreasing reserve requirements expands the money supply and decreases interest rates. (3) It sets the discount rate of interest it charges for loans to member banks, and it moves money into or out of commercial banks by buying or selling bonds.

Content Outline—Types of Loans

V. Financing
   B. Types of Loans
      1. Security for loans
      2. Repayment methods
      3. Forms of financing
      4. Secondary mortgage markets
      5. Other types of mortgage loans

SECURITY FOR LOANS

Security Instruments

Security instruments are used to provide collateral for the loan. They consist of

- mortgages, primarily used in lien-theory states;
- trust deeds, primarily used in title-theory states; and
- land contracts, used when the seller is financing the property.

Lien-Theory State

The lender's interest in the property can be a lien interest or a title interest. In a **lien-theory state,** the borrower receives the deed to the property at the closing, and the lender establishes a lien position on the property by recording the note and mortgage. Should the borrower default, the mortgage gives the lender the right to foreclose on the property, the note determines how much money the lender can collect and the lien establishes the order in which the lenders are paid.

Title-Theory State

In a **title-theory state,** the law construes the lender to have legal title to the property and the borrower to have an equitable title. Because the lender holds the title to the property, the lender has the right to possession of the property on default.

Deed of Trust

- A **deed of trust** is also known as a **trust deed.** (See Figure 5.1.)
- Legal title is conveyed to the **trustee** for the benefit of the **beneficiary.**
- A **defeasance** clause stipulates that when the final payment is made, the lender's interest is defeated and a **deed of reconveyance** is given from the trustee to the **trustor.**
- If the borrower defaults, the trustee will initiate **foreclosure.**
- This is a **nonjudicial foreclosure** or foreclosure by advertisement

REPAYMENT METHODS

Definitions

- **Equity**—the difference between the market value and any liens on the property
- **Mortgage**—a pledge of property to a lender; collateral

FIGURE 5.1 *Deeds of Trust*

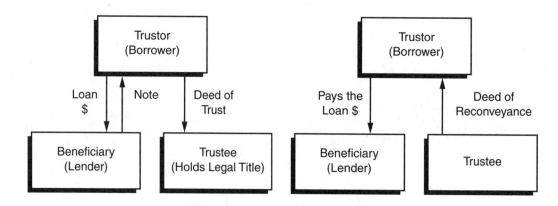

- **Mortgagor**—the borrower
- **Mortgagee**—the lender
- **Note**—gives evidence of the debt and states the terms of repayment
- **Obligor/promissor**—the borrower in a note
- **Obligee/promisee**—the lender in the note

Conventional and Unconventional Mortgages

- **Conventional mortgage**—Not insured or guaranteed by the government.
- **Conventional uninsured mortgage**—Typically, the borrower has a 20 percent or greater down payment and the lender accepts the creditworthiness of the borrower and the property as security for the loan.
- **Conventional insured mortgage**—Typically, the borrower has less than a 20 percent down payment and the lender requires private mortgage insurance.
- **Unconventional mortgage**—FHA is *insured* by the government and VA is *guaranteed* by the government.

Private Mortgage Insurance

If a borrower has less than a 20 percent down payment, the lender may require that the borrower purchase **private mortgage insurance (PMI).** Payment for PMI can be a one-time premium, but typically it is a percentage added to each monthly payment. When the loan balance is paid down to 80 percent of the total value, the PMI payment will be dropped. Should the borrower default, the lender may foreclose on the property. If the property sells at foreclosure for less than the mortgage balance, the PMI pays the lender up to the amount of the insurance, typically the top 20 percent to 25 percent of the loan.

Amortization

To *amortize* means to repay the loan in monthly or other periodic payments that include principal and interest. A portion of each payment is applied to the principal balance and a portion is kept by the lender as interest on the loan.

In a fully **amortized loan** or direct reduction loan, at the end of the loan period the principal balance is zero. A 30-year fixed-rate mortgage is a fully amortized loan. If the payments are paid each month, the loan is paid in full on final payment.

In a partially amortized loan, or balloon mortgage, the principal and interest payments do not pay off the entire loan. A balance remains when the final payment is made. Balloon mortgages may be negotiated when interest rates are high. For example, a borrower negotiates a loan in which the payments are amortized for 30 years, when in fact the note is due in 5 years. The borrower hopes the interest rate will drop during the five years and he or she can renegotiate the loan at that time.

In a nonamortized loan, periodic interest payments are made to the lender, but nothing is applied to the principal balance. These loans are called **term mortgages** or *straight mortgages.* A construction loan is one example. In a construction loan, the borrower receives the money in stages, called *draws,* and makes periodic payments of interest. When the construction is complete, the borrower must have secured long-term financing and will pay off the entire principal balance.

Types of Mortgages

An **adjustable-rate mortgage (ARM)** contains an **escalation clause** that allows the interest to adjust over the loan term. Adjustable-rate mortgages are tied to an index such as the cost of funds index or to U.S. Treasury Securities (T-bills).

The premium charged by the lender and added to the index to determine the interest is called the *margin.* Over the life of an adjustable-rate mortgage, the margin remains constant. A cap sets the maximum limit to which the interest rate can increase over the life of the loan.

A **blanket mortgage** may be used by a builder or developer. This mortgage covers more than one tract of land and contains a partial release clause, which allows the borrower to obtain a release of any one lot or parcel and thus to give the buyer a marketable title.

A **buydown mortgage** allows the borrower to "buy down" the interest rate, thus reducing the monthly payment for a number of years. To buy down the interest rate, the borrower must pay interest in advance. If interest rates are high, developers may buy down the interest rate to help buyers qualify for loans.

A **budget mortgage** includes principal, interest, taxes and insurance payments (PITI). The tax and insurance portions of each monthly payment are put into an escrow account and paid when those payments are due.

A **graduated-payment mortgage (GPM)** is also known as a *flexible-payment plan.* The borrower makes lower monthly payments for the first few years and larger payments for the remainder of the loan term. If the lower monthly payments do not cover all the interest charges, the lender adds the unpaid interest to the principal balance. This creates **negative amortization,** because the loan balance increases instead of decreases.

A borrower who has negotiated a **growing-equity mortgage (GEM)** realizes that there will be periodic increases in the monthly payment. However, the increase is applied directly to the principal, thus reducing the term of the loan.

Package mortgages are usually used in the sale of new homes in a subdivision or in condominium sales. Such a loan covers both real and personal property, such as a washer and dryer.

The **Nehemiah Grant Program** provides home buyers with gift money toward the down payment and closing costs. The gift can be from a non-profit organization or the seller.

In a **shared-appreciation mortgage (SAM),** the lender agrees to originate the loan at below market interest rates in return for a guaranteed share of the appreciation the borrower will realize when the property is sold. This typically is used in the financing of commercial projects.

A **reverse annuity mortgage (RAM)** allows elderly homeowners to borrow against the equity in their homes and receive monthly payments from the lender. The loan comes due on a specific date or on the occurrence of a specific event, such as the sale of the property or the death of the borrower.

A **wraparound mortgage** is also known as an *all-inclusive* or *overriding loan.* It is a junior loan that wraps around an existing senior loan. For example, an owner has an existing mortgage and equity in his property. When he goes to the lender to negotiate a loan against the equity, the lender agrees to do so and "wraps it around" the existing first mortgage. The borrower makes only one monthly payment to the lender that is applied to both mortgages. To create a wraparound mortgage, the original loan must be assumable.

FORMS OF FINANCING

FHA-Insured Loans

The **Federal Housing Administration (FHA)** was established in 1934 to encourage improvements in housing standards, to encourage lenders to make loans and to exert a stabilizing influence on the mortgage market after the Great Depression. FHA does *not* negotiate loans; FHA *insures* loans. FHA operates under the Department of Housing and Urban Development (HUD). An FHA-insured loan is backed by the government, meaning that should a borrower default and the lender foreclose on the property, the lender is insured against loss.

Lenders must be qualified to negotiate an FHA-insured loan. There are several FHA insured loan programs, with the most popular being the 203-B-1 for owner-occupied one- to-four family dwellings. The borrower must pay a mortgage insurance premium, or MIP. There is a one-time upfront insurance premium plus one-half percent is added to the monthly payments. There is a minimum down payment, and the borrower must have cash for it. Interest rates are negotiable, and as a rule, FHA does not set income limits for borrowers. Discount points may be paid by the buyer or seller on an FHA insured loan. Pre-payment penalties are not allowed under FHA, and the maximum origination fee a lender can charge is one percent.

VA-Guaranteed Loans

The *Serviceman's Readjustment Act of 1944* initially established the Department of Veterans Affairs (VA). One of its purposes was to make government-backed loans available to qualified veterans and unremarried widows or widowers of veterans. A qualified person can negotiate a loan with a 100 percent **loan-to-value** ratio, or with a minimum down payment, at relatively low interest rates. The VA guarantees loans to lenders and normally does not make loans. If financing is not readily available, such as in an isolated rural area, the VA may make a direct loan.

Other characteristics of a VA-guaranteed loan are as follows:

- A qualified person can secure a VA-guaranteed loan on a one- to four-family dwelling that will be owner occupied.
- The limit on the amount of loan that a veteran can obtain is determined by the lender.
- There is a limit on how much the VA will guarantee. Should the borrower default and the lender receive less than the mortgage balance after a foreclosure sale, the VA guarantees a certain amount based on a sliding scale of the value of the property.
- To determine the amount the VA will guarantee, a veteran must apply for a **certificate of eligibility,** which establishes the maximum guarantee entitlement of the veteran.
- A **certificate of reasonable value (CRV)** also is issued by the VA for the property being purchased. The CRV states the current market value based on a VA-approved appraisal and places a ceiling on the amount of a VA loan allowed for the property.
- The borrower or seller also must pay a funding fee to the VA. This is a percentage of the loan amount and depends on the eligibility status and down payment of the veteran. The funding fee may be financed as a part of the loan.
- Discount points may be paid by the buyer or seller when a VA-guaranteed loan is negotiated.
- No prepayment penalties are allowed on VA mortgages.
- A VA loan is assumable. If another qualified veteran assumes the loan, that veteran's certificate of eligibility may replace the existing certificate. The original borrower is granted novation by the lender, and his or her full eligibility is reinstated by VA.

- If a nonveteran assumes the loan, the original borrower remains liable for the loan. Novation from the lender does not reinstate the eligibility of the veteran. Only the VA can reinstate the eligibility.

SECONDARY MORTGAGE MARKETS

The secondary mortgage markets were created to stabilize the source of funds for lenders on the primary markets. Lenders on the primary markets can negotiate loans on a percentage of their deposits. When that percentage has been met, they can borrow money or sell the mortgages on the secondary market to create a source of funds to meet the mortgage demands. Secondary mortgage markets become especially desirable when money is in short supply.

A **nonconforming loan** is one that does not meet secondary market specifications.

Federal National Mortgage Association

The **Federal National Mortgage Association** (FNMA, or Fannie Mae) is the largest buyer of mortgages in the secondary market. Fannie Mae's original purpose was to buy FHA and then VA loans. Today, Fannie Mae is a quasi-governmental agency organized as a privately owned corporation. Fannie Mae buys any mortgage that meets its specifications. Mortgages purchased by Fannie Mae are funded through stock issued on the New York Stock Exchange.

Government National Mortgage Association

The **Government National Mortgage Association** (GNMA, or Ginnie Mae) is a federal agency created in 1968 when Fannie Mae was reorganized. It is owned by the government and is a division of the Department of Housing and Urban Development (HUD). Ginnie Mae specializes in high-risk and special assistance programs, such as housing for the elderly.

Ginnie Mae has a mortgage-backed securities program that sells guarantee certificates to investors. These Ginnie Mae pass-through certificates provide for a monthly "pass through" of principal and interest payments directly to certificate holders.

Through a tandem plan, Ginnie Mae also works with Fannie Mae in secondary market activities when money is tight. The tandem plan provides that Fannie Mae can purchase high-risk, low-yield loans at full market rates and Ginnie Mae will guarantee payment and absorb the difference between the low yield and current market prices. Ginnie Mae purchases FHA, VA and certain Rural Development loans.

Federal Home Loan Mortgage Corporation

The **Federal Home Loan Mortgage Corporation** (FHLMC, or Freddie Mac) was established to assist savings and loan associations as a secondary market for conventional mortgages. Freddie Mac is a publicly owned corporation that purchases mortgages, pools them and sells bonds in the open market as mortgage-backed securities. Freddie Mac does not guarantee payment of its mortgages. Freddie Mac also buys FHA and VA loans.

OTHER TYPES OF MORTGAGE LOANS

See page 117 for review.

Types of Loans—Key Point Review

1. A security instrument protects the lender's interest by providing collateral for the loan. Trust deeds and mortgages are standard security instruments. A land contract also is a security instrument.

2. In a lien-theory state, the borrower receives the deed to the property and the lender establishes a lien position by recording the note and mortgage.

3. In a title-theory state, the law construes the lender to have legal title to the property and the borrower to have an equitable title.

4. Under a deed of trust, the borrower transfers legal title to the trustee, who holds the title for the benefit of the beneficiary (the lender). When the borrower has made the final payment to the lender, the lender's interest in the property has been defeated. The lender sends the proper documents to the trustee, who uses a deed of reconveyance to convey the title to the trustor.

5. Under a deed of trust, should the borrower default on the loan, the lender sends the proper documents to the trustee showing the delinquency of the payments. Usually, the borrower is given some time to make the payments current, pay a reinstatement fee and reinstate the delinquent loan. If the borrower cannot, the trustee advertises and sells the property in a foreclosure by advertisement. This avoids the judicial foreclosure process found in title-theory states.

6. A mortgage is a pledge of property to the lender as security of the payment of debt. The mortgagor is the borrower and the mortgagee is the lender.

7. A note is evidence of the debt and states the terms of repayment. The borrower is the obligor, or promisor, because she or he is obligated or promises to repay the debt. The lender is the obligee, or promisee.

8. A conventional mortgage is not backed by the government, but can be insured or uninsured.

9. In conventional financing, if a borrower has a 20 percent or greater down payment, the lender may accept the creditworthiness of the borrower and the security of the property to ensure the payment of debt. If a borrower has less than a 20 percent down payment, the lender may require that the borrower purchase private mortgage insurance, usually a percentage added to each monthly payment. Should the borrower default, the lender may foreclose. If the property at the foreclosure sale sells for less than the mortgage balance, the private mortgage insurance pays the lender up to the amount covered in the policy.

10. An unconventional mortgage is backed by the government; for example, FHA-insured and VA-guaranteed loans.

11. To amortize means to repay a loan in periodic payments that include principal and interest.

12. In a fully amortized loan, the principal balance is zero at the end of the loan period. In a partially amortized loan, the principal and interest payments do not pay off the entire loan. In a nonamortized loan, periodic interest payments are made to the lender, but no part of the payments is applied to the principal balance.

Types of Loans—Key Point Review (Continued)

13. A construction loan is an example of a term mortgage. The borrower receives the money in stages, called *draws*, and makes periodic payments of interest. When the construction is complete, the borrower must have secured long-term financing and will pay off the entire principal balance.

14. An adjustable-rate mortgage (ARM) contains an escalation clause that allows the interest to adjust over the loan term. ARMs are tied to an index. The premium charged by the lender and added to the index to determine the interest charged is called the margin, which remains constant over the life of an ARM. A cap sets the maximum limit the interest rate can increase and the maximum limit of rate change at each adjustment interval.

15. In a graduated-payment mortgage, the borrower makes lower monthly payments for the first few years and then larger payments. If the lower monthly payments do not cover all the interest charges, the lender will add the unpaid interest to the principal balance, creating negative amortization.

16. In a growing-equity mortgage, there are periodic increases in the monthly payment that are applied directly to the principal, thus reducing the term of the loan.

17. In a shared-appreciation mortgage, the lender agrees to originate the loan at below-market interest rates in return for a guaranteed share of the appreciation the borrower will realize when the property is sold.

18. A reverse annuity mortgage allows elderly homeowners to borrow against the equity in their homes and receive monthly payments. The loan becomes due on a specific date or on the occurrence of a specific event.

19. Package mortgage loans on both real and personal property are usually used in the sale of new homes in a subdivision or in condominium sales.

20. A blanket mortgage covers more than one tract of land and contains a partial release clause that allows the borrower to obtain a release of any one lot or parcel.

21. A wraparound mortgage is a junior loan that wraps around an existing senior loan when the original loan is assumable.

22. A buydown mortgage allows the borrower to "buy down" the interest rate, thus reducing the monthly payment for a number of years.

23. A budget mortgage includes principal, interest, taxes and insurance payments. The tax and insurance portions of each payment are paid from an escrow account.

24. The FHA was established to encourage improvements in housing standards, to encourage lenders to make loans, and to exert a stabilizing influence on the mortgage market after the Depression of the 1930s. FHA does not negotiate loans.

25. With an FHA-insured loan, the borrower must pay an insurance premium, which may be a one-time fee or a percentage added to the monthly payments. A minimum down payment in cash is required. Interest rates are negotiable, and FHA does not set income limits for borrowers. No prepayment penalties are allowed on FHA-insured loans.

Types of Loans—Key Point Review (Continued)

26. One of the purposes of the VA is to make government-backed loans available for qualified veterans and unremarried widows or widowers of veterans. The VA guarantees loans but normally does not make loans.

27. A qualified veteran can negotiate a loan with 100 percent loan-to-value ratio, or with a minimum down payment, at relatively low interest rates. A qualified person can secure a VA-guaranteed loan on a one- to four-family dwelling when the property will be owner occupied.

28. Though the limit on the amount of loan that a veteran can obtain is determined by the lender, there is a limit that the VA will guarantee, based on a sliding scale of the value of the property. A veteran must apply for a certificate of eligibility, which establishes the maximum guarantee entitlement of the veteran. The VA also issues a certificate of reasonable value (CRV) for the property being purchased, which states the current market value based on a VA-approved appraisal and places a ceiling on the amount of a VA loan allowed. A veteran is not required to have a down payment unless the purchase price exceeds the amount cited in the CRV.

29. At the closing, the borrower or seller must pay a funding fee to the VA. This is a percentage of the loan amount and depends on the eligibility status and down payment of the veteran. The fee may be financed as a part of the loan. Discount points may be paid by the buyer or seller. No prepayment penalties are allowed on a VA loan.

30. A VA loan is assumable with VA approval. Another qualified veteran's certificate of eligibility may replace the existing certificate. The original borrower is granted novation by the lender, and full eligibility may be reinstated by the VA. If a nonveteran assumes the loan, the original borrower remains liable.

31. The secondary mortgage markets were created to stabilize the source of funds for lenders on the primary markets, especially when money is in short supply.

32. The Federal National Mortgage Association, or Fannie Mae, is a quasi-governmental agency organized as a privately owned corporation. Mortgages purchased by Fannie Mae are sold through stock issued on the New York Stock Exchange.

33. The Government National Mortgage Association, created when Fannie Mae was reorganized in 1968, specializes in high-risk and special assistance programs and has the management and liquidating functions of the old Fannie Mae. The Ginnie Mae pass-through certificate provides for a monthly "pass through" of principal and interest payments directly to the certificate holder.

34. Through a tandem plan, Ginnie Mae also works with Fannie Mae when money is tight. Under this plan, Fannie Mae can purchase high-risk, low-yield loans at full market rates and Ginnie Mae will guarantee payment and absorb the difference between the low yield and current market prices.

35. The Federal Home Loan Mortgage Corporation was established to assist savings and loans as a secondary market for conventional mortgages, and is a publicly owned corporation. Freddie Mac purchases mortgages, pools them and sells bonds in the open market as mortgage-backed securities. Freddie Mac does not guarantee payment of its mortgages.

Content Outline—Terms and Conditions

LOAN APPLICATION REQUIREMENTS

The loan process consists of filling out the application, analyzing the borrower and the property, processing the loan application and closing the loan. This process can be simplified if the borrower understands the steps and the information the lender requires.

To fill out the loan application properly, the lender must have a copy of the purchase and sale agreement, the residence, employment and credit histories of the applicants, as well as income information, assets and liabilities, and a copy of a gift letter (if applicable).

The borrower must be told that an appraisal and title report will be done on the property, and if everything is in order, a closing date will be set. The credit report and appraisal fee are usually paid by the borrower at the time of the loan application.

LOAN ORIGINATION COSTS

The loan origination fee is charged by the lender to cover the administrative costs of making the loan. The fee is a percentage of the loan amount.

> **O**ther costs the borrower pays to originate the loan are for the credit report and appraisal and points required by the lender. See pages 171–172 for more information on origination fees and discount points.

LENDER REQUIREMENTS

See pages 51–52 for review.

CONDITIONAL APPROVAL

Approval of every loan is conditional on some terms being met by the borrower. Typically, the loan commitment letter states the loan has been approved pending resolution of the following items before or at the closing:

- Satisfactory title report
- Mortgagee's title insurance
- Homeowner's insurance policy
- Survey
- Verification of job status
- Affidavit of marital status
- Copy of the settlement sheet of the house just sold
- Verification of bank accounts
- Payoff of a particular bill
- Inspection reports required by the lender
- Any repairs required by the appraiser

A lock-in clause in the loan application guarantees that the interest rate quoted the buyer on loan application is "locked" for a specific time.

PROVISIONS OF FEDERAL REGULATIONS

Lending laws provide protection to the consumer as well as to the lender. There are both state and federal laws that lenders must follow when negotiating loans.

Usury Laws

Usury laws in each state limit the maximum interest rate that a lender can charge on certain types of loans. Please note: Usury laws do not set the interest rates; they establish the maximum rate that can be charged. In times of emergencies, the federal government can set aside usury laws.

Truth-in-Lending Act

The **Truth-in-Lending Act** was passed as a part of the *Consumer Credit Protection Act*. This law, also known as *Regulation Z*, requires that lenders disclose the true cost of credit to borrowers, expressed as an annual percentage rate (APR).

The finance fees that must be disclosed include loan fees, finders' fees, service charges, interest and discount points. Fees that do not have to be disclosed by Regulation Z include attorneys' fees, escrow fees, appraisals, surveys, inspection fees, title fees and closing expenses.

Loans covered by Regulation Z include all real estate financing for borrowers who intend to purchase one- to four-family dwellings and who are natural persons. Loans *not* covered by Regulation

Z include loans for business, commercial or agricultural purposes; personal property credit transactions over $25,000; and loans to the owner of a dwelling containing more than four units.

When negotiating a home improvement loan or refinancing, there is a three-business-day right of rescission mandated by Regulation Z. This right of rescission does *not* apply to first mortgages and trust deeds, however.

Also under Regulation Z, full disclosure is required by the lender if any of the following trigger items appear in an ad:

- Amount of monthly payment
- Number of payments
- Amount of down payment
- Interest rate
- Term of payment

> **A**s used above, "full disclosure" means that if any of the above items are used in the ad, the same ad must include the cash price; required down payment; number, amounts and due dates of all payments; and the annual percentage rate.

Finally, according to Regulation Z, a *creditor* is an entity that extends consumer credit more than 25 times a year, or more than five times a year if the transaction involves a dwelling as security. The credit must be subject to a finance charge or payable in more than four installments by written agreement.

Equal Credit Opportunity Act

The **Equal Credit Opportunity Act** (ECOA) prohibits discrimination based on race, color, religion, national origin, sex, marital status, age or source of income in the granting of credit. This act requires that credit applications be considered only on the basis of income, net worth, job stability and credit rating. If the applicant is rejected, lenders have 30 days to inform the applicant of the reasons why credit was denied. (This 30-day notice also applies to creditors that terminate existing credit.)

Community Reinvestment Act

The **Community Reinvestment Act** was passed to prevent redlining and disinvestment in central city areas. This act requires that lenders delineate the communities in which their lending activities take place; make available listings of the types of credit they offer in the communities and make available appropriate notices and information regarding lending activities. It also gives lenders the option to disclose affirmative programs designed to meet the credit needs of their communities.

Terms and Conditions—Key Point Review

1. The loan process consists of filling out the application, analyzing the borrower and the property, processing the loan application and closing the loan.

2. To properly fill out the loan application, the lender must have a copy of the purchase and sale agreement; the residence, employment and credit histories of the borrower, income information; a report of the borrower's assets and liabilities; and a copy of a gift letter, if applicable.

3. The loan origination fee covers the administrative costs of making the loan and is a percentage of the loan amount.

4. The loan commitment letter states that the loan has been approved pending the resolution, before or at the closing, of a satisfactory title report, mortgagee's title insurance, home-owner's insurance policy, survey, verification of job status, affidavit of marital status, copy of the settlement sheet of the house sold, verification of bank accounts, payoff of a particular bill, inspection reports required by the lender and repairs required by the appraiser.

5. State usury laws limit the maximum interest rate that a lender can charge on certain types of loans. Usury laws do not set interest rates.

6. The Truth-in-Lending Act or Regulation Z, established by the Federal Reserve System, requires that lenders disclose to borrowers the true cost of credit expressed as an APR.

7. Finance fees that must be disclosed include loan fees, finder's fees, service charges, interest and discount points. These fees must be expressed as an APR. Fees that do not have to be disclosed by Regulation Z include attorneys' fees, escrow fees, appraisals, surveys, inspections fees, title fees and closing expenses. (RESPA does require the disclosure of these fees.)

8. Regulation Z covers all one- to four-family real estate financing for residential borrowers who are natural persons, but not loans that are used for business, commercial or agricultural purposes; personal property credit transactions involving more than $25,000; and loans to the owner of a dwelling containing more than four housing units.

9. A borrower negotiating a home improvement loan or refinancing (but not a first mortgage or trust deed) has a three-day right of rescission in which to cancel the transaction by notifying the lender.

10. Truth-in-Lending requires full disclosure by the lender if the following trigger items are used in an ad: amount of monthly payment, number of payments, amount of down payment, interest rate and the term of payment. If any of these items are used, the ad must include the purchase price; required down payment; number, amounts and due dates of all payments; and the annual percentage rate.

11. Regulation Z defines a creditor as a person or an institution that extends consumer credit more than 25 times a year or more than five times a year if the transaction involves a dwelling as security. The credit must be subject to a finance charge or payable in more than four installments by written agreement.

Terms and Conditions—Key Point Review (Continued)

12. The Equal Credit Opportunity Act prohibits discrimination based on race, color, religion, national origin, sex, marital status, age or source of income in the granting of credit. Credit applications must be considered only on the basis of income, net worth, job stability and credit rating.

13. Lenders have 30 days to inform a rejected applicant of the reasons why credit was denied.

14. The Community Reinvestment Act was passed to prevent redlining and disinvestment in central city areas. Lenders must delineate the communities in which their lending activities take place; make available a listing of the types of credit they offer; and provide appropriate notices and information regarding lending activities. The act gives lenders the opportunity to disclose affirmative programs designed to meet the credit needs of their communities.

Content Outline—Common Clauses and Terms in Mortgage Instruments

V. Financing

    D. Common Clauses and Terms in Mortgage Instruments

        1. Prepayment
        2. Interest rates
        3. Release
        4. Due-on-sale
        5. Subordination
        6. Escalation
        7. Acceleration
        8. Default
        9. Foreclosure and redemption rights
      10. Nonrecourse provision
      11. Rescission

PREPAYMENT

An **open mortgage** usually allows a borrower to pay off the loan at any time over the life of the loan without a penalty. This is allowed by a **prepayment privilege clause** in the mortgage. When a borrower repays the loan ahead of schedule, the lender collects less interest, so while some lenders allow the prepayment of the mortgage, they charge a prepayment penalty. This penalty may be a percentage of the remaining mortgage balance.

INTEREST RATES

The **interest** paid by the borrower is a charge for the use of money. A *fixed* interest rate is constant over the life of the loan. An *adjustable* interest rate can change over the life of the loan.

The lock-in clause in the note typically means that upon loan application, the lender has agreed to "lock" the rate for a specified time period; or it could mean that the loan cannot be prepaid unless all interest is paid. A lender normally computes simple interest on residential loans.

RELEASE

When the mortgage is paid in full, the lender must release its interest in the property. In **lien-theory states,** a mortgage release or satisfaction piece is recorded. In **title-theory states,** a defeasance clause provides that the lender release its interest in the title. If the mortgage document was a **trust deed,** the reconveyance deed must be recorded to release the lender's title interest.

If a lien is not released at settlement, the lien will "run with the land" or stay attached to the property. This is why a title search is conduced to protect the interest of the buyer and the lender.

DUE-ON-SALE

A **due-on-sale clause** in a mortgage allows the lender to collect full payment from the mortgagor when the property is sold. This clause prevents owners from selling the property to a buyer on a loan assumption or a land contract.

Alienation Clause

Mortgages may also contain an **alienation clause** providing that if the property is conveyed to any party without the lender's consent, the lender can collect full payment.

SUBORDINATION

Under certain circumstances, a lender with a first lien position will agree to switch positions (**subordination**) and take a second lien position on the property. For example, a borrower has a first mortgage with lender XYZ and a line of credit with lender ABC. The borrower decides to refinance her loan with XYZ. Because ABC's line of credit would be in first lien position after the existing first mortgage is paid in full, XYZ will agree to refinance only if ABC will subordinate. (Usually a subordination fee will be charged by a lender if it agrees to subordinate.)

ESCALATION

An **escalation clause** is found in an adjustable rate mortgage and in certain leases. In a mortgage, it allows the interest rate to adjust over the life of the loan. In a lease, it allows the lease payment to adjust over the life of the lease.

ACCELERATION

Notes, mortgages and security instruments contain an **acceleration clause** that allows the lender to call the note due and payable in advance of the loan term. Typical provisions that accelerate the payments are default of the mortgage, destruction of the premises or the sale of the property to another party. If this clause were not in the note and/or mortgage, the lender would have to sue the borrower for each individual monthly payment.

Please note that the acceleration clause allows the lender to call the *entire* balance due, not just the months the borrower is behind.

DEFAULT

The **default** clause in a note and mortgage protects the lender if there is a nonperformance of a duty or obligation on the part of the borrower. This clause requires the timely payment of the terms of the note, upkeep of the property, payment of property taxes and insurance, and permission from the lender for improvements to be made on the property. If the borrower defaults, the lender has the right to foreclose.

FORECLOSURE AND REDEMPTION RIGHTS

Foreclosure is the legal process whereby the property can be sold as security for the payment of a debt. State and local laws regulate foreclosure proceedings. The three types of foreclosure are judicial, nonjudicial and strict.

Foreclosure by **judicial sale** occurs in states that require that the lender go to court and prove that the borrower has defaulted. The judge orders an appraisal of the property and sets a foreclosure sale date. Creditors are notified, and the property is advertised. The property is sold, and when the paperwork is in order, the sale is confirmed. At that point, the owner's rights to the property have been foreclosed. A **deficiency judgment** is a personal judgment levied against the defaulted borrower when a foreclosure sale does not produce sufficient funds to pay the mortgage debt in full.

Nonjudicial Foreclosure

Nonjudicial foreclosure is used in states where the mortgage contains a power-of-sale clause. This clause allows the lender to sell the property without going through the court system. The defaulted borrower has a specified time in which to make up delinquent payments and costs. If the payments are not made, the property is advertised and sold.

FIGURE 5.2 *Redemption*

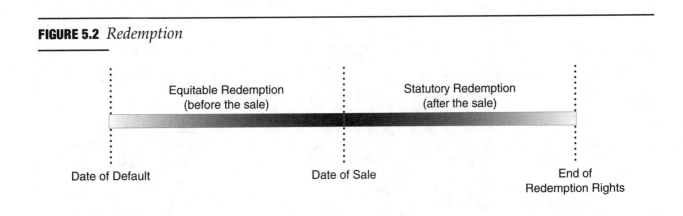

Equitable Redemption
(before the sale)

Statutory Redemption
(after the sale)

Date of Default

Date of Sale

End of
Redemption Rights

Strict Foreclosure

Strict foreclosure allows the lender to foreclose on the property after appropriate notice has been given to the delinquent borrower and the proper papers have been filed in court. If full payment is not made within a prescribed time, the borrower's equitable and statutory redemption rights are waived, the property is sold and the lender keeps all equity in the property, if there is any.

NONRECOURSE PROVISION

In a **nonrecourse loan,** the borrower is not held personally liable for the note. This may be used when the lender believes that the property used for collateral is adequate security for the loan. This type of loan could be made to real estate syndicates or other real estate investors.

RESCISSION

The process of **recession** means that the contract has been canceled, terminated or annulled and the parties have been returned to the legal positions they were in before they entered the contract. A contract may be rescinded due to mistake, fraud or misrepresentation. For example, if the seller cannot provide a marketable title, the buyer is not required to purchase the property, and the contract may be rescinded.

Common Clauses and Terms in Mortgage Instruments— Key Point Review

1. An open mortgage allows a borrower to pay off the loan at any time without a prepayment penalty, due to the prepayment privilege clause within the mortgage. Some lenders charge a prepayment penalty, a percentage of the remaining mortgage balance.

2. The interest paid by the borrower is a charge for the use of money. The interest rate is negotiated when the loan is negotiated. A fixed interest rate is constant over the life of the loan. An adjustable interest rate can change.

3. When the mortgage is paid in full, the lender must release its interest in the property. In lien-theory states, a mortgage release or satisfaction piece is recorded to release the lender's interest.

4. In title-theory states, a defeasance clause provides that the lender release its interest.

5. If the mortgage document was a trust deed, the reconveyance deed must be recorded to release the lender's title interest.

6. A due-on-sale clause in a mortgage allows the lender to collect full payment from the mortgagor when the property is sold. Mortgages may also contain an alienation clause, stipulating that if the property is conveyed to any party, the lender can collect full payment.

7. In a subordination agreement a lender with a first lien position agrees to take a second lien position on the property. Construction loans or interim loans often contain subordination agreements.

Common Clauses and Terms in Mortgage Instruments—
Key Point Review (Continued)

8. Notes, mortgages and security instruments contain an acceleration clause that allows the lender to call the note due and payable in advance of the loan term. Default of the mortgage, destruction of the premises or the sale of the property to another party may accelerate the payments.

9. The default clause in a mortgage protects the lender if there is a nonperformance of a duty or obligation on the part of the borrower. If the borrower defaults, the lender has the right to foreclose.

10. Foreclosure is the legal process whereby a property is sold as security for the payment of a debt. State and local laws regulate foreclosure proceedings.

11. Foreclosure by judicial sale occurs in states that require that the lender go to court and prove that the borrower has defaulted. The judge orders an appraisal of the property and sets a sale date. Creditors are notified and the property is advertised. When the sale of the property is confirmed, the owner's rights to the property have been foreclosed.

12. The defaulted borrower has an equitable right of redemption before confirmation of the foreclosure. In some states, the defaulted borrower has a statutory right of redemption to redeem the property after confirmation of the foreclosure.

13. Nonjudicial foreclosure is used in states where the mortgage contains a power-of-sale clause that allows the lender to sell the property without going to court. The defaulted borrower has a specified time in which to make up delinquent payments and costs, after which the property is advertised and sold.

14. Strict foreclosure allows the lender to foreclose after appropriate notice has been given to the delinquent borrower and the proper papers have been filed. If full payment is not made, the borrower's equitable and statutory redemption rights are waived, the property is sold and the lender keeps all equity.

15. In a nonrecourse loan, the borrower is not held personally responsible for the note because the lender believes that the property used for collateral is adequate security.

16. The process of recission means the contract has been canceled, and the parties have been returned to the legal positions they were in before they entered the contract.

17. When a property is refinanced, a title search is conducted, the property is appraised, the borrower must qualify for the loan and closing costs must be paid.

Questions

1. Who is the individual who obtains a real estate loan by signing a note and a mortgage?
   A. Mortgagor
   B. Mortgagee
   C. Optionor
   D. Optionee

2. Which of the following describes a mortgage that uses both real and personal property as security?
   A. Blanket mortgage
   B. Package mortgage
   C. Purchase-money mortgage
   D. Wraparound mortgage

3. Which of the following describes a mortgage that requires principal and interest payments at regular intervals until the debt is satisfied?
   A. Term mortgage
   B. Amortized mortgage
   C. First mortgage
   D. Balloon mortgage

4. What is the clause in a note, mortgage or trust deed that permits a lender to declare the entire unpaid sum due should the borrower default?
   A. Judgment clause
   B. Acceleration clause
   C. Forfeiture clause
   D. Escalator clause

5. A mortgage must include a power-of-sale clause to be foreclosed by
   A. action.
   B. advertisement.
   C. judicial procedure.
   D. the FHA.

6. In many states, by paying the debt after a foreclosure sale, the mortgagor has the right to regain the property. What is the right called?
   A. Equitable right of redemption
   B. Owner's right of redemption
   C. Vendee's right of redemption
   D. Statutory right of redemption

7. In a title-theory state, the
   A. mortgagee takes title to the mortgaged property during the term of the mortgage.
   B. mortgagor has a lien against the property for the full amount of the mortgage.
   C. mortgagor may foreclose only by court action.
   D. mortgagor holds title to the property during the term of the mortgage.

8. Gloria is qualified to obtain an FHA loan for the purchase of a new home. From which of the following may she obtain this loan?
   A. Federal Housing Administration
   B. Federal National Mortgage Association
   C. A qualified Federal Housing Administration mortgagee
   D. Federal Home Loan Bank System

9. A mortgage instrument may include a clause that prevents the assumption of the mortgage by a new purchaser without the lender's consent. What is this clause called?
   A. Alienation clause
   B. Power-of-sale clause
   C. Defeasance clause
   D. Certificate of sale

10. The defeasance clause in a mortgage requires that the mortgagee execute a(n)
    A. assignment of mortgage.
    B. satisfaction of mortgage.
    C. subordination agreement.
    D. partial release agreement.

11. John enters into a contract with Wally wherein John will sell his house to Wally for $40,000. Wally cannot get complete financing, and at the closing John and Wally enter into a contract for deed. On signing the contract for deed, Wally's interest in the property is that of
    A. legal title.
    B. equitable title.
    C. joint title.
    D. mortgagee in possession.

12. Which of the following is a lien on real estate?
    A. Easement
    B. Recorded mortgage
    C. Encroachment
    D. Restrictive covenant

13. What is a mortgage loan that requires monthly payments of $175.75 for 20 years and a final payment of $5,095 known as?
    A. Wraparound mortgage
    B. Accelerated mortgage
    C. Balloon mortgage
    D. Variable mortgage

14. Which of the following relates to a mortgage loan?
    A. Acceleration clause
    B. Covenant of further assurances
    C. Writ of execution
    D. Vested interest

15. In a sale-leaseback arrangement, the
    A. seller/vendor retains title to the real estate.
    B. buyer/vendee gets possession of the property.
    C. sale is disallowed in most states.
    D. buyer/vendee is the lessor.

16. In which of the following markets may a lender sell a loan that a bank had previously originated?
    A. Primary market
    B. Secondary market
    C. Mortgage market
    D. Investor market

17. Fannie Mae and Ginnie Mae
    A. work together as primary lenders.
    B. are both owned by the federal government.
    C. are both private agencies.
    D. are both involved in the secondary market.

18. A deficiency judgment can take place when
    A. a foreclosure sale does not produce sufficient funds to pay a mortgage debt in full.
    B. not enough taxes have been paid on a piece of property.
    C. a foreclosure sale is not completed.
    D. All of the above

19. When a buyer assumes the mortgage, which of the following is TRUE?
    A. If the mortgage has an alienation clause, this does not affect the assumption.
    B. Normally, the seller is released from all liability when the mortgage is assumed.
    C. The seller is primarily liable if the buyer defaults on an assumed mortgage.
    D. A buyer who assumes a mortgage is primarily liable for the debt and the original borrower becomes secondarily liable for the debt.

20. An eligible veteran made an offer of $50,000 to purchase a home to be financed with a VA-guaranteed loan. Four weeks after the offer was accepted, a certificate of reasonable value (CRV) for $47,000 was issued for the property. In this case, the veteran may
    A. withdraw from the sale with a 1 percent penalty.
    B. purchase the property with a $3,000 down payment.
    C. not withdraw from the sale.
    D. withdraw from the sale on payment of $3,000.

21. In an FHA transaction
    A. points may be paid by the seller or the buyer.
    B. an origination fee must be paid by the seller.
    C. the mortgage insurance premium must be paid in cash at settlement.
    D. the mortgage insurance premium must be paid by the seller.

22. A government-backed loan that guarantees the lender against a loss is a(n)
    A. FHA mortgage.
    B. VA mortgage.
    C. adjustable-rate mortgage.
    D. graduated-payment mortgage.

23. As an entity operating in the secondary mortgage market, the Federal Home Loan Mortgage Corporation was established to assist
    A. the Federal Housing Administration.
    B. the Federal National Mortgage Association.
    C. savings and loans associations.
    D. federal banks.

24. Which of the following is TRUE about a term mortgage?
    A. All interest is paid at the end of the term.
    B. The entire principal is due at the end of the term.
    C. The debt is partially amortized over the term.
    D. The term is limited by state statutes.

25. Which of the following is TRUE regarding a purchase money mortgage?
    A. The seller retains possession of the property.
    B. The seller executes and delivers a note at closing.
    C. The seller finances a portion of the purchase price and places a junior lien on the property.
    D. The seller agrees to repurchase the property if the buyer defaults.

26. Regulation Z applies to
    A. business loans.
    B. residential loans made to a person.
    C. commercial loans under $10,000.
    D. installment sales.

27. Terence lent money to Rena and in return took a mortgage as security for the debt. Terence immediately recorded the mortgage. Thereafter, Omar lent money to Rena, took a mortgage and recorded it. Rena later defaulted, and a court determined that Omar's interest had priority over Terence's interest. Under these circumstances, chances are
    A. Terence knew Omar was going to make a loan prior to making his own loan.
    B. Omar's loan was larger than Terence's loan.
    C. Terence had signed a subordination agreement in favor of Omar.
    D. Omar had signed a satisfaction.

28. All of the following are agencies operating in the secondary market EXCEPT the
    A. Federal National Mortgage Association.
    B. Federal Savings and Loan Insurance Corpo-ration.
    C. Government National Mortgage Association.
    D. Federal Home Loan Mortgage Corpo-ration.

29. Brice and Judy Jones purchased their home three years ago. They made a $20,000 down payment and obtained a mortgage loan to finance the balance of their purchase. The Joneses have paid $14,400 in mortgage payments over the last three years, $10,000 of which has been used to pay the mortgage interest. The $24,400 that the Joneses have invested in their home over the last three years is referred to as their
    A. homestead.
    B. profit.
    C. redemption.
    D. equity.

30. A mortgagor can get direct financing from all of the following EXCEPT
    A. mortgage banking companies.
    B. savings and loan associations.
    C. commercial banks.
    D. Fannie Mae.

31. Which of the following would be the beneficiary in the deed of trust security instrument used in a title-theory state?
    A. Buyer
    B. Seller
    C. Lender
    D. Attorney

32. What is the MAJOR DIFFERENCE between conventional and unconventional loans?
    A. A conventional loan is guaranteed or insured by the government while an unconventional loan is not.
    B. An unconventional loan is guaranteed or insured by the government while a conventional loan is not.
    C. A conventional loan is sold on the secondary market while an unconventional loan is not.
    D. An unconventional loan is sold on the secondary market while a conventional loan is not.

33. On an adjustable rate mortgage a margin is added to the index to determine the new interest rate. This margin will
    A. change every six months.
    B. decrease as the term of the loan decreases.
    C. change as the index changes.
    D. remain constant over the life of the loan.

34. A defaulted borrower's right to redeem property before a foreclosure is known as the
    A. statutory right of redemption.
    B. equitable right of redemption.
    C. borrower's right of redemption.
    D. lender's right of redemption.

35. Laws that determine the maximum interest rate a lender can charge are known as
    A. maximum interest rate laws.
    B. usury laws.
    C. truth-in-lending laws.
    D. borrower protection laws.

36. Developer Emil placed a mortgage on his housing development. When he sold a lot to purchaser Sandy, a partial release was obtained for the lot she purchased. The mortgage Emil obtained was a(n)
    A. blanket mortgage.
    B. purchase-money mortgage.
    C. package mortgage.
    D. open-end mortgage.

37. Which of the following instruments is given by the purchaser to a seller who takes back a note for part or all of the purchase price of the property?
    A. Installment contract
    B. Purchase-money mortgage
    C. FHA mortgage
    D. Contract for deed

38. Which of the following requires that finance charges be stated as an annual percentage rate?
    A. Regulation Z
    B. Real Estate Settlement Procedures Act
    C. Equal Credit Opportunity Act
    D. Fair Housing Act

39. In determining whether to extend a loan to the purchaser of a house, lending institutions MOST LIKELY consider MOST IMPORTANT the
    A. sale price.
    B. stability of the purchaser's financial position.
    C. appraised value.
    D. term of the loan.

40. The act that requires that lenders inform both buyers and sellers of all fees and charges is the
    A. ECOA.
    B. REIT.
    C. RESPA.
    D. Truth-in-Lending.

41. A recorded lien was not removed from the property at a settlement table. What is the status of the lien?
    A. It follows the seller of the property because it was his or her debt.
    B. It remains on record against the property.
    C. It is no longer valid because the property has transferred.
    D. It must be recorded again by the debtor since the property has transferred.

42. According to Truth-in-Lending, a lender must reveal all of the following EXCEPT
    A. discount points.
    B. interest rate.
    C. title fees.
    D. origination fee.

43. A buyer obtained a loan in which the interest can fluctuate and, if it does, there will be an adjustment in the monthly payment. The buyer MOST LIKELY has secured a(n)
    A. partially amortized loan.
    B. unconventional loan.
    C. fixed-rate mortgage.
    D. adjustable-rate loan.

44. A buyer purchases a property through a loan assumption. The seller has requested that the old note and mortgage be substituted for a new note and mortgage in the buyer's name. If the lender allows this change, it is known as the granting of a(n)
    A. attachment.
    B. release of mortgage.
    C. satisfaction piece.
    D. novation.

45. A mortgage that has been sold to another party is said to have been
    A. assigned.
    B. transferred.
    C. deferred.
    D. purchased.

46. The financial market is made up of primary and secondary intermediaries. Which of the following is NOT a financial intermediary?
    A. Credit unions
    B. Pension funds
    C. FNMA
    D. HUD

47. An owner negotiated a home equity loan on his property. The owner's right to rescind this agreement within three days is provided by
    A. FHA.
    B. Regulation Z.
    C. Regulation B.
    D. VA.

48. Which of the following would restore a veteran's benefits?
    A. Novation from the lender
    B. Loan assumption by a buyer
    C. Subject-to mortgage taken by a buyer
    D. Substitution of eligibility by another veteran on a loan assumption

49. A borrower negotiated a second mortgage on her property. This mortgage is subordinate to the first mortgage and the borrower makes one monthly payment. She MOST LIKELY secured a
    A. shared-appreciation mortgage.
    B. purchase-money mortgage.
    C. wraparound mortgage.
    D. growing-equity mortgage.

50. Which of the following mortgages MOST LIKELY creates negative amortization?
    A. Graduated-payment mortgage
    B. Shared-appreciation mortgage
    C. Adjustable-rate mortgage
    D. Growing-equity mortgage

51. A retired couple would like additional spendable income. They talked to their financial adviser and learned that they could use the equity in their property to negotiate a loan in which they will receive a monthly check from the lender for the next five years. This arrangement is known as a(n)
    A. open mortgage.
    B. closed mortgage.
    C. reverse annuity mortgage.
    D. open-end mortgage.

52. A borrower has secured a guarantee from the lender that the interest rate quoted on loan application would not change prior to closing. This is known as a(n)
    A. fixed-rate mortgage.
    B. anaconda agreement.
    C. extender clause.
    D. lock-in agreement.

53. Which of the following parties must sign the note and the mortgage?
    A. Mortgagor/promisee
    B. Mortgagee/promisor
    C. Mortgagor/promisor
    D. Mortgagee/promisee

54. A buyer assumes and agrees to pay an existing loan on the property. Who is liable for the loan?
    A. The seller is primarily liable.
    B. The buyer is primarily liable.
    C. The buyer is primarily liable and the seller is secondarily liable.
    D. The seller is primarily liable and the buyer is secondarily liable.

55. A trust deed or mortgage can be used to finance property. What is the MAJOR DIFFERENCE between these instruments?
    A. Both are security instruments.
    B. Both involve the buyer's signing a note.
    C. Both can be foreclosed on.
    D. A trust deed transfers a title interest, and a mortgage allows the lender to place a lien on the property.

56. Mr. Chalk is purchasing a duplex as a qualified veteran. Under these circumstances the VA will
    A. set the rate of interest.
    B. determine the maximum loan amount.
    C. set the limit on the guarantee.
    D. determine the term of the loan.

57. Keith is a first time home buyer seeking advice from an agent regarding the difference between a mortgage broker and a mortgage banker. The agent will tell her that
    A. free checking is a typical incentive to negotiate a loan through a mortgage banker, but not a mortgage broker.
    B. mortgage bankers normally deal in conforming loans, but mortgage brokers deal in non-conforming loans.
    C. mortgage bankers normally hold their loans in portfolio, but mortgage brokers sell their loans on the secondary mortgage market.
    D. mortgage bankers originate loans, package and sell them to investors, while mortgage brokers bring borrowers and lenders together and are paid a percentage on the loan amount.

58. Branham is negotiating a home loan and the lender is requiring him to set up an escrow account for taxes and insurance. This is known as a
    A. buydown mortgage.
    B. budget mortgage.
    C. balloon mortgage.
    D. blanket mortgage.

59. An FHA insured or VA guaranteed loan is an example of a(n)
    A. conventional mortgage.
    B. conventional uninsured mortgage.
    C. conventional insured mortgage.
    D. unconventional mortgage.

60. The federal act that prohibits a lender from discriminating based on race, color, religion, national origin, sex, marital status, age or source of income is the
    A. Federal Fair Housing Act.
    B. Equal Credit Opportunity Act.
    C. Community Reinvestment Act.
    D. Truth-in-Lending Act.

ANSWERS

1. A The mortgagor is the borrower, the mortgagee is the lender.
2. B By definition of package mortgage.
3. B By definition of amortization.
4. B By definition of acceleration clause.
5. B A power-of-sale clause is found in mortgages or trust deeds in title-theory states. This clause gives the lender the right to sell the property by advertisement when the borrower defaults and other stipulations are met.
6. D Statutory right of redemption is the right a delinquent borrower has after the foreclosure sale to redeem the property, if all costs are paid.
7. A By definition of title-theory state.
8. C A lender must qualify to negotiate FHA-insured loans. FHA, FNMA and FHLBS do not negotiate loans.
9. A The alienation clause allows the lender to call the note due if the property is transferred to another person.
10. B When the final payment is made, the lender must release its interest in the property. A deed of reconveyance would transfer the deed back to the buyer.
11. B When property is purchased under a land contract, the buyer's interest is an equitable title interest.
12. B A recorded mortgage places a lien on a property.
13. C By definition of a balloon mortgage.
14. A An acceleration clause in a mortgage allows the lender to call the entire balance due and payable on default of the borrower.
15. D The buyer or vendee becomes the lessor in a sale-leaseback agreement.
16. B Loans are bought and sold in the secondary mortgage market.
17. D FNMA and GNMA are both members of the secondary mortgage market.
18. A When a foreclosure sale does not produce sufficient funds to pay a debt in full, a deficiency judgment may be filed against the borrower.
19. D By definition of loan assumption.
20. B If the sale price was $50,000 but the CRV was $47,000, the veteran does not have to purchase. He could, however, purchase at $50,000 with a $3,000 down payment.
21. A Discount points may be paid by the buyer or seller in an FHA-insured loan. The origination fee and MIP are paid by the buyer. The MIP may be a one-time fee or a percentage added to the monthly payment.
22. B VA makes a guarantee to the lender; FHA insures the lender against a loss.
23. C FHLMC was established to buy mortgages from savings and loans.
24. B In a term mortgage, periodic interest payments are made and the principal is due at the end of the term.
25. C By definition of purchase-money mortgage.
26. B Regulation Z applies to residential loans made to a person, not to loans made for business, commercial or agricultural purposes or properties sold under land contracts.
27. C By definition of subordination agreement.
28. B The FSLIC is not a member of the secondary market.
29. D Equity is the difference between the market value and any liens on the property.
30. D Fannie Mae is not a source of funds on the primary market.
31. C In the deed of trust document, the lender is the beneficiary, the trustor is the borrower and the trustee holds the legal title for the lender.
32. B FHA and VA loans are unconventional loans that are backed by the government.
33. D The index may change on an adjustable rate mortgage, but the margin will remain constant over the life of the loan.
34. B Equitable right of redemption is the right to redeem the property BEFORE foreclosure. Statutory right of redemption is the right to redeem the property AFTER foreclosure.
35. B Usury laws determine the maximum interest rate that lenders can charge. They are normally state laws, but the federal government could set these rates as well.
36. A Blanket mortgages cover more than one tract of land and contain a partial release clause.
37. B By definition of purchase-money mortgage.

38. A Regulation Z, or Truth-in-Lending, requires the disclosure of the APR.
39. B Of these answers, the buyer's financial position is the major factor in determining if the lender should underwrite the loan.
40. C RESPA requires that a settlement sheet be given to the buyers and sellers, disclosing the fees paid by the parties.
41. B A lien not resolved at the closing remains with the property.
42. C Regulation Z does not require the disclosure of title fees. (RESPA does.)
43. D By definition of adjustable-rate mortgage.
44. D By definition of novation.
45. A A mortgage that has been sold is said to have been assigned to another party.
46. D HUD is a federal agency, but it is not a financial intermediary.
47. B Regulation Z provides for a three-day right of rescission on home equity loans and refinancing of property.
48. D The substitution of eligibility by another veteran on a loan assumption or the payoff of the loan would release the veteran's eligibility; then the VA could restore the veteran's benefits.
49. C By definition of wraparound mortgage.

50. A A graduated-payment mortgage can create negative amortization.
51. C By definition of reverse annuity mortgage.
52. D By definition of lock-in agreement.
53. C The buyer is the mortgagor in the mortgage and the promisor in the note. The buyer is required to sign these documents.
54. C When the buyer assumes a loan, the buyer is primarily liable and the seller is secondarily liable.
55. D A trust deed transfers a title interest to the lender (the beneficiary), while a mortgage allows the lender to place a lien on the property.
56. C The VA will set the limit on the guarantee to the lender.
57. D By definitions of mortgage bankers and mortgage brokers.
58. B A budget mortgage includes monthly payments of principal, interest, taxes and insurance.
59. D Unconventional mortgages are backed by the government.
60. B The Equal Credit Opportunity Act prohibits lenders from discriminating when negotiating loans.

6

Professional Responsibilities/
Fair Practice/Administration

This chapter covers the following information regarding the real estate brokerage business: professional responsibilities, fair practice and administration. *The topics bracketed by bullet points (•) appear on the brokers' exam only.*

Content Outline—Professional Responsibilities and Fair Practice

VI. Professional Responsibilities/Fair Practice/Administration

A. Professional Responsibilities and Fair Practice

1. Brokerage Relationships
2. Laws, rules and regulations pertaining to real estate
3. Resolving misunderstandings
4. Need to seek expert advice

BROKERAGE RELATIONSHIPS

Listing

When the owner of property hires a broker to help her or him find a buyer, an agency relationship is created. The owner (**principal**) has delegated to the broker (**agent**) the right to act on the owner's behalf. This creates a **fiduciary relationship** wherein the agent owes the seller certain duties. Sales associates represent their brokers, and their primary fiduciary relationship is with their broker. In most states sales associates act as subagents for their brokers. However, in states where brokers may designate salespeople to be the agents of buyers or sellers, the agency responsibility passes to the designated agents.

A **listing agreement** is a personal service contract securing the employment of a brokerage firm to find a ready, willing and able buyer. The types of listing agreements are exclusive-right-to sell, exclusive agency, open, net, and option. See page 28 for a review of these listings.

FIGURE 6.1 *Agency*

Types of Agents

1. **General agent**—When the principal delegates a broad range of powers. Examples: a property manager or a real estate agent with his or her broker.
2. **Special agent**—When the principal delegates a specific act or business transaction. Example: a listing agent or a party with a durable power of attorney.
3. **Universal agent**—A party given full power of attorney to represent another person.
4. **Designated agent**—One who has been appointed by a broker to act for a specific principal or client.

Creation of an Agency Relationship

1. **Express agency**—When the parties state the contract's terms and express their intention either orally or in writing. Example: a listing agreement.
2. **Implied agency**—When the actions or conduct of the parties communicate that there is an agreement. Example: an implied agency established by the agent when talking with a buyer. "Take this deal. It's the best one for you."

Types of Agencies

1. **Single agency**—When a broker is representing the seller or the buyer in the transaction, but not both.
2. **Dual agency**—When an agent represents two principals in the same transaction. This can occur only with the permission of both parties. Both parties are clients.

The payment of compensation or its source does not determine agency relationships. A contract creates the agency relationship.

Responsibilities of an Agent

The acronym COALD represents the duties of the agent to the principal. The broker must act with care, obedience, accountability, loyalty and disclosure.

- **Care**—A broker is to exercise reasonable care and skill as a professional while transacting the business of the principal. For a client who is a seller, this includes establishing the correct list price, properly representing the property, informing the seller of tax consequences and properly marketing the property. For a client who is a buyer, this means helping the buyer to find suitable property and negotiating the price offered, then directing the buyer to a lender for the loan.
- **Obedience**—The agent is to act in good faith and obey the principal's instructions given in the contract; however, the agent may not obey illegal instructions.
- **Accountability**—The agent is accountable for all funds or property of others that comes into his or her possession.
- **Loyalty**—The agent must be loyal, putting the principal's interests above those of all others. This includes obtaining the best offer from a buyer when representing a seller, explaining offers to a client, and representing only the interests of the client.

- **Disclosure**—The agent must keep the principal informed, disclosing all facts and information that could affect the transaction. If representing a seller, the agent must disclose if the buyer is willing to offer more for the property. If representing the buyer, an agent needs to disclose all defects and if the seller would take less for the property.

An agent must deal fairly and honestly with all parties, regardless of whom they are representing.

Ministerial acts are those acts that a licensee may perform for a consumer that are informative in nature and do not rise to the level of active representation.

Puffing is the exaggeration of a fact.

Each state now has mandatory agency disclosure laws that stipulate when, how and to whom disclosures must be made. Generally, the agency disclosure statement must be in writing. The purpose is to make sure buyers and sellers understand whether they are customers or clients in the transaction. Agency disclosure usually occurs before confidential information is given.

Selling

Once the listing is obtained, the agent will begin marketing and showing the property. The sellers' instructions are to be followed such as the placement of a for sale sign in the yard or a lockbox on the property. The seller may look to the agent for suggestions in how to make the property more marketable. All offers are to be presented to the seller. The agent may need to explain any contract terms the seller may not understand.

Most sales contracts contain contingencies or conditions that must be satisfied before the contract is fully enforceable. Common contingencies include property inspection, pest inspection, loan approval, and a marketable title. The sales contract should have provisions for canceling the contract. If the buyer defaults, the seller may be able to retain the earnest money as liquidated damages. If the seller defaults, the earnest money is returned to the buyer. The contract may contain other steps to be followed when canceling the contract.

Buyer Agency

When a real estate broker enters into a contract with a buyer, a buyer agency relationship is established. When a written agreement is secured, the buyer becomes the client and the seller becomes the customer in the transaction (unless the sellers have their own agent).

The three basic buyer agency agreements are an exclusive buyer agency, exclusive-agency buyer agency, and open buyer agency. When entering into a buyer agency agreement, the agent explains the parties' rights and responsibilities, including the agreement of compensation. The buyer's agent may be paid a flat fee or a commission, which could be paid by the buyer or seller, or both.

Types of Buyer Agency Agreements

1. **Exclusive Buyer Agency**—In this completely exclusive agency relationship, the buyer is legally bound to pay the agent when the buyer purchases the property described in the contract. This is true even if the buyer finds the property.

2. **Exclusive-Agency Buyer Agency**—This also creates an exclusive contract between the buyer and the agent. However, the broker is entitled to payment only if he or she locates the property purchased by the buyer. The buyer can find suitable property without the obligation to pay the agent.

3. **Open Buyer Agency Agreement**—In this nonexclusive contract with the agent, the buyer can enter into similar agreements with any number of agents. The agent who finds the suitable property will be compensated.

Property Management

The **property manager has a fiduciary relationship** with the owner of the property, which means that the property manager is placed in a position of trust and confidence. This fiduciary relationship includes the following duties:

- The manager must work with *care and skill* while managing the property and binding the owner to contracts, and must be responsible in every way to the owner. A manager negligent in his or her duties to the owner can be liable for any damages created for the owner.
- The duty of *obedience* means that the manager must carry out, in good faith, the owner's instructions. Should the owner ask the manager to do something that is illegal or unethical, the property manager should immediately terminate the relationship.
- The duty of *accounting* means the manager must maintain and accurately report to the owner the status of all funds received on behalf of or from the property owner. The manager should never commingle funds; that is, combine trust funds with business or personal accounts.
- The duty of *loyalty* means that the manager must put the property owner's interests first and act without self-interest in every transaction.
- The manager must *disclose* to the owner all material facts regarding the management of the property.

For additional review, see Chapter 3, page 62.

LAWS, RULES AND REGULATIONS PERTAINING TO REAL ESTATE

Real estate licensees must abide by federal, state and local laws. Federal laws include the federal fair housing laws and the recent Americans with Disabilities Act. State and local laws also regulate licensees. The National Association of REALTORS® (NAR) Code of Ethics establishes standards for its members.

Americans with Disabilities Act

The **Americans with Disabilities Act (ADA)** was signed into law in 1990 and became effective in 1992. It is intended to enable individuals with disabilities to become a part of the social and economic mainstream by mandating equal access to

- public accommodations,
- jobs,
- public transportation,
- telecommunications and
- government services.

A handicap is a physical or mental impairment or history of such impairment that substantially limits one or more of a person's major life activities. An individual with AIDS or a person in an addiction recovery program is protected. The law does not protect anyone using an illegal drug or a controlled substance. The law covers both temporary and chronic conditions. A disabled individual is to be given full and equal enjoyment of goods and services in places of public accommodation, including hotels, shopping centers, commercial properties and professional offices.

Private clubs and religious organizations are exempt from the Americans with Disabilities Act.

ADA stipulates that employers with 15 or more employees must adopt nondiscriminatory employment procedures, such as making reasonable accommodations to allow a qualified person with a disability to perform essential job functions. Any changes made are to be reasonable and are not to impose an undue burden on the business. Also, changes cannot cause a direct threat to the safety or health of others.

Property owners and managers need to know the priority guidelines for making buildings accessible to disabled individuals. All existing architectural and communication barriers must be removed, if doing so can be accomplished in a readily achievable manner at a low cost. Priorities have been set for these readily achievable changes.

ADA has affected the real estate business in several areas. Real estate brokerage firms must make the necessary changes to provide full and equal opportunities to disabled individuals. Property managers must have a solid understanding of the ADA so they can advise owners of necessary changes. Licensees should advise investors to seek professional advice in regard to the ADA.

Civil Rights and Fair Housing Policy

The *Civil Rights Act of 1866* was the first law written to prohibit discrimination based on race. The law reads:

> All citizens of the United States shall have the same right in every state and territory
> as is enjoyed by white citizens thereof to inherit, purchase, lease, sell, hold, and convey
> real and personal property.

Currently, the federal Fair Housing Act prohibits discrimination based on race, color, religion, sex, national origin, familial status and handicap. Many state laws are stricter than the federal regulations, and a licensee should be aware that failure to comply with these laws is a criminal act and grounds for disciplinary action.

The **Federal Fair Housing Act** regulates the sale or rental of most dwellings and any vacant land offered for sale for residential construction or use. Exclusions to the law are covered later in this section.

The following actions have been found to be discriminatory:

- Refusing to sell, rent, negotiate or deal with a person, or telling a person that a dwelling is not available for inspection, sale or rent when it is
- Changing or misrepresenting the terms or services for buying or leasing housing
- Discriminating through any statement or advertisement that indicates a preference for a certain race, color, sex, familial status, religion, national origin or handicap
- Blockbusting, or panic peddling, which means inducing owners to sell or rent now because minority groups are moving into the neighborhood
- Steering or channeling, which is directing buyers into or out of certain neighborhoods
- Denying or altering any terms or conditions for a loan to purchase, construct, repair or improve a dwelling
- Limiting or denying membership in any real estate organization, such as the MLS or any other facilities related to the selling or renting of housing
- Any act considered intimidation or influence by using fear, such as threatening or evicting a tenant who filed a complaint against the management for possible discriminatory acts
- Charging higher rents and higher deposits to families with children
- Deliberately slowing down the processing of a contract to hinder the sale or lease of a property
- Recording racially restrictive covenants in order to screen out minorities
- Checking the credit of a member of a minority group only
- Eviction of tenants because of interracial marriage
- Appraisal reports that state that population transitions are illegal
- Failure to display the equal housing opportunity poster

Familial Status

Familial status protects the head of a household from discrimination when she or he is responsible for a minor child or children. This protection also includes a pregnant woman. Unless exempt, a landlord cannot say "no children" can live in his or her building. The prospective tenant may be rejected if the number of people occupying the apartment exceeds occupancy codes.

The exemptions to the familial status law are: Any housing occupied or intended to be occupied solely by persons aged 62 or older; or if 80 percent of the units are occupied by someone 55 years of age or older, the building is exempt.

Exemptions to the Federal Fair Housing Act

The sale or rental of a single family home is exempt if

- the owner who is not occupying his or her home has only one sale in 24 months
- no more than three homes are owned at any one time

- the services of a broker or any other person who is engaged in the business of selling or leasing real estate are not used and
- no discriminatory advertising is used.

Other exemptions include the following:

- A one- to four-family dwelling is exempt if the owner occupies one of the units, no discriminatory advertising is used and no agent is used.
- A nonprofit religious organization can discriminate on a religious basis only. Membership in that religious organization cannot be discriminatory.
- A nonprofit private club may restrict rentals or occupancy of lodgings to members only. Membership in that private club cannot be discriminatory.

There are no exemptions to the Civil Rights Act of 1866 and there are no limits to punitive damages against those found guilty of discrimination because of race. *Jones v. Mayer* is a 1968 Supreme Court case that upheld the Civil Rights Act of 1866.

Complaints of violation of the federal Fair Housing Act may be filed with the Department of Housing and Urban Development (HUD) or taken directly to a federal district court. Action also may be taken by the Attorney General of the United States. An aggrieved party or the Secretary of HUD must file a complaint *within one year* of the discriminatory act.

Penalties include:

- A fine of up to $100,000 and imprisonment for up to one year for failure to attend or provide testimony at a hearing or failure to answer lawful inquiries.
- An offender can be fined up to $11,000 for the first offense; up to $27,500 for the second offense within five years of the filing date of the complaint; and up to $55,000 for the third offense within seven years.
- A fine of up to $1,000 and/or up to one year in jail for intimidation.
- A fine of up to $10,000 and/or up to 10 years in jail for bodily injury; for death, the penalty can be any jail term for up to life.

Affirmative Marketing

An affirmative marketing program is designed to inform all buyers in a minority community of the homes for sale without discrimination. The purpose of affirmative marketing is to encourage the integration of minority groups into housing.

HUD has published specific advertising guidelines to prevent discrimination. Policy guidelines from HUD provide the information that follows.

Real estate advertisements should state no **discriminatory preference** or limitation on account of race, color or national origin. Use of words describing the housing, the current or potential residents, or the neighbors or neighborhood in racial or ethnic terms (e.g., white family homes, Irish neighborhood) will create liability under this section. Advertisements that are racially neutral will NOT create liability. Thus, complaints over the use of phrases such as master bedroom, rare find or desirable neighborhood should NOT be filed.

Advertisements should not contain an explicit preference or imply any limitation or discrimination on account of religion (e.g., no Jews, Christian home). Advertisements that use the legal name of an entity that contains a religious reference, such as Roselawn Catholic Home, or those that contain a religious symbol, such as a cross, MAY indicate a religious preference. If such an advertisement includes a disclaimer (e.g., This home does not discriminate on the basis of race, color, religion, national origin, sex, handicap or familial status), it does NOT violate the act (fair housing law). Advertisements containing descriptions of properties (e.g., apartment complex with chapel) or services (e.g., kosher meals available) DO NOT on their face state a preference for persons likely to make use of those facilities, and are not violations of the act. The use of secularized terms or symbols relating to religious holidays, such as Santa Claus, the Easter Bunny or St. Valentine's Day images, or phrases such as Merry Christmas and the like, DOES NOT constitute a violation of the act.

Advertisements for single-family dwellings or separate units in a multifamily dwelling should contain no explicit preference, limitation or discrimination based on sex. Use of the term "master bedroom" DOES NOT constitute a violation of either the sex discrimination provisions or the race discrimination provisions. Terms such as "mother-in-law suite" and "bachelor apartment" are commonly used as physical descriptions of housing units and DO NOT violate the act.

Advertisements SHOULD NOT contain explicit exclusions, limitations or other indications of discrimination based on handicap (e.g., no wheelchairs). Advertisements containing descriptions of properties (e.g., great view, fourth floor walkup, walk-in closets), services or facilities (jogging trails), or neighborhoods (e.g., walk to bus stop) DO NOT violate the act. Advertisements describing the conduct required of residents (e.g., non-smoking, sober) DO NOT violate the act. Advertisements containing descriptions of accessibility features are lawful (e.g., wheelchair ramp).

Advertisements MAY NOT state an explicit preference, limitation or discrimination based on familial status. Advertisements MAY NOT contain limitations on the number or ages of children or state a preference for adults, couples or singles. Advertisements describing the properties (e.g., two-bedroom, cozy, family room), services and facilities (e.g., no bicycles allowed), or neighborhoods (e.g., quiet streets), ARE NOT racially discriminatory and DO NOT violate the act.

Equal Credit Opportunity Act

The **Equal Credit Opportunity Act** (ECOA) prohibits discrimination based on race, color, religion, national origin, sex, marital status, source of income or age in the granting of credit. This act requires that credit applications be considered only on the basis of income, net worth, job stability and credit rating. The practice by lenders or insurance companies of refusing to make loans or issue insurance policies in specific areas for reasons other than the financial qualifications of the applicant is known as redlining. Redlining is illegal.

IRS Form 8300 - Cash Payment Reporting Requirements

Each person engaged in a trade or business who, in the course of that trade or business, receives more than $10,000 in cash in one transaction or in two or more related transactions must file Form 8300 with the Internal Revenue Service. Any transactions conducted between a payer (or its agent) and the recipient in a 24-hour period are related transactions. Transactions are considered related even if they occur over a perod of more than 24 hours if the recipient knows, or has reason to know, that each transaction is one of a series of connected transactions. A copy of Form 8300 must be kept for five years from the date it is filed.

Form 8300 requires the identity of the individual/s from whom the cash was received, the person on whose behalf the transaction was conducted, a description of the transaction and method of payment, and the business that received the cash. The form must be filed by the fifteenth day after the date the cash was received. If that date falls on a Saturday, Sunday, or legal holiday, the form must be filed by the next business day.

Penalties may be imposed for

- failure to file a correct and complete form on time, unless a reasonable cause can be shown;
- failure to furnish a correct and complete statement to each person named in a required form;
- causing, or attempting to cause a trade or business to fail to file a required report;
- causing, or attempting to cause a trade or business to file a required report containing a material omission or mistatement of fact; or
- structuring, or attempting to structure, transactions to avoid the reporting requirements.

A minimum penalty of $25,000 may be imposed if the failure is due to an intentional disregard of the cash reporting requirements. These violations may result in imprisonment of up to five years or fine of up to $250,000 for individuals and $500,000 for corporations or both.

See the Appendix for a copy of Form 8300.

RESOLVING MISUNDERSTANDINGS

From time to time, disputes occur in any real estate office. A dispute may be between two agents, between the agent and the company or between real estate firms. Issues vary, but often revolve around commission splits.

Whenever possible, the agent and management should resolve such disputes as quickly as possible. Usually a dispute can be quickly resolved by a review of the agent's employment agreement.

In other cases, company policy and the procedures manual should be reviewed. When neither of these items exists, advice or even binding arbitration by an impartial, disinterested party from outside the firm may be sought. Many local boards of REALTORS® have a board of arbitration that can be used. If all else fails, the dispute can be settled through the court system.

If the dispute involves a real estate transaction, the parties will be looking to the agent/s for professional advice. The agent's knowledge and expertise should be used every step of the way to avoid ambiguities and misunderstandings.

NEED TO SEEK EXPERT ADVICE

Unless an agent is also an attorney, appraiser, accountant, property inspector, termite inspector or any other professional that may be involved in a transaction, the agent should not give his or her opinion. The agent needs to have a basic knowledge in such fields to know when to advise an expert's opinion.

Professional Responsibilities and Fair Practice—Key Point Review

1. When the owner of property hires a broker to help find a buyer, an agency relationship is created. The owner (principal) delegates to the broker (agent) the right to act on the owner's behalf, creating a fiduciary relationship wherein the agent owes the seller certain duties.

Professional Responsibilities and Fair Practice— Key Point Review (Continued)

2. Representing only one party in a transaction creates a single agency. Representing both parties creates a dual agency. A dual agency must be disclosed to all parties. In a dual agency, both parties would have a client status.

3. A facilitator or transaction broker does not represent either party in the transaction. Both parties are treated as customers.

4. A designated seller's agent would be the only agent representing the seller. A designated buyer's agent would be the only agent representing the buyer.

5. Ministerial acts are those acts that a licensee may perform for a consumer that are informative in nature and do not rise to the level of active representation.

6. A general agency is created when the principal delegates a broad range of powers to the agent. A special agency is created when the principal delegates only a specific act or business transaction with detailed instructions.

7. In an express agency, the parties state the contract's terms and express their intention either orally or in writing. An implied agency occurs when the actions or conduct of the parties communicate that there is an agreement.

8. The acronym COALD represents the duties of the agent to the principal: care, obedience, accountability, loyalty and disclosure.

9. The three types of buyer agency agreements are exclusive buyer, exclusive-agency buyer agency, and open buyer agency. In the exclusive buyer agency, the agent is due a commission whenever a property is purchased. In an exclusive-agency buyer agency, the broker is entitled to payment only if he or she locates the property purchased by the buyer. In an open buyer agency, the buyer may have contracts with several agents, and only pays the agent who finds suitable property.

10. The property manager has a fiduciary relationship with the owner, which includes the duties of care, obedience, accounting, loyalty and disclosure.

11. The duty of care means to use care and skill while managing the property and binding the owner to contracts and to be responsible in every way to the owner.

12. The duty of obedience means to carry out, in good faith, the owner's instructions. The property manager should immediately terminate the relationship if asked to do something illegal or unethical.

13. The duty of accounting means to maintain and accurately report to the owner the status of all funds received on behalf of or from the property owner. The manager should never commingle funds.

14. The duty of loyalty means to put the property owner's interests first and act without self-interest in every transaction.

Professional Responsibilities and Fair Practice—
Key Point Review (Continued)

15. The duty of disclosure means to keep the owner informed of all material facts regarding the management of the property.

16. The Americans with Disabilities Act is intended to enable individuals with disabilities to become a part of the mainstream by mandating equal access to public accommodations, jobs, public transportation, telecommunications and government services. Private clubs and religious organizations are exempted.

17. ADA stipulates that employers with 15 or more employees adopt nondiscriminatory employment procedures for the disabled, including making reasonable accommodations to allow a qualified person to perform job functions.

18. Property owners and managers need to know the priority guidelines for making buildings accessible. Existing architectural and communication barriers must be removed, if this can be accomplished in a readily achievable manner. Priority one for making changes is called get the party to the door. Priority two is providing equal access to all areas where goods and services are available to the public. Priority three is making restroom facilities accessible. Priority four is providing free access to all remaining areas.

19. The Civil Rights Act of 1866 was the first law written to prohibit discrimination based on race. There are no exceptions to this law and no limits on punitive damages for racial discrimination.

20. A landlord must make reasonable accommodations in rules, policies, practices, and services when those accommodations may be necessary to afford the handicapped person equal opportunity to use and enjoy a dwelling. An owner cannot refuse to permit a handicapped person to modify a dwelling, but the handicapped person may be required to restore the unit to its original condition.

21. After March 12, 1991, multifamily dwellings must be designed to allow accessibility to the building and through units by persons in wheelchairs; new apartment buildings with elevators must be built so that the entire building is accessible; and new apartment buildings without elevators must be built so that the ground levels are accessible.

22. *Jones v. Mayer* is a 1968 Supreme Court case that upheld the Civil Rights Act of 1866.

23. Currently, federal fair housing laws prohibit discrimination based on race, color, religion, sex, national origin, familial status and handicap. Many state laws are stricter than federal regulations. Failure to comply with these laws is a criminal act and grounds for disciplinary action.

24. Blockbusting (panic peddling) occurs when an agent induces the owners to sell or move because minority groups are moving into a neighborhood. Steering (channeling) occurs when an agent directs buyers into or out of certain neighborhoods. All these activities are illegal.

Professional Responsibilities and Fair Practice—
Key Point Review (Continued)

25. Familial status protects from discrimination the head of a household responsible for a minor child or children, and also a pregnant woman. Housing occupied or intended to be occupied by persons aged 62 or older is exempt from the law. If 80 percent of the units are occupied by someone 55 years of age or older, then the building also is exempt.

26. The sale or rental of a single-family home is exempt if the owner who is not occupying a home has only one sale in 24 months; no more than three homes are owned at any one time; the services of a broker or any other person engaged in the business of selling or leasing real estate is not used; and no discriminatory advertising is used.

27. Other exemptions include a one- to four-family dwelling if the owner occupies one of the units, no discriminatory advertising is used and a broker is not used. A nonprofit religious organization can discriminate on a religious basis, so long as membership in the organization is not discriminatory; a nonprofit private club may restrict rentals or occupancy of lodgings to members, so long as membership in the private club is not discriminatory.

28. Complaints for violations of the federal Fair Housing Act may be filed with HUD or taken directly to a federal district court. Action may also be taken by the Attorney General of the United States. An aggrieved party or the Secretary of HUD must file a complaint within one year of the discriminatory act.

29. Any person who fails to attend or provide testimony at a hearing or fails to answer lawful inquiries may be fined up to $100,000 and/or imprisoned for up to one year. An offender can be fined up to $11,000 for the first offense; $27,500 for the second offense within five years; and $55,000 for the third offense within seven years. Penalties for intimidation are up to $1,000 and/or up to one year in jail. Penalties for bodily injury are up to $10,000 and/or up to 10 years in jail; for death, the penalty can be any jail term up to life.

30. Refusing to make loans or issue insurance policies in specific areas for reasons other than the financial qualifications of the applicant is known as redlining. Redlining is illegal.

31. A handicap is a physical or mental impairment or history of such impairment that substantially limits one or more of a person's major life activities. The law does not protect anyone using illegal drugs or controlled substances.

32. An affirmative marketing program informs all buyers in a minority community of the homes for sale without discrimination and encourages the integration of minority groups into housing.

33. Real estate ads should state no discriminatory preference or limitation on account of race, color or national origin. Ads that are racially neutral will not create liability.

34. Ads should contain no explicit preference, limitation or discrimination on account of religion. Ads using the legal name of an entity that contains a religious reference or a religious symbol may indicate a religious preference. If the ad includes a disclaimer, it does not violate the act. The use of secularized terms or symbols relating to religious holidays does not constitute a violation of the act.

Professional Responsibilities and Fair Practice— Key Point Review (Continued)

35. Ads for single-family dwellings or separate units in a multifamily dwelling should contain no explicit preference, limitation or discrimination based on sex.

36. Ads should not contain explicit exclusions, limitations or other indications of discrimination based on handicap. Ads describing the conduct required of residents do not violate the act. Ads containing descriptions of accessibility features are lawful.

37. Ads may not state an explicit preference, limitation or discrimination based on familial status.

38. The Equal Credit Opportunity Act (ECOA) prohibits discrimination against anyone in the protected classes in the granting of credit. Credit applications must be considered only on the basis of income, net worth, job stability and credit rating.

39. Each person engaged in a trade or business, who receives more than $10,000 in cash in one transaction, or in two or more related transactions, must file Form 8300 with the Internal Revenue Service. The form must be filed by the fifteenth day after the date the cash was received. A copy of the form must be kept for five years.

Content Outline—Administration

VI. Professisonal Responsibilities/Fair Practice/Administration

   B. Administration

      1. Terms of contract between licensee and broker
      2. Complete and accurate records
      3. Company policies, procedures and standards
      4. Calculating commissions for real estate transactions
      5. • Notifications and reports required by the real estate regulatory agency. •
      6. • Trust accounts. •
      7. • Supervising and Educating Salesforce. •
      8. • Accounting procedures for the office.•

TERMS OF CONTRACT BETWEEN LICENSEE AND BROKER

For a salesperson to be **active,** a broker must hold the salesperson's license. The salesperson is authorized to perform real estate activities on behalf of the broker, and all activities must be carried out in the name of the broker. The broker is responsible for all of the agent's activities.

Independent Contractors

Most agents work as **independent contractors.** According to the Internal Revenue Code, the three requirements to meet the independent contractor status are (1) the individual must have a current real estate license; (2) he or she must have a written contract with the broker that contains the following clause: "The salesperson will not be treated as an employee with respect to the services performed by such salesperson as a real estate agent for federal tax purposes"; and (3) 90 percent or more of the individual's income as a licensee must be based on sales production, not on the number of hours worked. An independent contractor assumes responsibility for paying his or her own income tax and Social Security. The agent cannot receive any employee benefits from the broker.

The broker *can* regulate the working hours, office routine and attendance at meetings of *employees*. The broker withholds income tax and Social Security for the employee, and the employee may receive benefits from the broker.

COMPLETE AND ACCURATE RECORDS

State laws determine the length of time that brokers must retain complete and accurate records of all business transactions. The documents that must be kept include but are not limited to copies of sales contracts, deeds, title searches, title insurance policies, homeowners' insurance policies, surveys, inspection certificates, appraisals and warranties or guarantees of heating, electrical or plumbing systems.

COMPANY POLICIES, PROCEDURES AND STANDARDS

Company policies, procedures and standards are set to establish a clear understanding of the relationship between the broker and the sales associate, to communicate the "rules of the game" to the sales associate to resolve as many controversies as possible before they arise and to provide a framework and atmosphere in which people can work together and succeed.

A manual of procedures, policies and standards should include but not be limited to advertising and promotion, compensation, cooperative sales with outside brokers, escrow, floor duty, interoffice exchange of clients, listing, open houses, sales meetings, screening prospects, signs and termination.

CALCULATING COMMISSIONS FOR
REAL ESTATE TRANSACTIONS

Federal and state **antitrust laws** prohibit two or more brokers fixing commission rates. The source and the amount of each commission is negotiated between the broker and each client.

A **listing agreement** should state that the seller is responsible for the payment of the commission and whether the payment is to be paid from the proceeds of the sale. Because the brokerage fee is not a lien on the property, the broker has to take other legal recourse to collect the commission when the net proceeds are not sufficient to pay the commission.

When a buyer agency relationship is created, the agreement should state who is responsible for paying the commission. Typically, the seller still pays the commission on the purchase of a listed property. However, if the buyer purchases a for-sale-by-owner property, the seller is under no contractual obligation to pay the commission, and the buyer may be required to pay.

Each listing broker establishes the division of commission with cooperating brokers when information on the listing is shared or submitted and advertised in the brokers' local multiple-listing service. Usually, the cooperating broker receives the agreed-upon commission at the time of settlement.

Each broker should have a written agreement with his or her licensees on how commissions received will be divided. Commissions may be divided in different ratios between listing and selling agents and brokers. A salesperson is allowed to receive a commission only from her or his broker. For calculations of the commission, see page 168.

Most state laws require that in order to earn a commission, an agent must be licensed at the time of the transaction, have an employment contract (listing) and be the procuring cause of the sale. When a brokerage firm has secured a qualified buyer on the seller's terms, the broker is due a commission.

· NOTIFICATIONS AND REPORTS ·

Brokers must supply any notifications or reports that the real estate commission or federal or state regulations require. For example, brokers are required to display an Equal Opportunity poster. Failure to comply with the laws and requests of the commission can result in disciplinary action.

· TRUST ACCOUNTS ·

A trust account also is known as an *escrow account* or *impound account*. The account is set up by a broker to hold the money of others, until a transaction is closed. This includes earnest money checks in sales transactions and security deposits in property management. State laws regulate the establishment, maintenance and auditing of the account or accounts that a broker is required to have.

Should the broker *deposit* the client's money into his or her personal, operating or general account, **commingling** has occurred. Commingling is not allowed in most states. Should the broker *spend* the client's money, *embezzlement* has occurred. Embezzlement is illegal.

· SUPERVISING AND EDUCATING THE SALES FORCE ·

The training of a new agent is often done by formal classroom instruction, on-the-job training and attendance at sales meetings. The trainer must be able to show new agents how to succeed in the real estate business.

The success of a real estate office or company depends on the skill and knowledge of the sales force. It is the broker's responsibility to supervise the licensees under his or her control. The broker must ensure that the sales staff is well acquainted with the laws of agency and with federal, state and local fair housing laws, as well as with state laws covering the general conduct of the licensee.

Depending on the severity of the infraction committed by the salesperson, the broker also may have his or her own license suspended or revoked.

In some states, if the broker's license is suspended or revoked, all of the licenses held by the broker are immediately suspended until those licensees associate with another broker. *Check with your state to determine the status of an agent's license should a broker's license be suspended or revoked.*

A salesperson or broker who fails to adequately comply with required laws and regulations may be subject to disciplinary action by the real estate commission or by state or local courts. Actions against licensees may be brought by a buyer, a seller, another broker or the real estate commission itself.

• ACCOUNTING PROCEDURES FOR THE OFFICE •

A broker operating a real estate office must maintain accurate accounting records. A broker's trust or escrow account may contain funds such as deposits for agreements of sales, finders' fees, marketing funds, operating funds, rents and security deposits. *Marketing funds* are paid by the seller to help in the expense of marketing the property under a marketing agreement. *Operating funds* are used to maintain and repair a property or run credit checks and screen prospective tenants.

The broker must provide an owner with a statement showing the receipt and disbursement of any funds. Records of settlements that indicate the disbursement of funds at the time of settlement on behalf of the seller and the buyer should be maintained by the broker. These records balance the trust account with the funds received.

Escrow accounts are subject to the state real estate commission's regulation and examination. Mismanagement of escrow accounts can be cause for disciplinary action by the real estate commission.

The broker also must maintain records showing the receipt and the disbursement of commission funds to and from other brokers as well as to salesperson licensees.

Administration—Key Point Review

1. For a salesperson to be active in the real estate business, a broker must hold his or her license. The salesperson is authorized to perform real estate activities on behalf of and in the name of the broker.

2. An independent contractor pays his or her own income tax and Social Security and may not receive any employee benefits from the broker. The broker can regulate the working hours, office routine and attendance at meetings of employees and withholds income, Social Security, FICA and state taxes.

3. State laws determine the length of time that brokers must keep complete and accurate records of all business transactions.

4. Brokers must supply any notifications and reports that the real estate commission requires. Failure to comply can result in disciplinary action.

5. Company policies, procedures and standards establish a clear understanding of the relationship between brokers and sales associates, communicate the "rules of the game" to the sales associates to avoid as many controversies as possible and provide a framework and atmosphere where people can work together and succeed.

6. Federal and state antitrust laws do not allow groups of brokers to fix commission rates among or between them. Payments of commissions are negotiated between brokers and their clients.

Administration—Key Point Review (Continued)

7. Most state laws require that an agent be licensed at the time of the transaction, have an employment contract (listing) and be the procuring cause of the sale to earn a commission. When the brokerage firm has secured a qualified buyer, the broker is due a commission.

8. If a buyer agency relationship has been created, agreement should state who is responsible for the payment of the commission.

9. A trust account, also known as an escrow or impound account, is set up by a broker to hold the money of others. State laws regulate the establishment, maintenance and auditing of the account(s) that a broker is required to have.

10. Commingling a client's money with a broker's personal or business account is not allowed in most states. Embezzlement or using someone else's money is illegal.

11. The training of a new agent may include formal classroom instruction, on-the-job training and attendance at sales meetings. An appropriate timetable for the sales training course must be determined and pertinent instructional materials developed.

12. If the broker's license is suspended or revoked, all of the licenses held by the broker are also usually suspended until such time as the other licensees associate with another broker. Actions against the salesperson licensee or the broker may be brought by a buyer, seller, another broker or the real estate commission.

13. Each broker should have a written agreement with his or her licensees on how commissions will be divided. A salesperson may receive a commission only from her or his broker.

14. A broker operating a real estate office must maintain accurate accounting records and provide an owner with statements showing the receipt and disbursement of funds at the time of settlement and disbursement of commission funds to and from other brokers and licensees.

15. A broker who operates an office should maintain adequate insurance coverage, including errors and omissions insurance, which insures a licensee for mistakes made during the normal conduct of business. Some states require that the errors and omissions insurance payments be made directly through that state's real estate commission as a part of yearly license renewal. The cost of the insurance coverage usually is paid by the licensee.

16. All listed properties should be advertised through the broker.

17. Parties should receive a copy of all documents they sign.

Questions

1. The federal Fair Housing Act prohibits discrimination based on which of the following?
   A. Race, color and age
   B. Race, color and marital status
   C. Religion, military status and national origin
   D. National origin, sex and handicap

2. Which of the following is exempt under the federal Fair Housing Act?
   A. A real estate agent or broker selling his or her own home is exempt if the property is not listed with a brokerage firm.
   B. An owner not occupying a duplex is exempt when she or he refuses to rent to a potential tenant because of race.
   C. A private club operating a senior citizens home for profit is exempt.
   D. A religious organization is exempt if it gives preference to its members in leasing church-owned property, as long as discrimination does not occur in becoming a member of the organization.

3. Which of the following laws give an individual full and equal enjoyment of goods and services in places of public accommodation?
   A. Equal Credit Opportunity Act
   B. Regulation Z
   C. Americans with Disabilities Act
   D. Federal Fair Housing Act

4. Buyer Tina entered into buyer agency agreements in which the broker who finds her suitable property is paid. Tina has MOST LIKELY entered into a(n)
   A. exclusive buyer agency agreement.
   B. exclusive-agency buyer agency agreement.
   C. open buyer agency agreement.
   D. net buyer agency agreement.

5. Which of the following BEST describes an independent contractor in the real estate business?
   A. An independent contractor has a current real estate license, and he or she can receive employee benefits from the broker.
   B. An independent contractor has a current real estate license, and the broker assumes the responsibility for paying his or her income tax and Social Security tax.
   C. An independent contractor has a current real estate license, a written contract with the broker, and 90 percent or more of the individual's income as a licensee is based on sales production and not on the number of hours worked.
   D. An independent contractor has a current real estate license and a written contract with the broker, and the broker can regulate the working hours of the agent.

6. Which of the following laws prohibit price-fixing and the regulation of commission rates?
   A. The federal Sherman Antitrust Act and state antitrust laws
   B. The federal Truth-in-Lending Act and state antitrust laws
   C. The federal Usury Act and state antitrust laws
   D. The federal Regulation B Act and state antitrust laws

7. Broker *M* received an earnest money check from Mr. and Mrs. Buyer. Broker *M* took the check and placed it in his business account. Broker *M* is guilty of
   A. embezzlement.
   B. commingling.
   C. fraud.
   D. misrepresentation.

8. The broker is accountable for which of the following?
   A. The payment of agents' income taxes
   B. The training and supervision of licensees under his or her control
   C. The office hours that agents work
   D. The number of cold calls each agent makes each day

9. A principal broker's license has just been revoked, so all licenses held by the broker are MOST LIKELY
   A. revoked.
   B. suspended.
   C. placed on probation.
   D. canceled.

10. Mr. and Mrs. Buyer just entered into an exclusive buyer agency agreement. The agency relationship that has been created can be BEST described as a(n)
    A. general agency.
    B. universal agency.
    C. dual agency.
    D. special agency.

11. Agent Amelia just received a $500 bonus check from a seller. What should she do with the check?
    A. The check is considered commission, and it should be written to and given to her principal broker.
    B. Tell the seller she can accept only cash and the broker cannot know about the bonus.
    C. Tell the seller that her broker does not allow any of the agents to accept bonus checks.
    D. Cash the check and say nothing to her broker.

12. Agent Jordon works for ABC Realty. She was the buyer's agent in a real estate transaction that was listed by XYZ Realty. The seller has agreed to pay the commission. Jordon will receive her commission check from the
    A. principal broker of XYZ Realty.
    B. principal broker of ABC Realty.
    C. seller.
    D. buyer.

13. To earn a commission, an agent must be
    A. licensed at the time of the transaction.
    B. licensed at the time of the transaction, have an employment contract and be the procuring cause of the sale.
    C. licensed at the time of the transaction, be the procuring cause of the sale and have met all continuing education requirements.
    D. licensed at the time of the transaction, be the procuring cause of the sale and be a member of the multiple-listing service.

14. Under what circumstances may salespeople advertise a property for sale?
    A. If they personally listed the property
    B. If the name of their broker is listed in the ad
    C. If they personally pay for the ad
    D. If they are members of the local real estate board

15. Mary and Dick are salespeople in the brokerage firm of Farnsworth-Schmidt Realty. One day over coffee, they decide that Mary will specialize in houses on the east side of town and Dick will specialize in houses on the west side of town. Such a practice is
    A. legal, because the prohibition against allocation of market does not apply to salespeople working for the same broker.
    B. legal, because the agreement was not in writing.
    C. illegal, because only brokers may agree to restrict competition.
    D. illegal, because state laws prohibit such a division of the market.

16. Broker Carol has several salespeople employed at her office. Early one day, one member of the sales staff brings in a written offer with an earnest money deposit on a house listed with the broker. Later the same day, another salesperson brings in a higher written offer on the same property, also including an earnest money deposit. Carol, in accordance with the policy of her office, does not submit the second offer to the seller until the first has been presented and rejected, so the seller is not informed of the second offer. In this situation, the broker's actions are
    A. permissible, providing the commission is split between the two salespeople.
    B. permissible, if such an arrangement is written into the salespeople's employment contracts.
    C. not permissible, because the broker must submit all offers to the seller.
    D. not permissible, because the broker must notify the second buyer of the existence of the first offer.

17. Broker Sandra represents a buyer interested in a house listed with broker Jack. Sandra feels that Jack is often very difficult to negotiate with. Therefore, Sandra may inform her client to
    A. carry on negotiations with the seller directly.
    B. inform the buyer that Jack is difficult to deal with and to find another house.
    C. write an offer below the listed price.
    D. say nothing about Jack being difficult to deal with and tell the buyer that the house just sold.

18. All of the following statements are false regarding a real estate broker's acting as the agent of the seller EXCEPT the broker
    A. can lower the sale price of the property without the seller's approval.
    B. must follow the legal instructions of the seller.
    C. can disclose the seller's personal information to a buyer if it helps secure an offer on the property.
    D. can accept a commission from the buyer without the seller's approval.

19. An exclusive-right-to-sell listing is BEST described as an
    A. executed express contract.
    B. executed bilateral contract.
    C. executory unilateral contract.
    D. executory bilateral contract.

20. The government agency established to control the supply and reserves of money as well as to establish a discount rate is
    A. Fannie Mae.
    B. Ginnie Mae.
    C. Federal Reserve.
    D. FDIC.

21. For a broker to open an office, he or she must hold a minimum of how many licenses?
    A. One
    B. Two to three
    C. Four to six
    D. None

22. Who must be licensed in a real estate office?
    A. The owner
    B. Anyone engaged in listing real estate
    C. All personal assistants
    D. Anyone giving information from the newspaper

23. What is the difference between an appraisal and a competitive market analysis?
    A. One is used for financing and the other for refinancing.
    B. One is used to determine market value and the other for land.
    C. They are the same.
    D. One is used for fair market value and the other for marketing.

24. When listing a property with a fee simple defeasible title, which of the following appurtenances should be in the listing agreement?
    A. House and furniture
    B. House and car
    C. House and landscaping
    D. House and deed conditions

25. Which of the following legal descriptions must include air space above a datum?
    A. Survey of a cemetery plot
    B. Survey of a condominium
    C. Survey of a single-family home
    D. Survey of mineral rights

26. The principle of appraising that says the whole is worth more than the sum of its parts is referring to
    A. regression.
    B. progression.
    C. assemblage.
    D. plottage.

27. Which of the following is NOT true regarding a real estate settlement?
    A. Closing is the time when the title to real estate is usually transferred in exchange for payment of the purchase price and can be known as *passing papers*.
    B. The primary issues of a face-to-face closing are fulfilling the promises made in the sales contract, closing the buyer's loan and the mortgage lender's dispersing the loan funds.
    C. An escrow agent is a disinterested third party who is authorized to act for both the buyer and seller and to coordinate the closing activities; the agent also may be called the *escrow holder*.
    D. If the buyer is assuming the seller's existing mortgage loan, the buyer will want to know the exact balance of the loan as of the closing date, and the lender will issue an estoppel certificate to verify the loan balance.

28. A buyer purchased a property, but did not record the deed. By taking possession of the property, the buyer is giving
    A. possessory notice.
    B. constructive notice.
    C. actual notice.
    D. implied notice.

29. Which of the following is a lis pendens notice?
    A. A recorded notice that allows all lienholders to collect before a judgment
    B. A recorded notice that is filed only when a property is in foreclosure
    C. A recorded notice that is filed on final determination of a suit to quiet title
    D. A recorded notice that a property is in litigation that could result in a future lien being placed on the property

30. Which of the following is NOT found in an abstract of title?
    A. Any restrictions found within the deed
    B. Guarantee of title
    C. Property description
    D. Existing mortgage on the property

31. What law requires that a real estate broker make her office accessible to all individuals?
    A. The Building Accessible Law of 1995
    B. The Federal Fair Housing Act
    C. The Americans with Disabilities Act
    D. The Civil Rights Act of 1968

32. Which of the following would NOT be a factor influencing supply and demand in a real estate market?
    A. A new law regulating real estate agents
    B. The demographics of the area
    C. Interest rates increasing
    D. The announcement of a new factory moving to the area

33. Which of the following statements is FALSE regarding the Federal Reserve?
    A. When the reserve requirements are increased, the money supply shrinks, thus increasing interest rates.
    B. When the reserve requirements are decreased, the money supply grows, thus decreasing interest rates.
    C. An oversupply of money creates inflation, and an undersupply can cause a recession.
    D. The Federal Reserve does not regulate the reserve requirements for depository institutions.

34. Which of the following is exempt from the ADA?
    A. Hotels, motels and restaurants
    B. A church or synagogue
    C. A residential apartment building that is owner-occupied
    D. A shopping center

35. Which of the following is true regarding a trust account?

A. A trust account must be opened by a new agent within seven days of the receipt of his or her license.

B. A trust account is set up by a broker to hold the money of others until a transaction is closed.

C. Money from the trust account can be used by the broker at any time.

D. If the buyer defaults on a sales contract, the agent may withdraw money from the trust account and pay the seller.

36. Which of the following deeds is MOST LIKE-LY used to transfer property at a foreclosure sale?

A. General warranty

B. Trustor's

C. Special warranty

D. Quitclaim

37. A father gave each of his six children quitclaim deeds to the same property with the instructions that the deed not be recorded until his death. None of the deeds was acknowledged or attested. His instructions were followed. In his will, the father left the property to his second wife. Who most likely has ownership rights to the property?

A. The six children because they received deeds first.

B. The first child that received the quitclaim deed to the property.

C. The second wife because the deeds were not acknowledged.

D. The last child that received the quitclaim deed to the property.

38. The broker places a buyer's earnest money check into the firm's business account. This act is known as

A. embezzlement.

B. standard practice.

C. commingling.

D. redlining.

39. Broker Dee entered into an exclusive-right-to-sell listing with a seller and found a qualified buyer who agreed to buy the property at the listed price. The seller refused to sell. Which of the following is true?

A. The seller can refuse the offer and has no legal liability to anyone.

B. The seller can refuse to sell, but a commission is owed the broker.

C. The seller cannot refuse to sell because the listed price was offered.

D. The seller cannot refuse to sell because he signed an exclusive-right-to-sell listing agreement.

40. A violent crime was committed in a home, and as a result the property is stigmatized. When listing the property, the agent should

A. ignore the fact that the crime occurred and say nothing to the sellers.

B. be aware of the status of the property but say nothing to potential buyers.

C. show the property to out-of-town buyers who probably will not know to ask any questions.

D. discuss the situation with the broker and seek competent counsel about how to best deal with the property.

41. Which of the following is NOT a responsibility of the agent when the agent is representing the buyer in a real estate transaction?

A. To show properties that protect the broker's commissions and select the best times to show those properties

B. To be fair and honest with the seller but safeguard the buyer's interest under all circumstances

C. To suggest the minimum amount of earnest money deposit to be made and suggest that forfeiture of the deposit be the sole remedy if the buyer defaults

D. To require that a seller sign a property condition statement and confirm representations of the condition of the property

42. Which of the following is the responsibility of a seller's agent to the buyer?
    A. Disclosure of any material fact pertinent to the property
    B. Disclosure of the lowest offer the seller will accept on the property
    C. Disclosure that the seller is near bankruptcy or foreclosure
    D. Disclosure that the seller has AIDS

43. A buyer made an offer and gave the seller three days to accept. On the following day, she found a FSBO property she liked better. The buyer called the agent to revoke her previous offer. The agent had no communication of acceptance from the seller. Regarding this situation, the buyer must
    A. make an immediate offer on the FSBO property before it is purchased by someone else.
    B. make sure the seller is notified of the revocation before making an offer on the FSBO property.
    C. do nothing more because she has notified the agent of her decision to rescind the offer.
    D. give the seller three days to accept or reject, as stated in the offer.

44. An agent involved in conducting a single business transaction under detailed instructions of a principal is considered a(n)
    A. general agent.
    B. special agent.
    C. implied agent.
    D. universal agent.

45. Which of the following is NOT true regarding an exclusive agency agreement?
    A. It may contain a broker protection clause.
    B. It excludes the seller from selling the property.
    C. It excludes other brokers from listing the property.
    D. It excludes the property from being placed in the MLS unless permission is granted by the seller.

46. A seller agreed to list his house for $90,000, but he was not informed that the actual value of the property was $100,000. The agent purchased the property the next day. This is an example of a violation of which of the agent's responsibilities?
    A. Obedience
    B. Accountability
    C. Loyalty
    D. Discovery

47. The principal to whom an agent gives advice and counsel is a
    A. subagent.
    B. customer.
    C. client.
    D. fiduciary.

48. A testator devised a parcel of real estate under the restriction that it be used for single-family dwellings only. Zoning in this area allows multifamily dwellings. Which of the following would be upheld?
    A. The devisee can build single-family or multi-family dwellings because the grantor is dead.
    B. The zoning ordinance takes precedence, and the devisee can build multi-family dwellings.
    C. The deed restriction takes precedence and prevents the owner from building multi-family dwellings.
    D. The devisee can sell the property to someone else and that grantee can build single-family or multi-family dwellings.

49. A church was purchasing a property from a business. At the closing table, the attorney representing the church refused to accept the deed. Which of the following would permit the church to refuse the deed?
    A. The deed did not contain the correct consideration.
    B. The sales contract stated that the business would provide a general warranty deed, but it presented a special warranty deed for acceptance.
    C. The deed presented at the closing did not contain the signature of the grantee.
    D. The sales contract did not state that time is of the essence; therefore the church could refuse the deed because it did not close in a timely manner.

50. The law that states that "All citizens of the United States shall have the same right in every state and territory as is enjoyed by white citizens thereof to inherit, purchase, lease, sell, hold and convey real and personal property" is
    A. President John Kennedy's executive order.
    B. the Civil Rights Act of 1964.
    C. the Civil Rights Act of 1866.
    D. Title VIII of the Civil Rights Act of 1968.

51. Which of the following is NOT an unlawful practice?
    A. Refusing to sell, rent or negotiate with any person or otherwise make a dwelling unavailable
    B. Displaying the Equal Housing Opportunity Poster and providing all clients and customers with pertinent information in a transaction
    C. Altering the terms or conditions for a loan for the purchase, construction, improvement or repair of a dwelling for a protected class
    D. Representing that a property is not available for sale or rent when in fact it is

52. Which of the following is NOT true regarding the ECOA?
    A. It prohibits discrimination based on race, color and religion.
    B. It prohibits discrimination based on national origin, sex, marital status or age.
    C. It requires that credit applications be considered only on the basis of income, net worth, job stability and credit rating.
    D. It requires that credit applicants disclose their child-bearing intentions if income could be interrupted in the future.

53. Which of the following is NOT true regarding the ADA?
    A. It is designed to eliminate discrimination against individuals with disabilities by mandating equal access to jobs, public accommodations, government services, public transportation and telecommunications.
    B. Public accommodations include hotels, shopping centers, professional offices, private clubs, religious organizations and private entities that own, lease or operate virtually all commercial facilities.
    C. Any employer with 15 or more employees must adopt nondiscriminatory employment procedures and make reasonable accommodations to enable an individual with a disability to perform essential job functions.
    D. The definition of a person with a disability is one who has a physical or mental impairment that substantially limits one or more major life activities and includes disfiguration due to an accident.

54. A borrower's right to rescind within three days an agreement to allow a lender to place a second mortgage on his or her property as security for the loan is provided by the
    A. Real Estate Settlement Procedures Act.
    B. Equal Credit Opportunity Act.
    C. Truth-in-Lending Act.
    D. Fair Credit Reporting Act.

55. The practice of lending institutions refusing to make loans in certain geographic areas is called
    A. blockbusting.
    B. redlining.
    C. channeling.
    D. steering.

56. Which of the following BEST defines the law of agency?
    A. The selling of another's property by an authorized agency
    B. The rules of law that apply to the responsibilities and obligations of a person who acts for another
    C. The principles that govern one's conduct in business
    D. The rules and regulations of the state licensing agency

57. Which of the following BEST defines blockbusting?
    A. Changing the zoning districts of a municipality
    B. Representing to homeowners that minorities are moving into the area
    C. Discriminating against minorities by limit-ing the housing available to them
    D. Removing property from the tax rolls

58. The federal Fair Housing Act applies to all of the following EXCEPT
    A. rental property.
    B. vacant land sales.
    C. single-family sales.
    D. commercial or industrial properties.

59. An offer was presented to a seller for acceptance one day prior to the expiration of the listing. The seller had three days to accept the offer. On day two, the seller did accept the offer. One day prior to closing the seller discovered the buyer was a relative of the listing agent and rescinded the contract. Does the seller have the right to rescind the contract?
    A. No. Disclosure of a relationship between the buyer and listing agent is not relevant.
    B. Yes. A seller can rescind a contract any time prior to closing.
    C. No. A seller cannot rescind a contract any time prior to closing.
    D. Yes. An undisclosed dual agency was created and the seller can rescind the contract.

60. Mr. and Mrs. Homeowner own their principal place of residence in Anytown, U.S.A. They own a condominium in Resort Beach, U.S.A. They are now 65 years of age and decide to retire. Under Federal Fair Housing Laws they may discriminate in the sale of their home if
    A. they use the services of a small broker.
    B. they own four or fewer properties and do not discriminate because of race in the transaction.
    C. they own no more than three homes at one time, do not use the services of a broker and do not use discriminatory advertising.
    D. they are no longer living in the home and have not discriminated in the sale of a property within the last 36 months.

ANSWERS

1. D The classifications protected under federal fair housing are race, color, religion, national origin, sex, familial status and handicap.

2. D Religious organizations can give preference to members only.

3. C The Americans with Disabilities Act was passed in 1990 to enable individuals with disabilities to become a part of the social and economic mainstream.

4. C In an open buyer agency agreement, the agent is paid who finds suitable property.

5. C By definition of independent contractor.

6. A By definition of antitrust laws.

7. B A client's money must be placed in a separate escrow or trust account. When it is placed in the business account, commingling has occurred.

8. B A broker is liable for the training and supervision of activities of licensees under his or her control.

9. B When a principal broker's license is revoked or suspended, all licenses held by the broker are most likely suspended.

10. D A special agency is created when the principal delegates a specific act or business transaction.

11. A All commission checks must be given to the principal broker.

12. B An agent is paid by her or his principal broker.

13. B The three requirements for collecting a commission are (1) to be licensed at the time of the transaction, (2) have an employment contract and (3) be the procuring cause of the sale.

14. B Properties listed by an agent must be advertised in the name of the brokerage firm.

15. A The antitrust laws prohibit price-fixing in any way, but not how salespersons within a given office decide to divide a market.

16. C All offers must be presented to the seller.

17. C When representing the buyer, an agent must negotiate the best possible deal for the buyer. This includes offering less than the list price for the property.

18. B This is the true statement. A broker must follow the legal instructions of the seller.

19. D An exclusive-right-to-sell listing is an executory contract in that one or both parties have obligations to perform. It is a bilateral contract because both parties are obligated to perform.

20. C The Federal Reserve was established to control the supply of money to help stabilize the economy.

21. A A brokerage firm can be opened with the broker as the only licensee.

22. B Anyone engaged in listing, selling, property management or other activities regarded as the practice of real estate must be licensed.

23. D The appraisal is used to determine market value, while a CMA is a marketing tool that helps the seller determine the asking price of the property.

24. D If a fee simple defeasible title is being transferred, the deed conditions should be in the listing contract.

25. B A survey of a condominium must contain the legal description of the elevations of floor and ceiling surfaces and the vertical boundaries in reference to an official datum. Thus, it must include the air space above the datum.

26. D The principal of plottage states that the whole should be worth more than the sum of its parts. The process of merging adjacent lots held by separate landowners into a larger lot is assemblage.

27. D When the buyer is assuming the seller's existing mortgage, the lender issues a mortgage reduction certificate to verify the loan balance, not an estoppel certificate.

28. B Constructive notice is notice that certain facts can be discovered by due diligence or inquiry. Even though the deed was not recorded, possession of the property grants constructive notice.

29. D By definition of lis pendens.

30. B An attorney will give certificate of title, but there is no guarantee of title.

31. C The Americans with Disabilities Act requires that all properties provide accessibility to the public.

32. A A new real estate school would NOT influence supply and demand in the real estate market.

33. D The Fed does regulate the reserve requirements for depository institutions.

34. B Private clubs and religious organizations are exempt from the ADA.

35. B By definition of trust account.

36. D A quitclaim deed most likely transfers property at a foreclosure.

37. C The second wife would most likely receive the property because most states require a document to be acknowledged before it can be introduced as evidence in a court of law. Most states will not allow a document to be recorded at the court house without it being acknowledged.

38. C By the definition of commingling.

39. B A listing contract is an employment contract. When the broker found the qualified buyer, the commission had been earned.

40. D State laws vary as to how to handle the sale of stigmatized properties, and the agent should discuss the situation with the broker and an attorney immediately.

41. A When an agent is representing a buyer, the agent must search for the best properties for the buyer to inspect, including FSBO.

42. A A seller's agent is responsible for being honest and fair with the buyer and for disclosing all pertinent and material facts about the property.

43. C An offer can be revoked at any time before acceptance. Because the agent had no communication of acceptance from the seller, the buyer has no responsibilities for the offer once the revocation was communicated.

44. B By definition of special agent.

45. B An exclusive agency permits the seller to sell the property and not pay a commission if the buyer was procured without the assistance of the broker.

46. C Loyalty means placing the principal's interest above the interest of all others, including self-interest. Because the agent did not disclose the true market value of the property, the agent did not fulfill his responsibility of loyalty.

47. C A client is a person to whom the agent gives advice and counsel.

48. C Whenever a deed restriction and a zoning ordinance conflict, the most restrictive is upheld.

49. B If a deed other than a general warranty deed is to be given by the grantor, it must be stated in the sales contract and should be stated in the listing contract.

50. C The efforts of the federal government to guarantee equal housing opportunities to all U.S citizens began more than 100 years ago with the passage of the Civil Rights Act of 1866.

51. B It is not unlawful to display the Equal Housing Opportunity Poster and to provide clients and customers with pertinent information.

52. D Credit applicants cannot be asked about their childbearing intentions or capabil- ity or about their birth control practices.

53. B Private clubs and religious organizations are not included in the definition of public accommodations and are exempt from the ADA.

54. C Truth-in-Lending or Regulation Z provides the three-day right of rescission when a borrower is negotiating a second mortgage or refinancing the property.

55. B By definition of redlining.

56. B The rules of law that apply to the responsibilities and obligations of a person who acts for another is the law of agency.

57. B Blocking is representing to sellers that minorities are moving into a neighborhood.

58. D Federal fair housing laws do not apply to) 1 commerical properties.

59. D An undisclosed dual agency has been created and the seller would have the 5 right to rescind the contract.

60. C Under Federal fair housing laws the owners of a single family home may discriminate in the sale of the home if they own three or fewer homes, and do not use the services of a broker or discriminatory advertising.

Math Review

Depending on which test you receive, there could be between 8 and 20 math questions on your state examination. This chapter will show you how to use the "T" method for working math questions. It is a simple formula that can be used to solve most of the math questions that you could encounter on the exam. The formulas for brokerage, financing, appraising, area and settlement math will also be reviewed.

THE "T" METHOD

Here is a math question that you can work in your head. If an agent sold a property for $100,000 and the broker was paid a 7 percent commission, what was that commission? That's right. $7,000. Let's use this question to learn how the "T" formula works.

$$\frac{\text{Part}}{\text{Total} \mid \text{Rate}}$$

In the "T", the total is placed on the bottom left, the rate on the bottom right, and the part at the top. Using the "T" for the above question, it gives us this:

$$\frac{\$7,000 \text{ Commission } \$}{\$100,000 \mid 7\%}$$

Sale Price × Commission Rate

Rule 1

When given the two numbers in the bottom of the "T", which are the total and the rate, the mathematical function is multiplication. $100,000 × 7 percent = $7,000.

Rule 2

When given the part at the top of the "T" and the rate at the bottom, the mathematical function is **division.** It helps to remember TGIF: **T**op **G**oes **I**nto the calculator **F**irst.

Example: If a broker received a $7,000 commission check and the selling price was $100,000, what was the commission rate?

The $7,000 is the part and goes at the top of the "T." $100,000 is the sale price or total and goes in the lower left. Thus, $7,000 ÷ $100,000 = 7 percent.

÷ $7,000 Commission $	
$100,000 Sale Price	.07 or 7% Commission Rate

Rule 3

When given the part at the top of the "T" and the total at the bottom, the mathematical function is division. Remember TGIF.

Example: The seller received $100,000 and the commission paid was 7 percent. What was the sale price of the property?

Notice how this question is different. Is the $100,000 a part or a total? It's a part, so it goes at the top of the "T". It is equal to 93 percent of the selling price, so 93 percent goes in the lower right of the "T". $100,000 ÷ 93% = $107,526.88.

$100,000 Seller's Net ÷	
$107,526.88 Sale Price	.93 or 93% Seller's %

Rule 4

When solving for the total, take the part and divide by the percent to which that part is equal. For example: Commission $ ÷ Commission Rate = Sale Price and Seller's Dollars $ ÷ Seller's % = Sale Price.

BROKERAGE MATH FORMULAS

Brokerage math questions include computing commissions and determining the sale price when given the seller's dollars and the commission rate

÷ Commission $ ÷	
Sale Price	Commission Rate

Sale Price × Commission Rate = Commission $
Commission $ ÷ Commission Rate = Sale Price
Commission $ ÷ Sale Price = Commission Rate

÷ Seller's Dollars $ ÷	
Sale Price	Seller's %

Sale Price × Seller's % = Seller's Dollars $
Seller's Dollars $ ÷ Seller's % = Sale Price
Seller's Dollars $ ÷ Sale Price = Seller %

Brokerage Math Questions

1. A broker sold a property for $250,000. She was paid 6 percent on the first $100,000, 5 percent on the next $100,000 and 4 percent on the balance. How much was the broker paid?

   A. $6,000
   B. $5,000
   C. $13,000
   D. $24,000

2. A broker and sales associate split commissions on a 60/40 basis. How much commission will the sales associate earn if he sells a property for $125,000 and a 6 percent commission is paid?

   A. $7,500
   B. $3,000
   C. $4,500
   D. $3,500

3. An agent was paid $2,500, which was half of the 7 percent that the broker collected. What was the sale price of the property?

   A. $71,248
   B. $35,714
   C. $35,417
   D. $71,428

4. A broker and a sales associate split commissions on a 60/40 basis. If the broker's share of the commission was $3,500 and the sale price was $83,333, what was the commission rate?

   A. 6 percent
   B. 10.5 percent
   C. 7.5 percent
   D. 7 percent

5. Ms. Seller agreed to pay a 6 percent commission to a brokerage company. At the closing table, she received a check for $94,500. What was the selling price of the property?

   A. $100,170
   B. $100,710
   C. $100,532
   D. $100,352

6. Mr. Seller wants to net a profit of $20,000 and agrees to pay a 7 percent commission. He also has selling expenses of $400 and a mortgage of $35,250. What is the minimum offer he could accept on the property?

   A. $59,839
   B. $59,545
   C. $58,565
   D. $59,656

7. Mr. and Mrs. Seller want to net a 12 percent profit after paying the brokerage firm a 6.5 percent commission. If the original purchase price was $104,500, what is the minimum offer they can accept?

   A. $125,716
   B. $117,040
   C. $125,176
   D. $124,647

PROPERTY MANAGEMENT MATH FORMULAS

An agent acting as a property manager may be paid a percentage of the gross or net income as commission. Normally, the manager is paid a percentage of the gross income, but read the question carefully.

Example: The annual gross rent collected on a building is $124,000. If the property manager is paid a 6 percent commission on the rents collected, how much is he paid annually?

$7,440 Commission $

| $124,000 | 6% |

Gross Rent × Commission Rate

Gross or Net Rent × Commission Rate = Commission $
Commission $ ÷ Commission Rate = Gross or Net Rent
Commission $ ÷ Gross or Net Rent = Commission Rate

Read the question carefully to determine if you are solving for the annual, semiannual, quarterly or monthly commission.

The commission may also be computed as so many dollars per square footage of the space leased.

Example: A tenant leased a 60' × 100' space for $8 per square foot annually. If the property manager is paid 8 percent of the rent collected, how much is she paid annually?

Step 1   60' × 100' = 6,000 square feet

Step 2   6,000 square feet × $8 = $48,000 annual rent

Step 3
$$\frac{\$3{,}840 \text{ Commission } \$}{\$48{,}000 \quad | \quad 8\%}$$
Gross Rent × Commission Rate

Though there are several types of percentage leases, this is usually how they are negotiated: the tenant pays a fixed monthly rent or base rent, plus a percentage of all income over a certain amount. The rent could also be paid on all income.

Example: A shop owner entered into a percentage lease with the lessor in which she agreed to pay a fixed rental of $650 per month, and when gross sales reached $175,000, she pays 5 percent of sales over that amount. This year, her gross sales were $225,000. What was the total rent paid at the end of the year?

Step 1 $650 × 12 = $7,800 fixed rent

Step 2 $225,000 − 175,000 = $50,000 gross sales over $175,000

Step 3
$$\frac{\$2{,}500 \text{ Commission } \$}{\$50{,}000 \quad | \quad 5\%}$$
Gross Sales × Commission Rate

Step 4 $7,800 + 2,500 = $10,300 Total Commission Paid

In a graduated lease, the rents increase or "step up" on a gradual basis over the life of the lease.

Example: A tenant entered into a 12-year graduated lease with the owner of a building. He agreed to pay $400 per month for the first four years, $450 per month for the next four years, and $500 per month for the remaining term. If the property manager is paid 6 percent of the total rent collected, how much will he be paid at the end of the leasing term?

Step 1 $400 × 12 × 4 = $19,200
$450 × 12 × 4 = $21,600
+$500 × 12 × 4 = $24,000
$64,800

Step 2 $64,800 gross rent collected in 12 years

Step 3
$$\frac{\$3{,}888 \text{ Commission } \$}{\$64{,}800 \quad | \quad 6\%}$$
Gross Rent × Commission Rate

Property Management Questions

8. A space was leased for $1,200 per month. The owner pays a property manager 8 percent of the gross income as commission. How much does the owner pay annually?
   A. $1,512
   B. $1,152
   C. $1,215
   D. $96

9. A tenant rented a 20′ × 25′ office space for $10.25 per square foot annually. If a property manager is paid 7.5 percent of the rent collected, what is her quarterly income?
   A. $96.09
   B. $384.38
   C. $348.38
   D. $192.19

10. The XYZ store leased a space in the mall with the following agreement: $575 fixed monthly rent, plus a 5.25 percent commission on all sales over $225,000. The gross sales were $389,250 for the year. What was the total rent paid by XYZ?
    A. $15,523
    B. $8,623
    C. $9,600
    D. $15,253

11. The KLM store leased a space in the mall with a percentage lease and agreed to pay $425 monthly fixed rent and 6 percent on all sales over $175,000. This year, the total rent paid was $9,321. What were the gross sales?
    A. $184,849
    B. $213,350
    C. $213,530
    D. $245,350

12. A property manager negotiated a 15-year graduated lease with the following terms. The lessee will pay $550 per month for the first five years, with a $50 a month increase every five years thereafter. If the property manager is paid a 6.75 percent commission, what will be the total commission paid at the end of the term?
    A. $7,290
    B. $7,087
    C. $7,429
    D. $7,920

FINANCING MATH FORMULAS

Financing math questions include computing the loan amount, annual interest dollars, discount points, loan origination fees and amortization of a loan. Remember, the lender negotiates the loan on the sale price or appraised value, whichever is less.

Example: A seller agreed to pay $85,000 for a property, but it appraised for $83,500. The lender agreed to negotiate a 90 percent loan. What was the loan amount?

$$\frac{\$75,150 \text{ Loan}}{\$83,500 \mid 90\%}$$

Appraised Value × Loan-to-Value Ratio

Sale Price or Appraised Value × Loan-to-Value Ratio = Loan
Loan ÷ Sale Price or Appraised Value = Loan-to-Value Ratio
Loan ÷ Loan-to-Value Ratio = Sale Price or Appraised Value

A question may ask for the annual, semiannual, quarterly, monthly or daily interest that is due on a loan.

Example: Sterling negotiated a $125,000 loan at 8.75 percent annual interest. How much interest will she pay the first year?

$$\frac{\$10,937.50 \text{ Annual Interest } \$}{\$125,000 \mid 8.75\%}$$

Loan × Interest Rate

$$\text{Loan} \times \text{Interest Rate} = \text{Annual Interest \$}$$
$$\text{Annual Interest \$} \div \text{Loan} = \text{Interest Rate}$$
$$\text{Annual Interest \$} \div \text{Interest Rate} = \text{Loan}$$

Discount points are computed as a percentage of the loan amount: 1 point = 1% of the loan, 2 points = 2% of the loan.

Example: Fred secured an $89,000 loan and was required to pay three discount points. How much did he pay in points?

$$\frac{\$2,670 \ \text{Discount Points \$}}{\$89,000 \ | \ 3\%}$$

Loan × Discount Points %

$$\text{Loan} \times \text{Discount Points \%} = \text{Discount Points \$}$$
$$\text{Discount Points \$} \div \text{Loan} = \text{Discount Points \%}$$
$$\text{Discount Points \$} \div \text{Discount Points \%} = \text{Loan}$$

A lender's cash outflow is the loan minus the discount points percent.

Example: Ms. Buyer secured an $89,000 loan and had to pay one point. What was the cash outflow of the lender?

$89,000	Loan
− 1%	Discount Points %
$88,110	Cash Outflow

Loan
− Discount Points %
Cash Outflow

To determine the effective yield to the lender, remember this rule of thumb: For each discount point that the lender charges, the lender's yield is increased by 1/8 percent on a 30-year loan.

Example: Warren negotiated an $80,000 loan for 30 years at an 8.25 percent rate of interest and had to pay two points. What was the effective yield to the lender?

Step 1   1 ÷ 8 = .125%

Step 2   .125% × 2 = .25% increase

Step 3   8.25% interest + .25% increase = 8.5% effective yield

.125 percent × Discount Points = Increase
Interest Rate + Increase = Effective Yield

The loan origination fee is also computed as a percentage of the loan amount.

Example: The buyer secured a $50,000 loan and had to pay a 1.5 percent origination fee. How much did the buyer have to pay for the origination fee?

$$\frac{\$750 \ \text{Origination Fee \$}}{\$50,000 \ | \ 1.5\%}$$

Loan × Origination Fee %

$$\text{Loan} \times \text{Origination Fee \%} = \text{Origination Fee \$}$$
$$\text{Origination Fee \$} \div \text{Loan} = \text{Origination Fee \%}$$
$$\text{Origination Fee \$} \div \text{Origination Fee \%} = \text{Loan}$$

The word *amortize* means to reduce the debt by making payments that include both principal and interest. The principal and interest payment is normally given in the question about loan amortization.

Example: Sandy negotiated a $100,000 loan at 10 percent interest for 30 years. Her monthly payments are $877.58 per month. What is her loan balance after the first payment?

Step 1 $10,000 Annual Interest $
$$\frac{\$10{,}000 \text{ Annual Interest \$}}{\$100{,}000 \quad | \quad 10\%}$$
Loan × Interest Rate

Step 2 $10,000 Annual Interest $ ÷ 12 months = $833.33 Monthly Interest

Step 3 $877.58 P&I – $833.33 Monthly Interest = $44.25 Principal

Step 4 $100,000 – 44.25 = $99,955.75 Loan Balance after First Payment

Financing Questions

13. A lender negotiated an $82,250 loan, which was 80 percent of the appraised value. What was the appraised value of the property?
    A. $65,800.50
    B. $68,500.50
    C. $82,250.50
    D. $102,812.50

14. What is the rate of interest if the mortgagor makes quarterly interest payments of $1,340.63 on a $65,000 loan?
    A. 2.06 percent
    B. 8.25 percent
    C. 7.75 percent
    D. 9.25 percent

15. To secure a $100,000 loan, the buyer paid $3,000 in discount points and the seller paid $2,000 in discount points. How many points were charged?
    A. 3
    B. 2
    C. 5
    D. 4

16. The lender negotiated a $55,000 loan and charged three discount points. What was the cash outflow of the lender?
    A. $56,560
    B. $56,650
    C. $53,530
    D. $53,350

17. A savings and loan agreed to make a $65,000 mortgage at 8 percent interest for 30 years, and charged three points to negotiate the loan. What was the effective yield to the lender?
    A. 8.375 percent
    B. 8.735 percent
    C. 8.25 percent
    D. 8.35 percent

18. Mr. and Mrs. Buyer applied for a VA loan to purchase a property for $79,500. The property appraised at $79,000. They agreed to pay a 1 percent loan origination fee. How much did they pay in origination fees?
    A. $790
    B. $970
    C. $975
    D. $795

19. The buyers secured an $82,000 loan at 9.25 percent interest for 30 years. Their monthly payment is $674.59. How much of their first payment will be applied to the principal balance?
    A. $42.51
    B. $632.08
    C. $7,585
    D. $7,855

20. The listing price of a property was $135,000. The buyer made an offer of 90 percent of the listing price, which was accepted by the sellers. The property appraised for $135,000 and the buyers secured an 85 percent loan at 9 percent interest for 30 years. How much interest will be paid in the first payment?

    A. $774.56
    B. $747.56
    C. $860.62
    D. $839.24

21. This month's interest payment is $585.70. If the buyer secured a 90 percent loan at an 8.75 percent annual rate of interest, what was the sale price?

    A. $80,325
    B. $80,235
    C. $89,250
    D. $89,500

22. A borrower secured an $80,000 loan at 8.25 percent interest and the lender's cash outflow was $77,600. What was the effective yield to the lender?

    A. 8.50 percent
    B. 8.625 percent
    C. 8.375 percent
    D. 8.85 percent

PROPERTY TAX MATH FORMULAS

The calculation of real estate property taxes involves two math formulas. Taxes are computed on the assessed value, which is a percentage of the market value. The assessed value is then multiplied by the tax rate to give the annual property tax.

Example: The market value of a property is $70,000 and it is assessed at 40 percent of the market value. If the tax rate is $5.50 per $100, what is the annual property tax?

The word *per* in a math question means divide. Thus, $5.50 ÷ $100 = .055 tax rate.

$$\frac{\$28,000 \text{ Assessed Value}}{\$70,000 \quad | \quad 40\%}$$

Market Value × Assessment Rate

$$\frac{\$1,540 \text{ Annual Property Taxes}}{\$28,000 \quad | \quad .055}$$

Assessed Value × Tax Rate

Market Value × Assessment Rate = Assessed Value
Assessed Value ÷ Market Value = Assessment Rate
Assessed Value ÷ Assessment Rate = Market Value

Assessed Value × Tax Rate = Annual Property Taxes
Annual Property Taxes ÷ Assessed Value = Tax Rate
Annual Property Taxes ÷ Tax Rate = Assessed Value

The above formulas can also use the appraised value instead of the market value of the property.

The tax rate can also be expressed as mills, which means 1/1000 of a dollar. Thus, whenever you see the tax rate expressed as mills, divide that number by 1,000.

Example: If the tax rate is 55 mills, that means 55 ÷ 1,000 = .055 for the tax rate.

If the tax rate is 555 mills, that means 555 ÷ 1,000 = .555 for the tax rate.

23. If the market value of a property is $169,000, it is assessed at 35 percent, and the tax rate is $4.25 per $100, what are the monthly property taxes?
    A. $2,513.88
    B. $2,531.88
    C. $409.49
    D. $209.49

24. The appraised value of a property is $52,350. It is assessed at 38 percent of the appraised value and the tax rate is 95 mills. What are the quarterly property taxes?
    A. $472.45
    B. $1,889.83
    C. $1,998.83
    D. $1,589.83

25. The market value of a property is $65,000 and is assessed for 45 percent of its value. If the owner's semiannual tax bill was $511.88, what was the tax rate per $100?
    A. $3.50
    B. 350 mills
    C. $1.75
    D. 175 mills

26. Mr. and Mrs. Homeowner received a semi-annual tax bill of $984.38. Property in the jurisdiction is assessed at one-fourth the market value. If the tax rate is $4.50 per $100, what is the estimated market value of the property?
    A. $43,750
    B. $175,000
    C. $195,000
    D. $53,750

APPRAISAL MATH FORMULAS

The appraisal formulas reviewed in this section are the income, cost and the gross rent multiplier approach to appraising. This section also includes a review of capital gains, appreciation and depreciation of property.

The income approach to appraising is used to convert the annual net operating income of investment property into a value by dividing it by the capitalization rate.

Example: Three apartments rent for $450 per month, three for $500 per month, and two for $550 per month. There is a 5 percent vacancy rate, $300 in monthly expenses, and $125 per month additional income. If the owner wants a 10 percent return on her investment, how much can she pay for the property?

$$3 \times \$450 \times 12 = \$16,200$$
$$3 \times \$500 \times 12 = \$18,000$$
$$2 \times \$550 \times 12 = \$13,200$$

	$47,400	Potential Gross Income
	− 5%	Vacancy Rate
	$45,030	
$125 × 12 =	+ 1,500	Additional Income
	$46,530	Effective Gross Income
$300 × 12 =	− 3,600	Expenses
	$42,930	Annual Net Operating Income ÷

$429,300	10%
Value	Cap Rate

$$\begin{array}{l} \text{Potential Gross Income} \\ -\quad \text{Vacancy Rate} \\ +\quad \text{Additional Income} \\ \hline \text{Effective Gross Income} \\ -\quad \text{Expenses} \\ \hline \text{Annual Net Operating Income} \div \\ \hline \text{Value} \quad | \quad \text{Cap Rate} \end{array}$$

The cost approach to appraising is used to determine the value of special purpose properties, but it can also be used to appraise new buildings.

Example: The replacement cost of a building is $125,000. It has an annual depreciation of 10 percent, and a site value of $35,000. What is the value of the property?

$$\begin{array}{ll} \$125,000 & \text{Replacement Cost} \\ \underline{\quad 10\%} & \text{Depreciation Rate} \\ \$112,500 & \\ \underline{+\ 35,000} & \text{Site Value} \\ \$147,500 & \text{Property Value} \end{array}$$

$$\begin{array}{l} \text{Replacement Cost} \\ -\quad \text{Depreciation Rate} \\ +\quad \text{Site Value} \\ \hline \text{Property Value} \end{array}$$

The gross rent multiplier formula is used to appraise small income-producing properties, such as a single family home or duplex that is investment property. If this method is used to determine the value of a small shopping center, it is called the gross income multiplier and the annual rent is used.

Example: An appraiser has determined that the gross rent multiplier of a house that rents for $650 is 110. What is the value of the property?

$$\dfrac{\$71,500\ \text{Value}}{110\quad |\quad \$650}$$

Gross Rent Multiplier × Rent

Gross Rent Multiplier × Rent = Value
Value ÷ Gross Rent Multiplier = Rent
Value ÷ Rent = Gross Rent Multiplier

Gross Income Multiplier × Rent = Value
Value ÷ Gross Income Multiplier = Rent
Value ÷ Rent = Gross Income Multiplier

A capital gain is the profit that an owner makes when selling an asset, such as real estate.

Example: Harry purchased a property for $90,000. He made $22,500 worth of improvements. Three years later he sold the property for $130,000 and paid a 6 percent commission. What were his capital gains on the sale?

Step 1 $90,000   Original Investment
          +22,500   Improvements
          ‾‾‾‾‾‾‾‾
          $112,500 Adjusted Basis

Step 2 $7,800 Commission $
          ‾‾‾‾‾‾‾‾‾‾‾‾‾‾‾‾‾‾‾‾‾
          $130,000 | 6%
          Sale Price × Commission %

Step 3 $130,000 – 7,800 = $122,200 Adjusted (Net)
          Sale Price (The sale price minus selling
          expenses equals the adjusted sale price.)

Step 4 $ 122,200   Adjusted Sale Price
          – 112,500   – Adjusted Basis
          ‾‾‾‾‾‾‾‾‾   ‾‾‾‾‾‾‾‾‾‾‾‾‾‾
          $ 9,700   Capital Gains

          Original Investment
       + Improvements
          ‾‾‾‾‾‾‾‾‾‾‾‾‾‾‾‾‾‾‾‾
          Adjusted Basis

          Selling Price
       – Selling Expenses
          ‾‾‾‾‾‾‾‾‾‾‾‾‾‾‾‾‾‾
          Adjusted Sale Price

          Adjusted Sale Price
       – Adjusted Basis
          ‾‾‾‾‾‾‾‾‾‾‾‾‾‾‾‾‾‾
          Capital Gains

The above formula is for computing the capital gains on an owner's principal place of residence. Under the new tax laws, which became effective May 7, 1997, first-time homebuyers may make a penalty-free withdrawal of up to $10,000 from their tax-deferred individual retirement fund or IRA for a down payment. Homeowners whose gain exceeds the maximum for exclusion must pay tax on the amount over the exclusion ($500,000 for married homeowners who file jointly, $250,000 for single filers). The exclusion can be taken more than once. However, the home must have been used as a principal place of residence for two of the preceding five years.

Appraisal math may deal with the appreciation or depreciation of property value.

Example: Mr. and Mrs. Homeowner paid $80,000 for their property. This year, their property appreciated in value 10 percent. What is the value of the property today?

          $88,000 Appreciated Value
       ‾‾‾‾‾‾‾‾‾‾‾‾‾‾‾‾‾‾‾‾‾‾‾‾‾‾‾
          $80,000 | 100%
          Original | +10% Appreciation Rate
          Investment × 110% Appreciated %

          Appreciated Value |
       ‾‾‾‾‾‾‾‾‾‾‾‾‾‾‾‾‾‾‾‾‾‾‾‾‾
          Original | 100% |
          Investment | + Appreciation Rate
                      × Appreciated %

Example: Mr. and Mrs. Homeowner paid $80,000 for their property. This year their property depreciated in value 10 percent. What is the value of their property?

$72,000 Depreciated Value

$80,000	100%
Original	− 10% Depreciation Rate
Investment ×	90% Depreciated %

Depreciated Value

Original	100%
Investment	− Depreciation Rate
×	Depreciated %

Appraisal Questions

27. Five apartments rent for $550 per month, and five others for $600 per month. There is an 8 percent vacancy rate and monthly expenses of $250. If a buyer wants to yield an 8 percent return, what should he pay for the property?
    A. $790,375
    B. $765,000
    C. $756,000
    D. $790,735

28. A building has a semiannual effective gross income of $250,000. If the annual expenses are 20 percent of the effective gross income, what is the net operating income?
    A. $500,000
    B. $200,000
    C. $100,000
    D. $400,000

29. If the gross rent multiplier of a property is 112 and the rent is $600 monthly, what is the value of the property?
    A. $76,200
    B. $62,700
    C. $27,600
    D. $67,200

30. Three years ago, Ms. Owner paid $65,000 for her property. During her period of ownership, she added a family room valued at $6,500, and $3,000 worth of other improvements. If she sells the property for $95,000 and pays a 7 percent commission, what capital gains may she exclude?
    A. $13,850
    B. $74,500
    C. $75,400
    D. $88,350

31. Mr. Howard purchased a home for $250,000. He added a tennis court at a cost of $10,000. Two years later, he sold his property for $325,000 and paid a 7 percent commission plus $250 in attorney fees. If he buys another property for $350,000, how much capital gains will he exclude?
    A. $22,750
    B. $42,000
    C. $42,250
    D. $42,520

32. A property is now worth $117,978. If it has appreciated 6 percent each year for the past two years, what was the original investment?
    A. $111,300
    B. $105,000
    C. $104,245
    D. $110,899

33. A property is now worth $98,250. If it has depreciated in value 5 percent each year for the past two years, what was the original investment?
    A. $103,421
    B. $103,241
    C. $108,864
    D. $108,320

SETTLEMENT MATH FORMULAS

To prorate an expense means to divide or distribute it proportionately. The settlement sheet is a history of the buyer's and seller's debits and credits in a sales transaction. If the entry is a debit, the party owes it at the closing table. If the entry is a credit, the party receives it at the closing table. The following worksheet shows the normal entries on a settlement sheet. Discount points can be paid by buyer or seller, so read the question carefully.

Settlement Date: February 18, 2001	Buyer's Statement		Seller's Statement	
	Debit	Credit	Debit	Credit
Sales Price	DB			CS
Earnest Money Deposit		CB		
New Loan		CB		
Interest—New Loan	DB			
Loan Balance			DS	
Assumed Loan		CB	DS	
Interest—Assumed Loan	CB		DS	
Purchase-Money Mortgage		CB	DS	
Interest—Purchase-Money Mortgage	DB			CS
Commission			DS	
Property Taxes—Paid in Advance	DB			CS
Property Taxes—Paid in Arrears		CB	DS	
Assumed Insurance Policy	DB			CS
Credit Report	DB			
Origination Fees	DB			
Survey	DB			
Title Expenses	DB			
Appraisal Fee	DB			
Recording Fee	DB			
Transfer Fee			DS	

Discount Points (Could be a DS or DB. Read the question to determine how it is to be entered.)

Some states use a 360-day year to compute interest and a 365-day year to compute taxes, insurance, etc. Please check to determine how they are computed in your state.

To compute the proration problems in this section, use a 360-day year, with each month having 30 days, unless the question states otherwise. Each proration question has a beginning date, prorate date and ending date.

- The beginning date is always January 1, unless the question states otherwise.
- The prorate date is normally the closing date, but can be the date of sale.
- The ending date is December 30, unless the question states otherwise.
- If paid in arrears, count from the prorate date to the ending date.
- If paid in advance, the entry is a debit to the buyer, a credit to the seller.
- If paid in arrears, count from the beginning date to the prorate date
- If paid in arrears, the entry is a debit to the seller and a credit to the buyer.
- When computing the interest on a new loan, count from the first of the month to the closing date. (Or the 15th of the month, if that date is given.)
- When computing the interest on an assumed loan, count from the closing date to the end of that month. (Or the 15th of the month, if that date is given.)

Example: The property taxes of $1,250 have been paid for the year. If the property closes on June 23, how much is credited to the seller on the settlement sheet?

Step 1 January 1   The taxes have been paid, so count from the prorate date
         June 23   to the ending date and credit the seller, debit the buyer.
         December 30   June 23 to June 30   =   7 days
                          July through December   = 180 days
                          Total   = 187 days CS, DB

Step 2 $1,250 ÷ 360 = $ 3.47   daily tax rate
Step 3   × 187   days
                        _____
                        $648.89   CS, DB

34. Semiannual property taxes of $450 were paid only for the first half of the year. The property sold on July 11 and closed on September 19. If the taxes were prorated between the buyer and seller as of the date of sale, which of the following is true?

    A. $252.50 CS, DB
    B. $252.50 DS, CB
    C. $27.50 DS, CB
    D. $497.50 CS, DB

35. A buyer negotiated a $75,000 loan at 8 percent interest for 30 years, with the first payment due in arrears on April 1. If the closing takes place on February 26, how much interest must the buyer pay on the day of closing?

    A. $566.78
    B. $656.78
    C. $56.68
    D. $66.68

36. The buyer assumed a loan of $50,000 at 8.25 percent interest. Payments are due on the first of the month, in arrears. The last payment was made on April 1 and the closing took place on April 20. Which of the following is true?

    A. $119.60 CS, DB
    B. $119.60 DB, CS
    C. $229.20 CS, DB
    D. $229.20 DS, CB

37. The buyer had a 20 percent down payment on a property she purchased for $89,500. She must also pay a 1 percent origination fee, $350 for title insurance, and one discount point. How much money will the buyer owe at the closing?

    A. $18,966
    B. $19,682
    C. $17,423
    D. $20,350

38. After the borrower made his payment on September 1, his loan balance was $12,259. His monthly payment is $124.34 per month paid in arrears on the first of the month. The interest rate on the loan is 9 percent. On October 1, he paid the lender for the October 1 payment, then paid off the entire mortgage balance. If the prepayment penalty was 2 percent, his prepayment penalty charge was approximately

    A. $244.53.
    B. $245.18.
    C. $232.40.
    D. $247.93.

INSURANCE PRORATION

Sometimes the buyer assumes the seller's insurance policy. Insurance is always paid in advance; thus, this entry is a debit to the buyer and a credit to the seller. The following shows a very simple way to compute the number of days to prorate when more than one calendar year is involved.

- The beginning date is the date the policy was written.
- The prorate date is the closing date.
- The ending date is the same day as the beginning date, for the term of the policy.

FIGURE 7.1 *HUD 1 Uniform Settlement Statement*

A.	U.S.DEPARTMENT OF HOUSING AND URBAN DEVELOPMENT		B.TYPE OF LOAN	
			1. [ ]FHA 2. [ ]FMHA 3. [ ]CONV. UNINS.	
			4. [ ]VA 5. [ ]CONV. INS.	
			6. FILE NUMBER: KAREN	7. LOAN NUMBER:
			8. MTG. INS. CASE NO.:	

C.NOTE: This form is furnished to give you a statement of actual settlement costs. Amounts paid to and by the settlement agent are shown. Items marked ("p.o.c.") were paid outside the closing: they are shown here for information purposes and are not included in the totals.

D. NAME OF BORROWER: JOHN SMITH, MARY SMITH

   ADDRESS:

E.   NAME OF SELLER: JOHN DOE, MARY DOE

   ADDRESS: , Florence, KY, 41042   **SELLER TIN:**

F.   NAME OF LENDER: NATIONAL LENDER, INC.
   1 Wall Street
   ADDRESS: New York, NY 10001

G.PROPERTY LOCATION: Lot
   17-B Happy Hills Subdivision FLORENCE KY 41042

H. SETTLEMENT AGENT ATI TITLE AGENCY OF OHIO,INC.   CLOSER: JAMES DWYER   PHONE NUMBER: NOT ON FILE
   ADDRESS: 3980 RACE ROAD
   CINCINNATI, OHIO 45211   **SETTLEMENT AGENT TIN:** 34-1766936

PLACE OF SETTLEMENT: ATI TITLE AGENCY   **I.SETTLEMENT DATE**
   ADDRESS: Closing date: 07/31/01
   Proration date: 07/31/01

J. SUMMARY OF BORROWER'S TRANSACTION		K. SUMMARY OF SELLER'S TRANSACTION	
100. GROSS AMOUNT DUE FROM BORROWER:		400. GROSS AMOUNT DUE TO SELLER:	
101. Contract sales price	100,000.00	401. Contract sales price	100,000.00
102. Personal property		402. Personal property	
103. Settlement charges to borrower(line 1400)	2,099.50	403.	
104.		404.	
105.		405.	
Adjustments for items paid by seller in advance:		Adjustments for items paid for seller in advance:	
106. City/town taxes to		406. City/town taxes to	
107. County taxes to		407. County taxes to	
108. Assessments to		408. Assessments to	
109.		409.	
110.		410.	
111.		411.	
112.		412.	
120. GROSS AMOUNT DUE FROM BORROWER:	102,099.50	420. GROSS AMOUNT DUE TO SELLER:	100,000.00
200. AMOUNTS PAID BY OR IN BEHALF OF BORROWER:		500. REDUCTIONS IN AMOUNT DUE TO SELLER:	
201. Deposit or earnest money		501. Excess deposit(see instructions)	
202. Principal amount of new loan(s)	97,000.00	502. Settlement charges to seller(line 1400)	6,150.00
203. Existing loan(s) taken subject to		503. Existing loan(s) taken subject to	
204.		504. Payoff of first mortgage loan	46,425.58
205.		505. Payoff of second mortgage loan	
206.		506.	
207.		507.	
208.		508.	
209.		509.	
Adjustments for items unpaid by seller:		Adjustments for items unpaid by seller:	
210. City/town taxes to		510. City/town taxes to	
211. County taxes 01/01/01 to 07/31/01	815.67	511. County taxes 01/01/01 to 07/31/01	815.67
212. Assessments to		512. Assessments to	
213.		513.	
214.		514.	
215.		515.	
216.		516.	
217.		517.	
218.		518.	
219.		519.	
220. TOTAL PAID BY/FOR BORROWER:	97,815.67	520. TOTAL REDUCTION IN AMOUNT:	53,391.25
300. CASH AT SETTLEMENT FROM/TO BORROWER:		600. CASH AT SETTLEMENT TO/FROM SELLER:	
301. Gross amount due from borrower(line 120)	102,099.50	601. Gross amount due to seller(line 420)	100,000.00
302. Less amounts paid by/for borrower(line 220)	97,815.67	602. Less total reductions in amount due seller(line 520)	53,391.25
303. CASH [X FROM] [TO] BORROWER:	4,283.83	603. CASH [X TO] [FROM] SELLER:	46,608.75

SUBSTITUTE FORM 1099 SELLER STATEMENT-The information contained in Blocks E,G,H and I and on line 401 (or, if line 401 is asterisked, lines 403 and 404) is important tax information and is being furnished to the Internal Revenue Service. If you are required to file a return, a negligence penalty or other sanction will be imposed on you if this item is required to be reported and the IRS determines that it has not been reported.
SELLER INSTRUCTION-If this real estate was your principal residence, file Form 2119, Sale or Exchange of Principal Residence, for any gain, with your income tax return; for other transactions, complete the applicable parts of Form 4797, Form 6252 and/or Schedule D (Form 1040).

You are required by law to provide _____ with your correct taxpayer identification number.

If you do not provide _____ with your correct taxpayer identification number, you may be subject to civil or criminal penalties.

Under penalties of perjury, I certify that the number shown on this statement is my correct taxpayer identification number.

_____   _____
Seller   ATI Contact Person and Phone Number for 1099 Information

FIGURE 7.1 *HUD 1 Uniform Settlement Statement (Continued)*

File KAREN	L. SETTLEMENT CHARGES		PAID FROM BORROWER'S FUNDS AT SETTLEMENT	PAID FROM SELLER'S FUNDS AT SETTLEMENT
700. TOTAL SALES/BROKER'S COMMISSION Based on $ 100,000.00 @ 6.00 % = 6,000.00				
Division of Commission (line 700) as follows:				
701. $3,000.00	to XYZ			
702. $3,000.00	to ABC			
703. Commission paid at settlement				6,000.00
704.				
800. ITEMS PAYABLE IN CONNECTION WITH LOAN.				
801. Loan Origination fee	%			
802. Loan Discount	%			
803. Appraisal fee	to APPRAISALS "R" US		325.00	
804. Credit Report	to NATIONAL LENDER, INC.		50.00	
805. Lender's inspection fee	to			
806. Mortgage Insurance application fee	to			
807. Assumption Fee	to			
808. Tax Service Fee TAX SERVICE FEE	to NATIONAL LENDER, INC.			75.00
809.	to			
810.	to			
811. Flood Certification	to NATIONAL LENDER, INC.		15.50	
812.	to			
900. ITEMS REQUIRED BY LENDER TO BE PAID IN ADVANCE.				
901. Interest from 07/31/01 to 08/01/01 @$ 21.26027 /day 1 day			21.26	
902. Mortgage insurance premium for 12 mo. to JOHN SMITH -POCB 223.00				
903. Hazard insurance premium for yrs. to				
904. yrs. to				
905.				
1000. RESERVES DEPOSITED WITH LENDER				
1001. Hazard Insurance 3 mo.@$ 20.00 per mo.			60.00	
1002. Mortgage insurance 2 mo.@$ 40.42 per mo.			80.84	
1003. City property taxes mo.@$ per mo.				
1004. County property taxes 3 mo.@$ 117.58 per mo.			352.74	
1005. Annual assessments (Maint.) mo.@$ per mo.				
1006. mo.@$ per mo.				
1007. mo.@$ per mo.				
1008. mo.@$ per mo.				
1009. Aggregate Reserve for Hazard & Flood Ins, City & County Prop. Taxes, Mortgage Ins. & Annual Assessments			(80.84)	0.00
1100. TITLE CHARGES:				
1101. Settlement or closing fee	to ATI TITLE AGENCY		250.00	
1102. Abstract or title search	to ATI TITLE AGENCY		175.00	
1103. Title examination	to			
1104. Title insurance binder	to ATI TITLE AGENCY		50.00	
1105. Document preparation	to			
1106. Notary fee	to			
1107. Attorney's fee to	to			
(includes above items No.:				
1108. Title insurance	to ATI TITLE AGENCY		569.00	
(includes above items No.:)				
1109. Lender's coverage 97,000.00 $ 339.50				
1110. Owner's coverage 100,000.00 $ 229.50				
1111. Deed Preparation	to STEPHEN G. BRINKER, ATTY			75.00
1112.	to			
1113.	to			
1114.	to			
1200. GOVERNMENT RECORDING AND TRANSFER CHARGES				
1201. Recording fees: Deed $ 14.00 Mrtg $ 42.00 Rel. $			56.00	
1202. City/county tax/stamps: Deed $ Mrtg $				
1203. State tax/stamps: Deed $ Mrtg $				
1204.	to			
1205.	to			
1206.	to			
1300. ADDITIONAL SETTLEMENT CHARGES				
1301. Survey	to ATI TITLE AGENCY		130.00	
1302. Pest inspection PEST CONTROL	to PEST CONTROL		45.00	
1303.	to			
1304.	to			
1305.	to			
1400. TOTAL SETTLEMENT CHARGES (entered on lines 103, Section J and 502, Section K)			2,099.50	6,150.00

CERTIFICATION: I have carefully reviewed the HUD-1 Settlement Statement and to the best of my knowledge and belief, it is a true and accurate statement of all receipts and disbursements made on my account or by me in this transaction. I further certify that I have received a copy of HUD-1 Settlement Statement.

Borrowers   Sellers

The HUD-1 Settlement Statement which I have prepared is a true and accurate account of this transaction. I have caused or will cause the funds to be disbursed in accordance with this statement.

Settlement Agent   Date

WARNING: It is a crime to knowingly make false statements to the United States on this or any other similar form. Penalties upon conviction can include a fine and imprisonment. For details see: Title 18: U.S. Code Section 1001 and Section 1010.

Example: A three-year policy was written on June 15, 1999, and the premium for the policy was $425. The property was sold and closed on November 23, 2000. What is the approximate credit to the seller on the settlement sheet?

Beginning Date	June 15, 1999
Prorate Date	November 23, 2000
Ending Date	June 15, 2002

Start with the ending date and convert the month, day and year to numbers in this order:

Year	Month	Day
2002	6	15

Then, convert the prorate day in the same way.

Year	Month	Day
2000	11	23

Next, subtract.

Year	Month	Day
2002	6	15
− 2000	11	23

Because 23 cannot be subtracted from 15, borrow 30 days from a month, leaving 5 months and 45 days

Year	Month	Day
	5	45
2002	6	~~15~~
2000	11	23
		22

$$45 - 23 = 22 \text{ days}$$

Because 11 cannot be subtracted from 5, borrow 12 months from a year.

Year	Month	Day
	17	
2001	~~5~~	45
~~2002~~	6	~~15~~
−2000	11	23
1	6	22

$$17 - 11 = 6 \text{ months}$$
$$2001 - 2000 = 1 \text{ year}$$

Next, convert 1 year, 6 months, and 45 days into days. (There are 1,080 days in three years.)

$$
\begin{aligned}
1 \text{ year} &= 360 \text{ days} \\
6 \text{ months} &= 180 \text{ days} \\
&+ \ \ 22 \text{ days} \\
\hline
&562 \text{ days to prorate}
\end{aligned}
$$

$$\$425 \text{ premium} \div 1{,}080 = .3935 \text{ cents per day}$$
$$\times 562$$
$$\overline{\$221.14 \ \ \text{CS, DB}}$$

Income Proration

39. Bentley purchased a home for $180,000 and insured 80 percent of its value. His premium on the three-year policy was $3.50 per $1,000, and he purchased the policy on September 14, 1999. If he sold the property on October 25, 2000, how much will he be credited at the closing?

A. $308.67
B. $316.90
C. $219.23
D. $175.73

AREA MATH FORMULAS

The formulas and rules that you must know to compute area math questions are:

- the area of a rectangle or square is found by multiplying length × width.
- the area of a triangle is found by multiplying ½ base × height.
- the area of a circle is found by multiplying pi (3.1416) × radius squared.
- the area of a trapezoid is found by adding the parallel lines, dividing by 2, and then multiplying by the height.
- to compute square feet, multiply length × width.
- to compute cubic feet, multiply length × width × height.
- there are 9 square feet in 1 square yard.
- to convert square feet to square yards divide by 9.
- there are 27 cubic feet in 1 cubic yard.
- to convert cubic feet to cubic yards, divide by 27.
- to convert square feet to acres, divide by 43,560.
- to convert acres to square feet multiply by 43,560.
- there are 5,280 feet in 1 mile.

Example: A lot measures 200′ × 250′ and sells for $55,000. Another lot in that same area measuring 150′ × 175′ would likely sell for what price?

Step 1   A = 200′ × 250′
         A = 50,000 square feet

Step 2 $55,000 ÷ 50,000 = $1.10 per sq. ft.

Step 3   A = 150′ × 175′
         A = 26,250 square feet

Step 4   26,250 × $1.10 = $28,875

Example: How many square feet are in a triangular-shaped area that has a base of 60′ and a height of 130′?

A = ½(b) × h
Step 1   A = ½ (60′) × 130′
         A = 30′ × 130′
         A = 3,900 square feet

Example: A circle has a diameter of 90'. How many square feet does it contain? (The radius is one half of the diameter.)

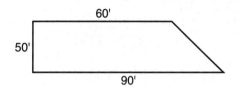

$$A = \pi r^2$$
Step 1 $A = 3.1416 \times 45' \times 45'$
$$A = 6{,}361.74 \text{ square feet}$$

How many square yards does it contain? 6,361.74 ÷ 9 = 706.86 square yards

Example: The two parallel sides of a trapezoid are 60' and 90'. The height is 50'.

How many square feet does it contain?

$$A = [(\text{parallel lines}) \div 2] \times h$$
Step 1 $A = [(60' + 90') \div 2] \times 50'$
$$A = 75' \times 50'$$
$$A = 3{,}750 \text{ square feet}$$

How many acres does it contain?
$$3{,}750 \div 43{,}560 = .0861 \text{ acres}$$

Example: A storage room that measures 20' × 30' × 10' contains how many cubic feet?

$$V = L \times W \times H$$
Step 1 $V = 20' \times 30' \times 10'$
$$V = 6{,}000 \text{ cubic feet}$$

How many cubic yards does it contain?
$$6{,}000 \div 27 = 222.22 \text{ cubic yards}$$

Area Math Questions

40. A two-story house measures 25' × 50'. A one-story family room was added that measures 20' × 20'. At a cost of $9.95 per square yard for carpet and $2.50 per square yard for installation, how much will it cost to carpet the house and family room?
    A. $2,282.50
    B. $36,105.00
    C. $20,542.50
    D. $4,011.67

41. A buyer purchased a property that is one mile square and another that measures 511.23' × 511.23'. At a cost of $2,000 an acre, how much did she pay for the property?
    A. $1,291,999
    B. $1,921,999
    C. $1,733,435
    D. $1,373,435

42. A building measures 30' × 80' × 15'. *B* made an offer of $35 per square foot on the property. The owner made a counteroffer of $2.75 per cubic foot. How much more will it cost *B* if he accepts the counteroffer?
    A. $18,000
    B. $15,000
    C. $17,000
    D. $16,000

43. A lot contains 9/10 of an acre. What is the depth of the lot if the front measures 150'?
    A. 216.36'
    B. 261.36'
    C. 322.67'
    D. 323.67'

44. How many cubic yards of concrete must a builder buy to pour a sidewalk that measures 45' × 3.25' and is five inches thick?

    A. 60.9375
    B. 2.2571
    C. .4167
    D. 6.7708

45. How many square feet of living area are in the following house?

    A. 2,087.5 square feet
    B. 2,150.0 square feet
    C. 2,775.0 square feet
    D. 2,990.5 square feet

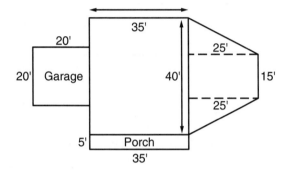

ADDITIONAL PRACTICE

46. Mr. Stewart's home is valued at $250,000. He insured 80 percent of its value. The three-year insurance policy was purchased on January 12, 2001, at a cost of $4.25 per $1,000. The property was sold and the buyer assumed his policy on December 23, 2002. How much will Mr. Stewart be credited at the closing?

    A. $5,831.67
    B. $2,998.47
    C. $298.27
    D. $583.16

47. Ms. Wilson offered 90 percent of the $120,900 list price of a property. Her offer was accepted and the lender agreed to negotiate an 80 percent loan at 8 percent interest for 30 years. Ms. Wilson had a $5,000 earnest money deposit, paid $350 for title expenses, $250 attorney fees, and had other expenses of $749. How much money does she need to close on the property?

    A. $18,111
    B. $23,111
    C. $10,159
    D. $15,159

48. Mr. and Mrs. Lloyd pay $137.81 in monthly property taxes. If the tax rate is $3.50 per $100 and the assessment rate is 35 percent, what is the value of the property?

    A. $153,998.69
    B. $143,997.45
    C. $166,532.72
    D. $134,997.54

49. Ms. Singleton assumed the seller's insurance policy on June 24, 2002. The owner paid $649.50 for a three-year policy on April 30, 2001. Which of the following is true?

    A. $249.90 DS, CB
    B. $249.90 CB, DS
    C. $399.60 DB, CS
    D. $399.60 CB, DS

50. An agent is managing a 15-unit apartment building and is paid 9 percent of the gross income. She leases five apartments for $500, five for $550, and five for $600. There is a 3 percent vacancy rate and additional income of $450 per month. The monthly operating expenses are $1,749 and the owner is generating an 8 percent return on the investment. What is the effective gross income on the building?

    A. $99,000
    B. $96,030
    C. $80,442
    D. $101,430

51. On September 20, 2001, Ms. Huwel closed on her new home, for which she paid $160,000, and she insured 80 percent of its value. Her premium on the two-year policy was $3.75 per $1,000. On November 11, 2002, she sold the property, and the buyer assumed the policy. How much will be debited the buyer at the closing, using a 360-day year?

    A. $480.00
    B. $273.99
    C. $206.01
    D. $274.01

52. Four units are renting for $450 each per month. There is a 5 percent vacancy factor, and annual expenses are $3,547. The owner wants an 8 percent return on her investment and the property has additional monthly income of $464. What is the effective gross income of the property?

    A. $21,796
    B. $21,976
    C. $20,984
    D. $26,088

53. Mr. and Mrs. Ben-Hur secured a loan with a 75 percent loan-to-value ratio. The interest rate was 7.125 percent and the term was for 30 years. The first month's interest payment was $477.82. What was the appraised value of the property?

    A. $107,300
    B. $80,475
    C. $103,700
    D. $79,239

54. A lot is 275 feet deep. It contains 2/3 of an acre. What is the length of the lot?

    A. 158.4'
    B. 106.5'
    C. 290.04'
    D. 105.6'

55. Mr. Smiley sold his property for $99,500. He paid a real estate commission of 6 percent, paid an attorney $250, paid a transfer tax of $99.50, and paid his existing mortgage of $50,140 and agreed to a purchase-money mortgage of $10,000. What were his net proceeds at the closing?

    A. $43,050.40
    B. $33,040.50
    C. $53,040.50
    D. $33,050.40

56. Ms. Feldkamp wants to receive a net of $82,000 after selling her home. She has an existing mortgage of $32,500 and will have selling expenses of $444. If the broker is to receive a 7 percent commission, what is the least offer that she can accept for the property?

    A. $122,990.08
    B. $122,515.08
    C. $123,595.70
    D. $123,959.70

57. Mr. and Mrs. First Time Homebuyers purchased a property for $79,000. They had to make a 10 percent down payment, and they negotiated a 30-year fixed rate loan for 7 percent. They paid $1,000 in earnest money, a .5 percent origination fee, $670 in other closing costs and $25 per month for hazard insurance. How much cash did the buyer need to bring to closing?

    A. $8,225.50
    B. $8,432.50
    C. $7,950.50
    D. $7,225.50

58. A homeowner has a property valued at $125,000 that is assessed at 35 percent of its value. If the local tax rate is 6,400 mills per $100 of the assessed value, what are the monthly taxes?

    A. $280.00
    B. $140.33
    C. $480.00
    D. $233.33

59. An owner of a fourplex has one unit that rents for $450 a month, one unit that rents for $475 per month and two units that rent for $500 per month. The vacancy rate is 4 percent and the monthly expenses average $350. If the return on the property is 10 percent, what is the value?

    A. $218,260
    B. $118,260
    C. $189,760
    D. $179,760

60. A house is now worth $105,000. The lot is now worth $50,000. If the house depreciated 4 percent each year for the past two years and the lot appreciated 6 percent each year for the past two years, what was the approximate combined original value of the house and lot?

    A. $156,544
    B. $113,932
    C. $109,375
    D. $158,432

MATH REVIEW ANSWERS

1. C

$6,000		$5,000		$2,000		$6,000
$100,000	6%	$100,000	5%	$50,000	4%	5,000
×		×		×		+ 2,000
						$13,000

2. B

$7,500		$3,000	
$125,000	6%	$7,500	40%
×		×	

3. D $2,500 × 2 = $5,000

$5,000 ÷	
$71,428.57	7%

4. D

$3,500 ÷		÷ $5,833.33	
$5,833.33	60%	$83,333	.07 or 7%

5. C   100%
    − 6%
    ——
    94%

$94,500 ÷	
$100,531.91	94%

6. A   100%
    − 7%
    ——
    93%

$20,000
35,250
+ 400
$55,650

$55,650 ÷	
$59,838.71	93%

7. C   100%
    −6.5%
    ———
    93.5%

$104,500
+ 12%
$117,040

$117,040 ÷	
$125,176.47	93.5%

8. B $ 1,200
    × 12
    ———
    $14,400

$1,152	
$14,400	8%
×	

9. A   A = 20′ × 25′
    A = 500 sq. ft.

    $10.25
    × 500
    ———
    $5,125

$384.38	
$5,125	7.5%
×	

    $384.38 ÷ 4 =
    $96.09

10. A $ 575
     × 12
     ———
     $6,900

    $389,250
    −225,000
    ————
    $164,250

$8,623	
$164,250	5.25%
×	

    $ 8,623
    +6,900
    ———
    $15,523

11. D

$$\begin{array}{r} \$\ 425 \\ \times\ 12 \\ \hline \$5,100 \end{array}$$

$$\begin{array}{r} \$9,321 \\ -5,100 \\ \hline \$4,221 \end{array}$$

$$\begin{array}{r} \$4,221 \div \\ \hline \$70,350 \ \big|\ 6\% \end{array}$$

$$\begin{array}{r} \$175,000 \\ +\ 70,350 \\ \hline \$245,350 \end{array}$$

12. A $\$550 \times 12 \times 5 = \ \$\ 33,000$
$\$600 \times 12 \times 5 = \ \$\ 36,000$
$\$650 \times 12 \times 5 = \ \$\ 39,000$

$$\begin{array}{r} \hline \$108,000 \end{array}$$

$$\begin{array}{r} \$7,290 \\ \hline \$108,000 \ \big|\ 6.75\% \\ \times \end{array}$$

13. D

$$\begin{array}{r} \$82,250 \div \\ \hline \$102,812.50 \ \big|\ 80\% \end{array}$$

14. B

$$\begin{array}{r} \$1,340.63 \\ \times\ 4 \\ \hline \$5,362.52 \end{array}$$

$$\begin{array}{r} \div\ \$5,362.52 \\ \hline \$65,000 \ \big|\ 8.25\% \end{array}$$

15. C

$$\begin{array}{r} \$3,000 \\ +2,000 \\ \hline \$5,000 \end{array}$$

$$\begin{array}{r} \div\ \$5,000 \\ \hline \$100,000 \ \big|\ .05 \text{ or 5 points} \end{array}$$

16. D

$$\begin{array}{r} \$55,000 \\ -\ 3\% \\ \hline \$53,350 \end{array} \text{ or }$$

$$\begin{array}{r} \$1,650 \\ \hline \$55,000 \ \big|\ 3\% \\ \times \end{array}$$

$$\begin{array}{r} \$55,000 \\ -\ 1,650 \\ \hline \$53,350 \end{array}$$

17. A $.125 \times 3 = .375\%$
$8\% + .375\% = 8.375\%$

18. A

$$\begin{array}{r} \$790 \\ \hline \$79,000 \ \big|\ 1\% \\ \times \end{array}$$

19. A

$$\begin{array}{r} \$7,585 \\ \hline \$82,000 \ \big|\ 9.25\% \\ \times \end{array}$$

$\$7,585 \div 12 = \$632.08$

$$\begin{array}{r} \$674.59 \\ -632.08 \\ \hline \$\ 42.51 \end{array}$$

20. A

$$\begin{array}{r} \$121,500 \\ \hline \$135,000 \ \big|\ 90\% \\ \times \end{array}$$

$$\begin{array}{r} \$103,275 \\ \hline \$121,500 \ \big|\ 85\% \\ \times \end{array}$$

$\$9,294.75 \div 12 = \$774.56$

$$\begin{array}{r} \hline \$103,275 \ \big|\ 9\% \\ \times \end{array}$$

21. C $ 585.70 $7,028.40 ÷ $80,324.57 ÷
         × 12 $80,324.57 | 8.75% $89,249.52 | 90%
      ‾‾‾‾‾‾‾‾‾
       $7,028.40

22. B $80,000   ÷ $2,400   .125 × 3 = .375%
       −77,600 $80,000 | 3%   8.25% + .375% = 8.625%
      ‾‾‾‾‾‾‾‾
       $ 2,400

23. D $4.25 ÷ 100 = .0425 $59,150 $2513.875 ÷ 12 = $209.49
                                  $169,000 | 35% $59,150 | .0425
                                         ×   ×

24. A 95 ÷ 1,000 = .095 $19,893 $1,889.83 ÷ 4 = $472.45
                                 $52,350 | 38% $19,893 | .095
                                        ×   ×

25. A $29,250 $ 511.88   ÷ $1,023.76   .035
        ‾‾‾‾‾‾‾‾‾‾‾‾‾‾   × 2 $29,250 | .035   ×100
        $65,000 | 45%   ‾‾‾‾‾‾‾‾   ‾‾‾‾‾‾‾
               × $1,023.75 $3.50

26. B $4.50 ÷ 100 = .045 $1968.76 ÷ $43,750 ÷
       $984.38 × 2 = $1,968.76 $43,750 | .045 $175,000 | 25%
       1 ÷ 4 = 25%

27. C 5 × $550 × 12 = $33,000
       5 × $600 × 12 = $36,000
                                ‾‾‾‾‾‾‾‾
                                 $69,000
                                 − 8%
                                ‾‾‾‾‾‾‾‾
                                 $63,480
       $250 × 12 =   − 3,000
                                ‾‾‾‾‾‾‾‾
                                 $60,480 ÷
                    $756,000 | 8%

28. D $250,000 $500,000
            × 2   − 20%
       ‾‾‾‾‾‾‾‾‾   ‾‾‾‾‾‾‾‾‾
       $500,000 $400,000

29. D $67,200
        ‾‾‾‾‾‾‾‾‾‾‾‾
        112 | $600
               ×

30. A $65,000
    + 6,500
    + 3,000
    $74,500

$6,650

$95,000 | 7%

     ×

$95,000
− 6,650
$88,350

$88,350
− 74,500
$13,850

31. B $250,000
    + 10,000
    $260,000

$325,000
−   7%
$302,250
−   250
$302,000

$302,000
−260,000
$ 42,000

32. B $117,978 ÷

$111,300 | 100%
          + 6%
          106%

$111,300 ÷

$105,000 | 100%
          + 6%
          106%

33. C $98,250 ÷

$103,421 | 100%
          − 5%
          95%

$103,421 ÷

$108,864 | 100%
          − 5%
          95%

34. C July 1 - 11 = 11 days $450 ÷ 180 = $2.50 $ 2.50
                                                           × 11
                                                      $27.50

35. D Feb. 26   Feb. 30 - 26 = 4 days
       Feb. 30

$6,000 ÷ 360

$75,000 | 8%
          ×

= $16.67

$16.67
   × 4
$66.68

36. D April 1   April 1 - 20 = 20 days
       April 20

$4,125 ÷ 360

$50,000 | 8.25%
          ×

= $11.46

$ 11.46
   × 20
$229.20

37. B $71,600

$89,500 | 80%
          ×

$89,500
−71,600
$17,900

$716

$71,600 | 1%
          ×

$ 716 discount points
     716 original fee
     350 insurance
+17,900 down payment
$19,682

38. A $1,103.31   ÷ 12 = $91.94 $124.34 $12,259.00 $244.53

         $12,259 | 9%   − 91.94   − 32.40 $12,226.60 | 2%

             × $ 32.40 $12,226.60   ×

39. B $144,000 $3.50 ÷ 1000 = $504 premium for 3 years

        $180,000 | 80%   .0035 $144,000 | .0035

             ×   ×

Sept. 14, 1999		8	44	2001	20	44
Oct. 25, 2000	2002	−9	14	2002	−9	14
Sept. 14, 2002	−2000	10	25	−2000	10	25
		1	10	19	1	10	19 = 679 days

$504 ÷ 1,080 = .4667

.4667 × 679 = $316.898

40. D   A = 25′ × 50′   A = 20′ × 20′   2,500   2,900 ÷ 9 =   322.222

     A = 1,250 square feet   A = 400 square feet   +400 $9.95 + 2.50 =   × 12.45

           × 2   2,900 $4,011.67

        2,500

41. A   5,280 × 5,280 = 27,878,400   511.23 × 511.23 = 261,356.1129

     27,878,400 ÷ 43,560 = 640   261,356.1129 ÷ 43,560 = 5.9999

     640 + 5.9999 = 645.9999   645.9999 × $2,000 = $1,291,999

42. B   A = 30′ × 80′   V = 30′ × 80′ × 15′ $99,000

     A =   2,400 square feet   V =   36,000 cubic feet   −84,000

         × $35   × $2.75 $15,000

       $84,000 $99,000

43. B   9 ÷ 10 = 90%   43,560 × 90% = 39,204   39,204 ÷ 150 = 261.36

44. B   5″ ÷ 12″ = .4167′   60.9423 ÷ 27 = 2.2571 cubic yards

     V = 45′ × 3.25′ × .4167′

     V = 60.9423 cubic feet

45. A   A = 35′ × 40′   A = [(15′ + 40′) ÷ 2] × 25′   1,400

     A = 1,400 square feet   A = 687.5 square feet   +687.5

                            2,087.5

46. C $4.25 ÷ 1,000 = .00425

$200,000			$850	
$250,000	80%		$200,000	.00425
×			×	

$850 ÷ 1,080 = .787

			12		
	0	42	2003	0	42
Jan. 12, 2001	2004	~~1~~ ~~12~~	2004	~~1~~ ~~12~~	
Dec. 23, 2002	− 2002	12 23	− 2002	12 23	
Jan. 12, 2004		19	1 0 19		

360 days + 19 days = 379   379 × .787 = $298.27

47. A

$108,810		$87,048		Debits	Credits
$120,900	90%	$108,810	80%	$108,810	$87,048
×		×		350	5,000
				250	
				749	
				$110,159	$92,048

$110,159 − 92,048 = $18,111

48. D $137.81 × 12 = $1,653.72 $1,653.72 ÷ $47,249.14 ÷
    $3.50 ÷ 100 = .035

$47,249.14	.035		$134,997.54	35%

49. C $649.50 ÷ 1,080 = .60

April 30, 2001	2004	4 30	2003	16 30	360 + 300 + 6 = 666
June 24, 2002	− 2002	6 24	2002	6 24	666 × .60 = $399.60
April 30, 2004		6	1 10 6		

50. D 5 × $500 × 12 = $30,000 $99,000 $450 × 12 = $5,400 $ 96,030
    5 × $550 × 12 = $33,000   − 3%   + 5,400
    5 × $600 × 12 = $36,000 $96,030 $101,430
    Total PGI = $99,000

51. C

				2002	21	
Sept. 20, 2001	2003	9	20	~~2003~~	~~9~~	20
Nov. 11, 2002	− 2002	11	11	− 2002	11	11
Sept. 20, 2003			9		10	9

$$10 \times 30 = 300 + 9 = 309 \text{ days}$$

$$\frac{\$128,000}{\$160,000 \mid 80\%} \qquad \$3.75 \div 1000 = .00375$$

$$\times$$

$$\frac{\$480}{\$128,000 \mid .00375}$$

$$\times$$

$$\$480 \div 720 = .6667$$

$$.6667 \times 309 = \$206.01$$

52. D

4 × $450 × 12 =	$21,600	PGI
	− 5%	VR
	$20,520	
$464 × 12 =	+ 5,568	AI
	$26,088	EGI

53. A $477.82 × 12 = $5,733.84   Annual Interest $

$$\frac{\$5,733.84 \div}{\$80,475 \mid 7.125\%} \qquad \frac{\$80,475 \div}{\$107,300 \mid 75\%}$$

54. D   43,560 ÷ 3 = 14,520 × 2 = 29,040 sq. ft.
         29,040 ÷ 275′ = 105.60 ft.

     OR 2 ÷ 3 = .6667
         43,560 × .6667 = 29,041.45 sq. ft.
         29,041.45 ÷ 275′ = 105.6052 ft.

55. B
Debits	Credits
$ 5,970.00	$99,500
250.00	
99.50	
$50,140.00	
$10,000.00	
$66,459.50	$99,500

$5,970

$99,500	6%
	×

$99,500 − 66,459.50 = $33,040.50

56. C

100%
- 7%
93%

$ 82,000
32,500
+ $444
$114,944

$114,944 ÷

$123,595.70	93%

57. A
Debits	Credits
$79,000.00	$71,100
$355.50	$1,000
$670.00	
$300.00	
$80,325.50	$72,100

$79,000

$355.50
− 10%

$25 × 12 = $300

$71,100	.5%
$71,100	×

$80,325.50 − $72,100 = $8,225.50

58. D 6,400 mills ÷ 1,000 = 6.40 ÷ 100 = .064

$43,750	
$125,000	35%
	×

$2,800	
$43,750	.064
	×

$2,800 ÷ 12 = $233.33

59. D
1 × $450 × 12 = $5,400
1 × $475 × 12 = $5,700
2 × $500 × 12 = $12,000
               $23,100   PGI
                 – 4%   VR
               $22,176   EGI
$350 × 12 =   – $4,200   EXP

               $17,975   ANOI
               $17,976 ÷
| $179,760 | 10% |

60. D

$105,000 ÷	
	100%
	– 4%
$109,375	96%

$109,375 ÷	
	100%
	– 4%
$113,932,29	96%

$50,000 ÷	
	100%
	+ 6%
$47,169.81	106%

$47,169.81 ÷	
	100%
	+ 6%
$44,499.82	106%

$113,932.29 + 44,499.82 = $158,432.11

1. A buyer working with an agent makes an offer on a property offered for sale by owner. The offer is contingent upon the buyer's securing an FHA loan. Does this loan have to follow RESPA guidelines?
   A. No, because FHA and VA loans do have to meet HUD guidelines, but not RESPA guidelines
   B. No, because the offer was made by a buyer working with a broker
   C. Yes, because an FHA loan is guaranteed by the government
   D. Yes, because it is a single-family residential property

2. Which of the following is a typical characteristic of an FHA or VA loan?
   A. They are backed by the government and are not assumable.
   B. The down payment on these loans can normally be financed.
   C. Prepayment penalties cannot be charged on these loans.
   D. Typically, these loans must be repaid within 15 years.

3. The current market interest rate is 17 percent. Mr. and Mrs. Homeowner want to transfer their property to their daughter. The loan balance is $75,000. The property can be transferred if the loan does NOT contain a(n)
   A. alienation clause.
   B. acceleration clause.
   C. defeasance clause.
   D. nondisturbance clause.

4. Mr. Buyer purchased two parcels of land. One was one mile square and the other contained ten acres. If the land cost $2,500 an acre, what was the cost of the land?
   A. $1,265,000
   B. $1,625,000
   C. $1,526,000
   D. $1,600,000

5. An offer has been accepted on a property. After the title search, who gives an opinion of title?
   A. An attorney
   B. The seller
   C. The buyer
   D. The broker

6. Mr. and Mrs. Buyer just purchased their first house, which sits on five acres. They intend to keep goats on the property. Which of the following would allow or disallow them to keep goats?
   A. Federal ordinances
   B. State ordinances
   C. Zoning
   D. Neighbors

7. A buyer made an offer of $250,000 on a property with no contingencies and the offer was accepted. The buyer planned to build a shopping center, but never mentioned it to the agent. Just before the closing, the buyer discovered that he could not build the shopping center. What is the status of the sales contract?
   A. Valid
   B. Void
   C. Voidable
   D. Unenforceable

8. A handicapped person moved into an apartment and at his own expense lowered the light switches, lowered the kitchen cabinets, installed handrails and widened the doorways. At the expiration of the lease, which of the following would the tenant LEAST LIKELY have to return to its original condition?
   A. Light switches
   B. Kitchen cabinets
   C. Handrails
   D. Doorways

9. Which of the following BEST describes physical depreciation?
   A. Functional obsolescence caused by a poor design
   B. External obsolescence caused by any outside factor
   C. Deterioration caused by the age of the building
   D. Deterioration caused by normal wear and tear of the property

10. Which of the following must be disclosed when an agent is showing a house?
    A. Mortgage balance
    B. The asking price of other homes in the neighborhood
    C. That the property is in a flood plain zone
    D. Original cost of the property

11. What type of interest is normally computed on a residential loan?
    A. Simple   C. Annual
    B. Compound   D. Monthly

12. Which of the following is an example of an emblement?
    A. A stand of walnut trees
    B. A field of corn
    C. An apple orchard
    D. A vineyard

13. A buyer's agent is usually considered to be in what relationship to the seller?
    A. Client   C. Agency
    B. Customer   D. Subagency

14. A mortgage document and mortgage note are
    A. nonnegotiable instruments.
    B. debt-releasing documents.
    C. used by mortgagors to secure liens on a property.
    D. standard security instruments.

15. Who is the optionee in an option contract?
    A. Vendor   C. Lessor
    B. Vendee   D. Lessee

16. J sells a property to H, then H leases it back to J. At the conclusion of this transaction, what is the status of J's interest in the property?
    A. Fee simple absolute
    B. Fee simple defeasible
    C. A freehold interest
    D. A nonfreehold interest

17. Which of the following is a physical characteristic of real estate?
    A. Mobility   C. Uniqueness
    B. Scarcity   D. Transferability

18. Which of the following normally purchases mortgages in the secondary mortgage market?
    A. Mortgage banking companies, savings and loans, commercial banks and mutual saving banks
    B. Fannie Mae, Ginnie Mae and Freddie Mac
    C. Federal Housing Administration
    D. Department of Veterans Affairs

19. Broker Alma had a listing agreement to sell Noah's house. Noah found a buyer for the house and Alma collected the brokerage fee. The type of listing agreement Alma had is a(n)
    A. exclusive-right-to-sell listing.
    B. exclusive agency listing.
    C. open listing.
    D. net listing.

20. The federal Truth-in-Lending Act
    A. requires a lender to estimate a borrower's loan closing charges on all mortgages.
    B. regulates advertising that contains information regarding mortgage terms.
    C. prevents brokers from using phrases like "FHA-VA financing available" in classified ads.
    D. dictates that all mortgage loan applications be made on specially prepared government forms.

21. Recording a deed provides the greatest benefit for the
    A. grantor.   C. attorney.
    B. public.   D. grantee.

22. Which of the following documents is only signed by one party to the transaction?
    A. Purchase agreement
    B. Listing agreement
    C. Option
    D. Warranty deed

23. The ability to pay for a home is the foremost consideration in choosing a home. What is the second consideration?
    A. Specification   C. Improvements
    B. Age   D. Location

24. The most important test in determining whether something is a fixture is
    A. the weight and/or size.
    B. its amount of utilization.
    C. its method of attachment.
    D. the intention of the party who attached it.

25. A section of real estate
    A. contains 460 acres.
    B. is 1 mile square.
    C. contains 43,560 acres.
    D. is numbered to indicate either north or south.

26. Mr. and Mrs. Mark have decided to list their house. Thirty minutes before the sales agent was scheduled to arrive, Mrs. Mark had to leave for an emergency. Mr. Mark stayed for the appointment and reached an agreement for the listing price of the property, which he owns in severalty. Who must sign the listing agreement?
    A. Mr. Mark now
    B. Mrs. Mark when she returns
    C. Mr. and Mrs. Mark before the listing is placed in the MLS
    D. Mr. and Mrs. Mark as soon as their schedules permit

27. Which of the following is NOT necessary in a listing contract?
    A. The signature of all parties on the deed
    B. The signature of the sellers
    C. The signature of the broker
    D. The signature of the buyer

28. Mr. and Mrs. Hampton own their property as tenants by the entirety. The agent secured the signature of one spouse on the listing contract. Which of the following is true?
    A. Both signatures are required.
    B. One spouse can sign because they each have an equal interest in the property.
    C. Only one spouse is required to sign because they are married.
    D. If it's an open listing, the agent has the proper signature.

29. A real estate tax lien takes priority over which of the following?
    A. Encroachment
    B. Encumbrance
    C. Mortgage lien
    D. Deed restrictions

30. The principles of appraising include which of the following?
    A. Reserves for replacement
    B. Operating expense ratio
    C. Highest and best use
    D. Holding period

31. Broker Sally of Happy Valley Realty recently sold Jack and Jill's home for $43,500. Smith charged Jack and Jill a 6.5 percent commission and paid 30 percent of that amount to the listing salesperson and 25 percent to the selling salesperson. What amount of the commission did the listing salesperson receive?
    A. $2,827.50
    B. $1,272.38
    C. $848.25
    D. $706.88

32. Harold is curious to know how much money his son and daughter-in-law still owe on their mortgage loan. He knows that the interest portion of their last monthly payment was $291.42. If they are paying interest at the rate of 8.25 percent, what was the outstanding balance of their loan before that last payment was made?
    A. $43,713.00
    B. $42,388.36
    C. $36,427.50
    D. $34,284.70

33. David's home on Dove Street is valued at $65,000. Property in their area is assessed at 60 percent of its value, and the local tax rate is $2.85 per hundred. How much are David's monthly taxes?
    A. $1,111.50
    B. $926.30
    C. $111.15
    D. $92.63

34. Andrew leases the 12 apartments in the Overton Arms for a total monthly rental of $3,000. If this figure represents an 8 percent annual return on Andrew's investment, what was the original cost of the property?
    A. $450,000
    B. $360,000
    C. $45,000
    D. $36,000

35. A broker receives a check for earnest money from a buyer and deposits the money in an escrow or trust account. He does this to protect himself from the charge of which of the following?
    A. Commingling
    B. Novation
    C. Lost or stolen funds
    D. Embezzlement

36. By paying the debt after a foreclosure sale, the mortgagor has the right to regain the property. What is this right called?
    A. Acceleration
    B. Redemption
    C. Reversion
    D. Recovery

37. Helen grants a life estate to her grandson and stipulates that, upon his death, the title will pass to her son-in-law. What is the second estate called?
    A. Estate in reversion
    B. Estate in remainder
    C. Estate for years
    D. Estate in recapture

38. Under joint tenancy
    A. there is a right of survivorship.
    B. only two people can own real estate.
    C. the fractional undivided interest may be different.
    D. the estate is inheritable.

39. In some states, a lender holds title to the mortgaged land. These states are known as
    A. title-theory states.
    B. lien-theory states.
    C. statutory share states.
    D. dower rights states.

40. A buyer is interested in making an offer on a property that has a deed restriction prohibiting the sale of alcoholic beverages. Which of the following documents would indicate that the buyer takes the title with this restriction?
    A. Original deed of the grantor
    B. Offer to purchase the buyer will make
    C. Listing agreement
    D. Counteroffer of the seller

41. Which of the following is NOT an example of a subdivision rule and regulation?
    A. The agreement that the property cannot be sold and used as a waste disposal site
    B. The agreement that a tree house cannot be built on the property
    C. The agreement that walls and fences shall not exceed four feet in height
    D. The agreement that no structure of a temporary character shall be constructed on any lot

42. Which of the following is NOT an example of an appurtenance that would transfer when the property is sold?
    A. Easement
    B. Lease
    C. Deed restriction
    D. License

43. A couple wants to list a home they have lived in for 38 years because they have decided to move to Florida before the winter storms arrive. The listing agent is aware that zoning may change in the area, which would greatly increase the value of their property. The agent should
    A. say nothing in case the zoning does not change.
    B. inform the sellers of all the facts she has regarding the zoning change, and let them make the decision about listing the property.
    C. list the property because she has a buyer that has already shown interest, and if it sells, then the sellers will be in Florida before the winter storms.
    D. list the property and say nothing because if the zoning does change, the listing contract will be void anyway.

44. Which of the following is NOT a depreciation factor when assessing the value of a property?
    A. A house with four bedrooms located on the second floor and the bath located on the first floor.
    B. A hog farm located one-half mile down the road from a $250,000 home.
    C. A house located next to a city park.
    D. A house, which cost $50,000 to build 40 years ago, with major cracks in the foundation.

45. What is a tenancy at will?
    A. A tenancy with the consent of the landlord
    B. A tenancy that expires on a specific date
    C. A tenancy created by the death of the owner
    D. A tenancy created by the testator

46. The value of a piece of land
    A. is the present worth of future benefits.
    B. includes a measure of past expenditures.
    C. is what a buyer pays for the property.
    D. is the same as the market price.

47. A seller wants to net $65,000 on his house after paying the broker's fee of 6 percent. What will the gross selling price be?

    A. $69,149   C. $67,035
    B. $68,900   D. $66,091

48. Wilma is buying a condominium in a new subdivision and obtaining financing from a local savings and loan association. Which of the following best describes Wilma?

    A. Vendor   C. Grantor
    B. Mortagee   D. Mortgagor

49. All of the following terminate an offer EXCEPT

    A. revocation of the offer before acceptance.
    B. death of the offeror before acceptance.
    C. a counteroffer by the offeree.
    D. an offer from a third party.

50. Ellen is purchasing a house under a contract for deed. Until the contract is paid, Ellen has

    A. legal title to the premises.
    B. no interest in the property.
    C. a legal life estate in the premises.
    D. equitable title in the premises.

51. Broker Len receives a deposit with a written offer that includes a ten-day acceptance clause. On the fifth day, and prior to acceptance by Carla, the seller; the buyer, Fergus, notifies the broker he is withdrawing his offer and demands that his deposit be returned. In this situation

    A. Fergus cannot withdraw the offer; it must be held open for the full ten days.
    B. Fergus has the right to revoke his offer and secure the return of the deposit at any time before he is notified of Carla's acceptance.
    C. Len notifies Carla that Fergus is withdrawing his offer, and Len and Fergus each retain one-half of the deposit.
    D. Len declares the deposit forfeited and retains it for his services and commission.

52. Amanda and George are joint tenants. George sells his interest to Percy. What is the relationship of Amanda and Percy with respect to the land?

    A. They are automatically joint tenants.
    B. They are tenants in common.
    C. There is no relationship, because the sale from George to Percy of joint tenancy property is ineffective.
    D. Each owns a divided one-half interest.

53. A homeowner who always maintains his house has just discovered that he has termite infestation. This is an example of

    A. incurable physical obsolescence.
    B. possible curable physical obsolescence.
    C. possible curable economic obsolescence.
    D. incurable internal obsolescence.

54. When appraising property, the appraiser considers which of the following?

    A. The original price paid for the property, if purchased within three years
    B. The reconciliation of the values determined by the different methods of appraising
    C. The average cost of the comparable properties, after adjustments are made
    D. The cost for updating the subject property, other than the cost of replacing the carpet

55. When appraising a property, the appraiser determines the most probable price that a buyer would be willing to pay for a property. This is known as a(n)

    A. objective value/fair market value.
    B. subjective value/fair market value.
    C. plottage value.
    D. use value.

56. On Monday, Victor receives an offer from Leona for $12,000 on a vacant lot he has for sale. On Tuesday, Victor rejects the offer, counteroffers at $13,000 and gives Leona 3 days to accept. On Friday, Leona rejects the counteroffer and Victor then accepts Leona's original offer. Under these conditions there is

    A. a valid agreement, because Leona accepted Victor's offer exactly as it was made.
    B. not a valid agreement, because Leona's offer was rejected, and once rejected, it cannot later be accepted.
    C. a valid agreement, because Leona accepted before Victor advised her that the offer was withdrawn.
    D. not a valid agreement, because Victor's offer was not accepted within 72 hours.

57. Due to the economic growth in an area, a house designed by a famous architect is now in a flight pattern from the nearby airport. This is an example of
    A. external obsolescence, and the owners could receive compensation through inverse condemnation.
    B. external obsolescence, and the owners will not under any circumstances receive any compensation.
    C. functional obsolescence because of the poor design.
    D functional obsolescence because of the noise from the planes.

58. In an appurtenant easement the property burdened by the easement is known as a
    A. prescriptive estate.
    B. dominant estate.
    C. condemned estate.
    D. servient estate.

59. Which of the following is NOT found in the appraisal report?
    A. Date of the inspection
    B. Condition of the subject property
    C. Adjustments of the subject property
    D. Signature of the appraiser

60. Unless stated otherwise in the listing contract, the buyer should receive upon the purchase of a property
    A. air rights, surface rights and subsurface rights.
    B. air rights and surface rights.
    C. air rights and subsurface rights.
    D. air rights and mineral rights.

61. A house sold for $84,500 and the commission rate was 7 percent. If the commission is split 60/40 between the selling broker and the listing broker, and each broker splits his share of the commission evenly with his salesperson, how much will the listing salesperson earn from the sale of the house, according to the sales contract?
    A. $1,774   C. $1,020
    B. $1,183   D. $2,366

62. Justin Time and Lotta Time enter into a purchase agreement with Henry and Susan Date to buy the Date's house for $84,500. The buyers pay $2,000 in earnest money and obtain a new mortgage of $67,600. The purchase agreement provides for a March 15, 2001, closing. The buyers and sellers prorate 2001 taxes of $1,880.96, which have been prepaid. The Times have closing costs of $1,250 and the Dates have closing costs of $850. How much cash must the buyers bring to the closing? (Use a 360 day year.)
    A. $17,239.09   C. $16,541.87
    B. $17,639.09   D. $19,639.09

63. If a mortgage on a house is 80 percent of the appraised value and the mortgage interest of 8 percent amounts to $460 per month, what is the appraised value of the house?
    A. $86,250   C. $69,000
    B. $71,875   D. $92,875

64. A building is 100′ by 150′ and sits on a lot valued at $25,000. If the replacement cost of the property is $25 per square foot and it has depreciated 5 percent, what is the value of the property?
    A. $375,000   C. $481,250
    B. $381,250   D. $318,250

65. Broker Mary took a listing and later discovered that her client had previously been declared incompetent by a court of law. The listing is now
    A. binding, as the broker was acting as the owner's agent in good faith.
    B. of no value to the broker because it is void.
    C. the basis for recovery of a commission if the broker produces a buyer.
    D. renegotiable.

66. Perry defaulted on his home mortgage loan payments, and the lender obtained a court order to foreclose on the property. At the foreclosure sale, however, Perry's house sold for only $29,000; the unpaid balance on the loan at the time of foreclosure was $40,000. What must the lender do to recover the $11,000 Perry still owes?
    A. Sue for damages
    B. Sue for specific performance
    C. Seek a judgment by default
    D. Seek a deficiency judgment

67. All of the following are exemptions to the federal Fair Housing Act of 1968 EXCEPT the
    A. sale of a single-family home where the listing broker does not advertise the property.
    B. rental of a unit in an owner-occupied, three-family dwelling where no advertisement is placed in the paper.
    C. restriction of noncommercial lodgings by a private club to members of that club.
    D. property is a state or local housing program designed specifically for the elderly.

68. A broker holds a listing on a vacant lot measuring 100' by 125' at a listing price of $250 per front foot. The commission that the broker will collect is 8 percent. If the property sells for its full asking price, what will be the broker's fee?
    A. $2,500   C. $1,500
    B. $2,000   D. $1,250

69. Sal has been offering Cathay's house for sale at the price of $47,900. Mr. and Mrs. Cortez, a Mexican couple, saw the house and were interested in purchasing it. When Mrs. Cortez asked Sal what the price of the house was, Sal said $53,000. Under the federal Fair Housing Act of 1968, such a statement is
    A. legal, because all that is important is that Mr. and Mrs. Cortez be given the right to buy the house.
    B. legal, because the representation was made by broker Sal and not by Cathay.
    C. illegal, because the difference in the offering price and the quoted price was greater than $5,000.
    D. illegal, because the terms of the sale were changed for Mr. and Mrs. Cortez.

70. The market rent for a duplex is $650 per month per unit. If the GRM is 125, what is the value of the property?
    A. $81,250   C. $126,500
    B. $162,500   D. $216,500

71. House keys are considered to be
    A. personal property because they are movable.
    B. personal property because they are not attached.
    C. real property because sale contracts stipulate that they will be transferred.
    D. real property because of the adaptation to the real estate.

72. In the lease agreement, a tenant has agreed to build out space to meet her needs at her expense. The chattel fixtures that she adds to the property are the
    A. property of the landlord upon the expiration of the lease because they are now attached to the property.
    B. tenants' as long as they are removed from the property on or before the expiration of the lease and she leaves the property in good repair.
    C. tenants' as long as they are removed from the property on or before the expiration of the lease because she paid for them.
    D. property of the landlord automatically upon their addition, and the property must be left in good repair.

73. *A, B* and *C* are co-owners of property. When *C* dies testate, *A* and *B* are the devisees to her one-third interest in the property. How do they own the property?
    A. Joint tenancy
    B. Tenancy in common
    C. Severalty
    D. Partnership tenancy

74. Which of the following is an example of a freehold inheritable estate?
    A. Life estate
    B. Dower estate
    C. Estate at will
    D. Fee simple defeasible estate

75. Frances moved into a condominium that boasted of many common facilities, including a swimming pool, tennis courts and a putting green. Under a typical condominium arrangement, these common elements are owned by
    A. an association of homeowners in the condominium.
    B. a corporation in which Frances and the owners of the other units own stock.
    C. Frances and the owners of the other units in the form of an undivided percentage interest.
    D. Frances and the owners of the other units in the form of divided interests.

76. In a graduated-payment loan
    A. mortgage payments decrease.
    B. mortgage payments balloon in five years.
    C. mortgage payments increase for a period of time and then level out.
    D. the interest rate on the loan adjusts annually.

77. Jack feels that he has been the victim of an unfair discriminatory practice by a local broker. His complaint must be filed with HUD within
    A. 3 months of the alleged discrimination.
    B. 6 months of the alleged discrimination.
    C. 9 months of the alleged discrimination.
    D. 12 months of the alleged discrimination.

78. A mortgage using both real and personal property as security is a
    A. blanket mortgage.
    B. package mortgage.
    C. dual mortgage.
    D. wraparound mortgage.

79. If a buyer obtains a mortgage for $50,000 with four points, how much will she be charged by the lender at closing for the points?
    A. $6,000   C. $2,000
    B. $200   D. $600

80. A borrower obtained a second mortgage loan for $7,000. The loan called for payments of $50 per month, including 6 percent interest over a period of five years, with the final installment made as a balloon payment including the remaining outstanding principal. What type of loan is this?
    A. Fully amortized loan
    B. Straight loan
    C. Partially amortized loan
    D. Accelerated loan

81. Michael bought property in a secluded area adjacent to the Atlantic Ocean. Shortly thereafter, he noticed that people from town often walked along the shore in front of his property. He later learned that the locals had been walking along this beach for years. Michael went to court to try to stop people from walking along the water's edge in front of his property. Michael is likely to be
    A. unsuccessful, because the local citizens were walking there before he bought the property, and thus had an easement.
    B. unsuccessful, because under the doctrine of littoral rights, he owns the property only to the high-water mark, and the public can use the land beyond that mark.
    C. successful, because of the doctrine of riparian rights.
    D. successful, because he has the right to control access to his own property.

82. All of the following are true about the concept of adverse possession EXCEPT
    A. the person taking possession of the property must do so without the consent of the owner.
    B. occupancy of the property by the person taking possession must be continuous over a specified period.
    C. the person taking possession of the property must compensate the owner at the end of the adverse possession period.
    D. the person taking possession of the property may end up owning the property.

83. Reconciliation is an appraisal term used to describe the
    A. appraiser's determination of a property's highest value.
    B. average values for properties similar to the one being appraised.
    C. appraiser's analysis and comparison of the results of each appraisal approach.
    D. method used to determine a property's most appropriate capitalization rate.

84. In consideration of $50, Jim gives Charles the right to purchase certain described real estate for $2,000. If Charles enters into an agreement to purchase it within 60 days, Charles is a(n)
    A. optionor.
    B. escrowee.
    C. optionee.
    D. grantor.

85. When a mortgage loan has been paid in full, which of the following is the most important thing for the borrower to do?
    A. Put the paid note and all canceled papers in a safe-deposit box
    B. Arrange to receive and pay future real estate tax bills
    C. Be sure the mortgagor signs a satisfaction of mortgage
    D. Record the satisfaction of mortgage

86. Normally, the priority of general liens is determined by the
    A. order in which they are filed or recorded.
    B. order in which the cause of action arose.
    C. size of the claim.
    D. court.

87. When property is held in tenancy by the entirety
    A. the owners must be husband and wife.
    B. either owner may sell his or her own interest separately to a third party by signing a quitclaim deed.
    C. there is no right of survivorship.
    D. the property may be partitioned.

88. The practice of directing potential buyers of one race into one area and potential buyers of another race into a second area is known as
    A. canvassing.
    B. blockbusting.
    C. redlining.
    D. steering.

89. A broker who is entitled to collect a commission when the sellers sell their own property has a(n)
    A. exclusive agency listing contract with the sellers.
    B. net listing contract with the sellers.
    C. exclusive-right-to-sell listing contract with the sellers.
    D. open listing contract with the sellers.

90. Sheila, a broker, listed a property under a valid written listing agreement. After the sale was completed, the owner refused to pay the broker's fee. Which of the following can Sheila do?
    A. She can take the seller to court and sue for the commission.
    B. She is entitled to a lien on the seller's property for the amount of the commission.
    C. She can go to court and stop the transaction until she is paid.
    D. She can collect the commission from the buyer.

91. All of the following are tests for determining a fixture EXCEPT
    A. intent of the parties.
    B. size of the item.
    C. method of attachment of the item.
    D. adaptation of the item to the particular real estate.

92. When real estate is sold under an installment land contract, possession is usually given to the buyer. The vendee's interest in the property is
    A. a legal title interest.
    B. an equitable title interest.
    C. kept by the seller until the full purchase price is paid.
    D. held by the mortgagee until the full purchase price is paid.

93. To start a condominium, a developer usually files which of the following?
    A. Judgment
    B. Lien
    C. Certificate
    D. Declaration

94. George agrees to buy Elaine's real estate for $53,000. George signs a sales contract and deposits $5,300 earnest money with broker Stuart. Elaine is unable to show good title, and George demands the return of his earnest money as provided in the contract. What should Stuart do?

    A. Deduct his commission and return the balance to George
    B. Deduct his commission and pay the balance to Elaine
    C. Return the entire amount of the earnest money to George
    D. Pay the entire amount to Elaine to dispose of as she sees fit

95. If the annual rate of interest on a mortgage loan is 8.5 percent, and the monthly interest payment is $201.46, what is the principal amount of the loan?

    A. $2,417.52   C. $2,844.14
    B. $28,441.41   D. $14,270.00

96. All of the following are contracts between an agent and a principal EXCEPT

    A. open listing.
    B. net listing.
    C. multiple listing.
    D. exclusive listing.

97. Mary and Dudley enter into a contract wherein Dudley will build a structure on some vacant land. Dudley begins work and finds that because of the nature of the soil, the supports for the structure must be dug much deeper than he had thought. The additional work will cause Dudley to lose money on the project. Under these circumstances

    A. Dudley does not have to continue with the contract, under the doctrine of impossibility.
    B. Dudley does not have to continue with the contract, because Mary does not have the right to force Dudley to lose money.
    C. Dudley can force Mary to renegotiate the contract because of Dudley's mistake, if the mistake was reasonable.
    D. Dudley is liable for breach of contract if he fails to perform, and the fact that the job is more difficult than Dudley had expected is irrelevant.

98. Allen offers to sell Naomi certain undeveloped land in the country and represents to her that a new freeway will run right by the land, even though Allen knows that the plans for the new freeway have been dropped. Naomi, relying on the representation, purchases the land from Allen. Under these circumstances

    A. Allen can be forced to proceed with the sale even though there was fraud.
    B. the contract is voidable at the option of Allen.
    C. the misrepresentation automatically voids the contract.
    D. Naomi must purchase the property and cannot sue Allen for fraud.

99. If the market value of a house is $84,500, the assessment ratio is 35 percent and the tax rate if 30 mills, what are the monthly taxes?

    A. $887.25   C. $73.94
    B. $942.50   D. $87.72

100. Richard seeks relief from zoning regulations on the ground of nonconforming use. Effective arguments to the zoning authorities would include all of the following EXCEPT that

    A. the nonconforming use existed prior to the passing of the zoning ordinance.
    B. he would earn more by using the property for purposes that do not conform with the zoning ordinance.
    C. the nonconforming use didn't harm the public health, safety and welfare.
    D. conforming to the zoning ordinance would create an undue hardship.

ANSWERS

For additional information please refer to the page number in parenthesis.

1. D RESPA covers one- to four-family residential loans financed by a federally related mortgage loan. (94)
2. C Prepayment penalties cannot be charged on FHA or VA mortgages. (118)
3. A The alienation clause in a mortgage document allows the lender to call the note due and payable upon the conveyance of the property. (128)
4. B 640 + 10 = 650 acres x $2,500= $1,625,000 (1 mile square = 640 acres). (4)
5. A An attorney gives an opinion of title and issues a title certificate. (88)
6. C The local zoning laws regulate the type of animals that can be kept on a property. (24)
7. A A contract with no contingencies is a valid, enforceable contract. (41)
8. D The tenant would least likely be responsible for returning the doorways to their original width. (120)
9. D Deterioration caused by normal wear and tear of the property best describes depreciation. (11)
10. C Any material fact or property defect must be disclosed to potential buyers of a property. (47)
11. A The lender normally computes simple interest on residential loans. (128)
12. B Emblements are crops that require annual planting. The crop that has been harvested is an emblement. (18)
13. B The seller is normally considered to be the customer to a buyer's agent. (142)
14. D By definition of mortgage document and mortgage note. (115)
15. B In an option contract, the optionee is the vendee or buyer. (42)
16. D In this sale-leaseback transaction *J* is the lessee and has a nonfreehold interest in the property. (70)
17. C Heterogeneity, immobility and durability are the physical characteristics of real estate. Heterogeneity, or nonhomogeneity, means that every parcel of land is unique. (17)
18. B Fannie Mae, Ginnie Mae and Freddie Mac buy and sell mortgages on the secondary market. (119)
19. A In an exclusive-right-to-sell listing, the broker collects a commission even if the seller sells the property. (28)
20. B Truth-in-Lending requires the disclosure of the cost of financing the loan expressed as an APR, and regulates the advertising of mortgage loans. (124)
21. D It is to the benefit of the buyer to give constructive notice to the world that she or he is the owner of the property. (8)
22. D A deed is a transfer of title, and the party currently holding title is required to sign. (96)
23. D The location of the property affects its price today and in the future. People purchase homes because of their preference for certain locations. (11)
24. D Courts have held that the intention of the parties is the most important factor in determining when an item is a fixture. (19)
25. B A section of land is one mile square. (4)
26. A Mr. Mark owns the property in severalty and he is the only party who must sign the listing. (2)
27. D The buyer is not a party to the listing contract. (2)
28. A Both signatures are required on the listing because it is owned as tenancy by the entirety. (2)
29. C Real estate taxes and special assessments take priority over all other liens. (91)
30. C The highest and best use of the property is its most profitable use. (13)

31. C
$$\frac{\$2,827.50}{\$43,500 \mid 6.5\%} \qquad \frac{\$848.25}{\$2,827.50 \mid 30\%} \qquad (168)$$
$$\times \qquad\qquad \times$$

32. B $\$291.42 \times 12 = \$3,497.04 \qquad \dfrac{\$3,497.04 \div}{\$42,388.36 \mid 8.25\%} \qquad (171)$

33. D $2.85 \div 100 = .0285$

$$\frac{\$39,000}{\$65,000 \mid 60\%}$$
$$\times$$

$$\frac{\$1,111.50}{\$39,000 \mid .0285}$$
$$\times$$

$\$1,111.50 \div 12 = \$92.625$

(174)

34. A $\$3,000 \times 12 = \$36,000$

$$\frac{\$36,000 \div}{\$450,000 \mid 8\%}$$
$$\times$$

(175)

35. A All money received in a fiduciary relationship must be placed in an escrow account to prevent commingling. (154)

36. B The equitable right of redemption is the owner's right to regain property before foreclosure. The statutory right of redemption is the owner's right to regain the property after foreclosure. (129)

37. B The son-in-law is a remainderman and his interest is an estate in remainder. (27)

38. A Joint tenancy is characterized by right of survivorship. (21)

39. A By definition of title-theory state. (120)

40. C The listing agreement indicates that the buyer is taking title with all recorded restrictions. (29)

41. A This is an example of a deed condition placed on the property by a grantor that is binding to all future owners. (2)

42. D A license is the revocable permission for a temporary land use granted to another, but it does not transfer with the property. (7)

43. B The agent must inform the sellers of all facts that she has regarding the possible zoning change and the consequences of their decision should they accept any offers on the property before the decision about the zoning is finalized. (47)

44. C Depreciation does not occur because a house is located next to a city park. (11)

45. A A tenancy at will is a lease that can be terminated at the will of the landlord or tenant. (70)

46. A By definition of value. (14)

47. A $100\% - 6\% = 94\%$

$$\frac{\$65,000 \div}{\$69,148.94 \mid 94\%}$$

(168)

48. D Wilma is the borrower or the mortgagor. (116)

49. D An offer from a third party does not terminate an offer. (43)

50. D When the legal title in the property is held by another party, the buyer's interest is an equitable interest. (45)

51. B An offer can be withdrawn at any time prior to acceptance. (70)

52. B When a joint tenant sells an interest in a property, the new owner becomes a tenant in common with the other joint tenants. (25)

53. B Unless termite infestation has occurred on the property for an extended period of time, it is curable. Because the question states that the homeowner always maintained his house and the termite infestation was just discovered, then the physical obsolescence is probably curable. (11)

54. B An appraiser reconciles the values as determined by the different methods of appraising, but they do not consider any of the factors in the other answers. (13)

55. A The appraiser determines the most probable price that a buyer will pay for the property. This is known as the fair market value and should be an objective value. (12)

56. B Once an offer has been rejected it cannot be accepted later. (43)

57. A A change outside the property has affected the property's value. This is external obsolescence, and the owners could receive compensation through inverse condemnation. (11)

58. D In an appurtenant easement, the servient estate is burdened by the easement and the dominant estate benefits from it. (6)

59. C Adjustments are never made in the subject property, only in the comparable properties. (16)

60. A Any rights that are not being transferred should be in the listing contract. (17)

61. B

$$\frac{\$5,915}{\$84,500 \quad | \quad 7\%} \qquad \frac{\$2,366}{\$5,915 \quad | \quad 40\%} \qquad \$2,366 \div 2 = \$1,183$$

$\times$ $\times$ (168)

62. B

Debit	Credit
$84,500.00	$ 2,000
$ 1,489.09	$67,600
$ 1,250.00	
$87,239.09	$69,600

Jan. 1
March 15—Count from March 15 through Dec. 30 = 285 days
Dec. 30
$1,880.96 ÷ 360 = $5.22489 per day
$5.22489 × 285 days = $1,489.09
$87,239.09 – 69,600 = $17,639.09 (179)

63. A $460 × 12 = $5,520

$$\frac{\$5,520 \div}{\$69,000 \quad | \quad 8\%} \qquad \frac{\$69,000 \div}{\$86,250 \quad | \quad 80\%} \qquad (171)$$

64. B A = 100′ × 150′ 15,000 × $25 =

A = 15,000 square feet

$375,000	(176, 184)
– 5%	
$356,250	
+ 25,000	
$381,250	

65. B The listing agent should enter into the listing agreement with the guardian of the incompetent party. (44)
66. D By definition of deficiency judgment. (129)
67. A Single-family homeowners under certain circumstances can discriminate when selling their property, but an owner who does cannot use the services of a broker. (145)

68. B 100′ × $250 = $25,000

$$\frac{\$2,000}{\$25,000 \quad | \quad 8\%} \qquad (168, 184)$$

$\times$

69. D It is discriminatory to change the terms of the listing agreement. (145)

70. B $650 × 2 = $1,300

$$\frac{\$162,500}{125 \quad | \quad \$1,300} \qquad (176)$$

$\times$

71. D House keys are adapted to the use of a specific property and are considered real property. (19)
72. B Trade fixtures must be removed from the property on or before the lease expires. The tenant is responsible for any damage caused by the removal of the fixtures. Those that are not removed become the property of the landlord. (18, 25)
73. B Tenancy in common is an inheritable estate. When *C* wrote her will she made the other co-owners her devisees. (21)
74. D Fee simple absolute and fee simple defeasible estates are freehold inheritable estates. (23)
75. C Common areas are owned by the condo owners in an undivided percentage interest. (20)
76. C By definition of graduated-payment mortgage. (117)
77. D Complaints must be filed with HUD within one year. (146)

78. B By definition of package mortgage. (117)

79. C $$\frac{\$2,000}{\$50,000 \mid 4\%} \quad (172)$$
$$\times$$

80. C By definition of partially amortized loan. (120)
81. B By definition of littoral rights. (19)
82. C The adverse possessor does not compensate the owner at the end of the adverse possession period. (100)
83. C By definition of reconciliation. (13)
84. C Charles is the buyer and thus the optionee. (42)
85. D The satisfaction of mortgage or mortgage release needs to be recorded to release the lender's interest in the property. (129)
86. A The priority of liens is usually determined by the order in which they are filed or recorded. (91)
87. A Tenancy by the entirety involves a husband and wife who own property. (21)
88. D By definition of channeling and steering. (145)
89. C By definition of exclusive-right-to-sell listing. (28)
90. A The broker must sue the seller for the commission. (42)
91. B The size of an item is not one of the tests to determine if it is a fixture. (19)
92. B The buyer's interest in the property in a land contract is an equitable title interest. (113)
93. D To develop a condominium community, the developer must file a declaration. (20)
94. C The earnest money check should be returned to the buyer. The broker must pursue the seller for the commission. (41)

95. B $\$201.46 \times 12 = \$2,417.52$
$$\frac{\$2,417.52 \div}{\$28,441.41 \mid 8.5\%} \quad (173)$$
$$\times$$

96. C The multiple-listing service is an agreement between brokers, not between an agent and a principal. (29)
97. D Because there were no contingencies in the contract, Dudley must fulfill the contract. (142)
98. A Allen committed fraud in selling the property. However, if Naomi still chooses to buy the property upon the discovery of that fact, Allen must sell. (40)

99. C $30 \div 1000 = .03$
$$\frac{\$29,575}{\$84,500 \mid 35\%} \qquad \frac{\$887.25}{\$29,575 \mid .03} \qquad \$887.25 \div 12 = \$73.94$$
$$\times \qquad\qquad\qquad \times \qquad\qquad (174)$$

100. B The fact that Richard could earn more money is not a valid reason to grant relief from zoning regulations. (24)

Broker Examination

1. A house sold for $37,500, and the buyers secured an FHA mortgage. The required down payment was set at 3 percent for the first $25,000 and 5 percent for any amount over $25,000. What was the amount of the mortgage?
   A. $1,375
   B. $1,425
   C. $36,125
   D. $35,850

2. After a neighborhood had been hit by vandals on a number of occasions, Nolan offered to pay $100 to anyone providing information leading to the arrest and conviction of the guilty party. Shortly thereafter, Eileen supplied the needed information and received the reward. This is an example of a(n)
   A. gift.
   B. option.
   C. unilateral contract.
   D. voidable contract.

3. Broker Kate pays her salespeople 20 percent of the commission for listing property and 40 percent of the commission for selling it. The commission rate is 5 percent. What was the selling price of a house if the salesperson who both listed and sold it received $3,600?
   A. $120,000
   B. $200,000
   C. $72,000
   D. $100,000

4. Which of the following is a loan in which only interest is payable during the term of the loan and all principal is payable at the end of the loan period?
   A. Amortized loan
   B. Flexible loan
   C. Fixed installment loan
   D. Term loan

5. A property owned solely by one spouse
   A. is owned in trust.
   B. is owned in severalty.
   C. is immune from seizure by creditors.
   D. cannot be homesteaded.

6. When a property fails to sell at a court foreclosure for an amount sufficient to satisfy the mortgage debt, the mortgagee may usually sue for which of the following?
   A. Judgment by default
   B. Deficiency judgment
   C. Satisfaction of mortgage
   D. Damages

7. Joe is purchasing a parcel of real estate registered as Torrens property. In connection with the purchase
   A. Joe should have an attorney review the abstract and render an opinion about prior transfers.
   B. the Torrens certificate is proof of ownership.
   C. Joe should check for adverse possession.
   D. the execution of the deed transfers title.

8. Sam is purchasing property from Harry and taking a quitclaim deed. Under the assurances of such a deed, Sam can be certain that
   A. Harry has a good title to the property.
   B. Harry's interest at that time in the property is being transferred to Sam.
   C. Harry will convey after-acquired title.
   D. there are no liens against the property that adversely affect marketable title.

9. Seller Henry and Broker Walter enter into an open listing agreement. Under such an agreement, Henry
   A. must inform Walter of all potential buyers.
   B. does not have to pay Walter a commission if Henry finds a buyer.
   C. must pay Walter a commission if Henry or Walter finds a buyer.
   D. must pay Walter a commission if anyone but Henry finds a buyer.

10. When a buyer signs a purchase agreement and the seller accepts, the buyer acquires an interest in the real estate, prior to closing, known as
  A. equitable title.
  B. equitable rights.
  C. statutory rights.
  D. servient tenement.

11. All of the following are intended to convey title to real estate that has been sold EXCEPT
  A. warranty deed. C. trustee's deed.
  B. deeds of trust. D. deed in trust.

12. The ABC Real Estate Company listed a property at $4.50 per square foot. The land dimensions were 50 feet by 137 feet. If the commission rate was set at 7.25 percent, how much did the seller pay the ABC Real Estate Company?
  A. $1,005.50 C. $22,348.12
  B. $2,234.81 D. $10,055.00

13. To purchase a home, a buyer obtained a $42,500 mortgage at 9.75 percent interest for 25 years. The mortgage was closed on June 15, with the first P&I payment in arrears due on August 1. At the closing, which of the following occurred?
  A. The buyer paid a $172.65 interest adjustment.
  B. The seller paid a $172.65 interest adjustment.
  C. The seller paid a $345.31 interest adjustment.
  D. The buyer paid a $345.31 interest adjustment.

14. To be valid, a deed must be signed by which of the following?
  A. Grantors C. Grantees
  B. Attorney at law D. Broker

15. In order to have a valid conveyance, all of the following are necessary EXCEPT
  A. legal capacity to execute.
  B. recital of consideration.
  C. designation of any limitations.
  D. proof of heirship.

16. Which of the following discriminatory acts is exempted from the Federal Fair Housing Act?
  A. Rental of rooms in an owner-occupied one- to four-family dwelling
  B. Alteration of the terms or conditions of mortgage
  C. Property for sale above $250,000
  D. Property sold on an installment sales contract

17. Thornton Enterprises manages a number of income-producing properties for a large landholder in the city. The management agreement provides that the property manager shall be responsible for finding new tenants and maintaining the properties. The fee Thornton Enterprises may charge for its services is MOST LIKELY a percentage of the
  A. net income earned from the properties.
  B. gross income earned from the properties.
  C. total expenses incurred in maintaining the properties.
  D. ROI.

18. On a settlement statement, the commission owed to the broker is a
  A. debit to the sellers.
  B. debit to the buyers.
  C. credit to the sellers and a debit to the buyers.
  D. credit to the buyers.

19. Mike and Joyce entered into an agreement to sell a rental property they own. The closing is to take place September 15. On September 1, Mike and Joyce received a rent payment for the month of September from the tenant. Under the terms of the purchase agreement, the buyers are entitled to any rent received covering the period subsequent to the closing. At the closing, the prepaid rent will appear as a
  A. credit to the sellers and a debit to the buyers.
  B. debit to the sellers and a credit to the buyers.
  C. credit to the buyers.
  D. debit to the sellers.

20. Under the provisions of the Real Estate Settlement Procedures Act, certain disclosures are required from the
    A. seller in a residential real estate transaction.
    B. buyer in a residential real estate transaction.
    C. lender in a residential real estate transaction.
    D. closer in a residential real estate transaction.

21. Which of the following real estate documents will LEAST LIKELY be recorded at the county recorder's office?
    A. Contract for deed
    B. Long-term lease
    C. Option agreement
    D. Purchase agreement

22. Salesperson Harry is proposing an advertisement for a house on which he obtained a listing for broker Wallace. In the ad, Harry
    A. need not show Wallace's name if Harry's phone number appears.
    B. must show his association with Wallace.
    C. must show the sale price of the property.
    D. All of the above

23. Broker Sally obtained a listing agreement on the sale of Hamilton's house. A buyer was found and purchase agreements signed. It is Sally's duty to make sure that the buyer
    A. will make a loan application.
    B. has a copy of all written agreements.
    C. is qualified for the mortgage.
    D. has inspected the home.

24. Sellers Fred and Margaret have executed three open listings with three brokers around town. All three brokers would like to place "For Sale" signs on the seller's property. Under these circumstances
    A. a broker does not have to obtain the seller's permission before placing a sign on the property.
    B. only one "For Sale" sign may be placed on the property at one time.
    C. upon obtaining the seller's written consent, all can place signs on the property.
    D. the first listing broker must consent to all signs.

25. For a parcel of real estate to have value, it must have
    A. utility.
    B. scarcity.
    C. transferability.
    D. All of the above

26. Under the income approach to estimating the value of real estate, the capitalization rate is the
    A. rate at which the property increases in value.
    B. rate of return the property earns on an investment.
    C. rate of capital required to keep a property operating by its most effective method.
    D. maximum rate of return allowed by law on an investment.

27. Robert was asked to value a single-family home in order to determine the proposed sale price. Robert found five comparable houses that had recently sold. Adjustments to the sale prices of the comparables should be made to reflect differences in
    A. location, physical condition and amenities of the property.
    B. gross rent multiplier of other properties.
    C. expired properties.
    D. current listed properties.

28. The final step in the appraisal process is to
    A. make copies for the lender.
    B. create an invoice.
    C. adjust the subject property.
    D. reconcile the differences.

29. If a landlord breaches the lease and the unit is uninhabitable, what action can the tenant take?
    A. Suit for possession
    B. Constructive eviction
    C. Tenancy at sufferance
    D. Covenant of quiet possession

30. How can tenancy at sufferance be created?
    A. By failure to surrender possession
    B. By payment of rent
    C. By bringing an unlawful detainer action
    D. By giving 30 days' written notice

31. If the title will pass to a third party upon the death of the life tenant, what was the third party's interest in the property?
    A. Remainder interest
    B. Reversionary interest
    C. Conditional interest
    D. Redemption interest

32. What is the interest of the grantee when real estate is conveyed only for as long as specified conditions are met?
    A. Defeasible fee   C. Restrictive fee
    B. Indefeasible fee   D. Base fee

33. FHA insurance regulations state that the
    A. FHA set the interest rate.
    B. buyer and/or seller may pay the points.
    C. mortgage insurance premium be paid by the seller.
    D. closing costs be paid by the buyer.

34. The United States uses both lien theory and title theory in mortgage law. Under the title theory the
    A. mortgagor has title to the property.
    B. mortgagee has title to the property.
    C. mortgagor and mortgagee jointly hold title.
    D. buyer holds title in trust.

35. Brokers who conspire to set commission rates or enter into an agreement to allocate a specific market are subject to which of the following?
    A. Sherman Antitrust Act
    B. Law of agency
    C. Blue-sky laws
    D. Securities Act of 1933

36. Which of the following affect the control and regulation of land use?
    A. Public and private land-use controls
    B. Zoning ordinances
    C. Deed restrictions
    D. All of the above

37. Under a percentage lease, the lessee pays $400 per month plus 2.75 percent of gross sales. Last month's gross sales were $198,210. How much is the rent?
    A. $5,450.78   C. $5,540.78
    B. $5,850.78   D. $5,580.78

38. What type of lease requires the lessee to pay taxes, insurance and repairs?
    A. Net lease   C. Variable lease
    B. Percentage lease   D. Gross lease

39. After signing a lease, the lessor obtains which of the following interests in real estate?
    A. Freehold estate
    B. Leased fee interest
    C. Leasehold interest
    D. Remainderman interest

40. If the market value of a property is $72,000 and it is assessed at 67 percent of value, what are the monthly taxes if the tax rate for the area is $6.50 per $100 of the assessed value?
    A. $3,157.38   C. $261.30
    B. $4,857.50   D. $48,575.00

41. A $50,000 mortgage on a property represents an 80 percent loan-to-value ratio. If the real estate was assessed at 82 percent, the taxes were based on $4 per $100 of assessed value and the taxes were $2,050 annually, what was the sale price of the home?
    A. $62,500   C. $41,000
    B. $51,250   D. $50,000

42. Which of the following is a method of foreclosure that does not require civil action?
    A. Judicial foreclosure
    B. Strict foreclosure
    C. Sheriff's foreclosure
    D. Nonjudicial foreclosure

43. If a home sells for $65,900, and the mortgage requires a 40 percent down payment and a 1 percent origination fee plus $450 in closing costs, how much does the buyer need to close?
    A. $26,623.60   C. $27,173.59
    B. $27,205.40   D. $26,360.00

44. If a building is 200 feet wide, 300 feet long and five stories high (each story 12 feet in height), how much does the building cost at $.79 per cubic foot?
    A. $237,000   C. $284,800
    B. $275,982   D. $2,844,000

45. Prorated items that represent prepaid expenses of the seller should be shown on the settlement statement as a
    A. credit to the seller and debit to the buyer.
    B. debit to the seller and credit to the buyer.
    C. credit to buyer.
    D. debit to seller.

46. A mortgagor can get direct financing from all of the following EXCEPT
    A. mortgage banking companies.
    B. savings and loan associations.
    C. commercial banks.
    D. Ginnie Mae.

47. After the statute of limitations has run out, a contract that has been breached is which of the following?
    A. Unenforceable   C. Terminate
    B. Rescinded   D. Discharged

48. In the event the parties to a contract wish to delete a provision in the printed agreement form, they should
    A. execute a supplement to the purchase agreement.
    B. cross out the provisions to be deleted.
    C. have their signatures notarized.
    D. arrive at an oral agreement to make the changes.

49. A licensed real estate broker
    A. becomes an agent of the vendee upon obtaining a valid listing.
    B. can disclose any truthful information received from the principal.
    C. becomes an agent of the vendor when a buyer is found.
    D. must disclose all material facts to the principal.

50. How many acres are in the S½ of the NW¼ of the SE¼ of a section?
    A. 10   C. 40
    B. 20   D. 120

51. Greg listed his home with the XYZ Brokerage Company under an open listing agreement. After the sale of the property, a dispute arose between XYZ Brokerage and Sunday Brokerage; each claimed to be entitled to a commission. In this situation, the commission should be paid to the broker who
    A. listed the property.
    B. advertised the property.
    C. obtained the first offer.
    D. was the procuring cause of the sale.

52. Broker Sam has an exclusive-right-to-sell listing with Ned. While Ned is out of town on business, Sam finds a buyer who is interested in the house if Ned will take a purchase-money mortgage. However, the buyer must have a commitment from the seller prior to Ned's scheduled return to the city. Under these circumstances
    A. Sam may enter into a binding agreement on behalf of Ned.
    B. Sam may collect a commission even if the transaction falls through due to Ned's absence from the city.
    C. the buyer is deemed to have an option until Ned signs.
    D. Sam must obtain the signature of Ned in order to get a commission.

53. Sandy and Gary, who are not married, jointly own a parcel of real estate. Each owns an undivided interest. Sandy's share is two-thirds and Gary's share is one-third. This form of ownership is
    A. tenancy in common.
    B. joint tenancy.
    C. tenancy by the entirety.

54. Jay, an unmarried man, signed a contract to purchase real estate. The contract included a clause providing that Jay's liability would terminate and his deposit be refunded if a duplicate of the contract signed by the seller is not delivered to him within two days of the contract date. Owner Saul signed the contract the next day. The broker attempted to deliver the signed copy to Jay, but learned that he had since died as the result of an accident. In these circumstances

    A. because the seller had accepted the offer within the time limit, the estate of the deceased buyer is liable for completion of the contract.

    B. the contract, by its terms, is void.

    C. death cancels all real estate contracts.

    D. the broker can collect a commission from the seller.

55. Sam leases a property to Henry under an oral one-year lease. If Henry defaults, Sam may

    A. not bring court action because of parol evidence rule.

    B. not bring court action because of the statute of frauds.

    C. bring a court action because one-year leases need not be in writing to be enforced.

    D. bring a court action because the statute of limitations does not apply to oral leases.

56. Acceleration is a term associated with which of the following?

    A. Listings   C. Mortgages

    B. Sales contracts   D. Leases

57. The federal Fair Housing Act of 1968 makes it illegal to discriminate because of

    A. age.

    B. marital status.

    C. public assistance.

    D. religion.

58. Barclay owns a large parcel of undeveloped property, in severalty, very near a large urban area. Developer Longworth, who believes the property could be developed for commercial purposes, enters into an agreement with Barclay to purchase the property. Longworth insists that Barclay's wife sign the deed. The purpose of obtaining Mrs. Barclay's signature is to

    A. terminate any rights Mrs. Barclay may have in the property.

    B. defeat any curtesy rights.

    C. provide the developer with a sale-lease-back agreement.

    D. subordinate Barclay's wife's interest to that of Longworth.

59. Broker Allen enters into a listing agreement with seller Bennett wherein Bennett will receive $12,000 from the sale of a vacant lot and Allen will receive any sale proceeds over and above that amount. The type of listing agreement into which Allen and Bennett entered is

    A. called a gross listing

    B. a highly popular method of listing property in most states.

    C. called an exclusive agency.

    D. called a net listing.

60. If the annual net income from certain commercial property is $22,000, and the capitalization rate is 8 percent, what is the value of the property using the income approach?

    A. $275,000   C. $200,000

    B. $176,000   D. $183,000

61. If a storage tank that measures 12′ × 9′ × 8′ was designed to store natural gas, and the cost of natural gas is $1.82 per cubic foot, what does it cost to fill the tank to one-half its capacity?

    A. $864.00   C. $786.24

    B. $1,572.48   D. $684.58

62. A real estate sales contract becomes valid or in effect when it has been signed by which of the following?

    A. Buyer

    B. Buyer and seller

    C. Seller

    D. Broker and seller

63. Sandy and Chris enter into an agreement wherein Chris will mow Sandy's lawn every two weeks during the course of the summer. Shortly thereafter, Chris decides to go into a different business. George would like to assume Chris' duties mowing the lawn. Sandy agrees and enters into a new contract with George. Sandy and Chris tear up the original agreement. This is known as a(n)
    A. assignment.
    B. novation.
    C. secondary agreement.
    D. sublease.

64. All of the following situations are in violation of the federal Fair Housing Act of 1968 EXCEPT the
    A. refusal of property manager Joe Kelley to rent an apartment to a Catholic couple who are otherwise qualified.
    B. general policy of the Locust Loan Company, which avoids granting home improvement loans to individuals in "changing" neighborhoods.
    C. intentional neglect of broker Harvey Hall to show a black family any property listings of homes in all-white neighborhoods.
    D. insistence of Agnes Taylor, a widow, on renting her spare bedroom only to another woman.

65. If a house sold for $40,000, and the buyer obtained an FHA mortgage in the amount of $38,500, how much money would be paid for four points?
    A. $1,500   C. $1,540
    B. $385   D. $1,600

66. What is a tenancy at will?
    A. Tenancy with the consent of the landlord
    B. Tenancy that expires on a specific date
    C. Tenancy created by the death of the owner
    D. Tenancy created by the testator

67. Which of the following BEST describes a datum?
    A. Undersized or fractional section
    B. Imaginary line from which heights are measured
    C. Primary township
    D. Imaginary line that measures longitude

68. A licensed salesperson is authorized by law to
    A. sign a closing statement.
    B. collect a commission directly from a principal for performing assigned duties.
    C. advertise listed property under his or her own name.
    D. act under the supervision of a real estate broker.

69. Which of the following BEST describes steering?
    A. Leading prospective homeowners to or away from certain areas
    B. Refusing to make loans to persons in certain areas
    C. A requirement to join MLS
    D. Practice of setting commissions

70. In establishing priorities for liens
    A. a mechanic's lien is always first in priority.
    B. the date on which the lien was recorded determines priority.
    C. the date on which the debt was incurred determines priority.
    D. a broker's lien is automatically in first priority.

71. A management agreement usually covers which of the following items?
    A. Statement of owner's purpose
    B. Estoppel certificates
    C. Joint and several liability
    D. Waiver of subrogation

72. If either party to a real estate sales contract defaults, usually the other party can
    A. bring an action of adverse possession.
    B. declare the sale canceled and has no legal recourse.
    C. serve notice of redemption.
    D. sue for specific performance.

73. The taxes for 2001 are $743.25 and have not been paid. If the sale is to be closed on August 12, 2001, which of the following is true?
    A. $284.91 DS,CB   C. $284.91 CB,DS
    B. $458.32 DS,CB   D. $458.32 CB,DS

74. The supply of mortgage credit for single-family homes is regulated by the Federal Reserve System through the use of which of the following?
    A. Reserve requirements and discount rates
    B. Federal National Mortgage Association
    C. Federal Housing Administration
    D. Housing and Urban Development Corporation

75. In estimating the value of commercial property, what is the appraiser's most important consideration?
    A. Reproduction cost
    B. Net income
    C. Gross rent multiplier
    D. Gross income

76. All of the following are examples of a specific lien EXCEPT
    A. real estate taxes.   C. mortgage.
    B. IRS lien.   D. mechanic's lien.

77. Which of the following types of ownership are characterized by the right of survivorship?
    A. Joint tenancy and tenancy by the entireties
    B. Joint tenancy and severalty
    C. Joint tenancy and tenancy in common
    D. Joint tenancy and condominium tenancy

78. The type of ownership that blends severalty and tenancy in common ownership is a
    A. periodic tenancy.   C. cooperative.
    B. condominium.   D. life estate.

79. If K grants a life estate to L based on the life of M, and L dies before M; what is the status of the life estate?
    A. It belongs to K in fee simple absolute ownership.
    B. It belongs to K's remainderman.
    C. It belongs to M and the heirs of M.
    D. It belongs to L's heirs until the death of M.

80. A subdivision has a deed restriction that does not allow tree houses. An architect moves into the subdivision and builds a tree house in the back yard. How many neighbors will it take to enforce the deed restriction and what action should be taken?
    A. 75 percent of the neighbors must sign a petition that will be given to the local zoning board for enforcement.
    B. Only one neighbor needs to take action through the local zoning board.
    C. Only one neighbor needs to take action through the court system.
    D. 75 percent of the neighbors must take action through private court action.

81. A developer discovers that a proposed swimming pool in a condominium community meets all local zoning requirements except for the side yard line on one side of the clubhouse. What should the developer do?
    A. Because it's only on one side of the clubhouse, no action is necessary on the part of the developer.
    B. The developer should file for a variance with the local zoning board.
    C. The developer should file for a nonconforming use with the local zoning board.
    D. The developer should continue with the construction and later file for an adverse possession claim to the property.

82. A lot has been valued at $25,000. If the owner of a two-story house that measures 30' × 50' wants to net $35 a square foot and is willing to pay a 6 percent commission, the agent should list the property for at least what amount?
    A. $82,447   C. $111,702
    B. $82,150   D. $138,298

83. Which of the following situations would terminate a listing agreement without legal liability?
    A. Death of the agent
    B. Destruction of the broker's office
    C. Death of the seller
    D. Bankruptcy of the agent

84. An exclusive listing is usually an
    A. executory bilateral contract.
    B. exculpatory bilateral contract.
    C. executed unilateral contract.
    D. executed implied contract.

85. An agent listed a property for $89,000 and five days later received an offer of $89,000. Which of the following is true?

  A. The seller must accept the offer because it is for the listed price.
  B. The buyer cannot withdraw the offer because it is for the listed price.
  C. The seller does not have to accept the offer or pay the broker's commission unless she or he accepts the offer.
  D. The buyer may withdraw the offer prior to its acceptance.

86. A contract that stipulates an offer can be accepted within a specified time and contains a specified price and specified terms, which may or may not include the right of assignment, in return for the payment of consideration is known as a(n)

  A. sales contract.   C. offer.
  B. lease.   D. option.

87. Which of the following statements is NOT true?

  A. A land contract is also known as an installment contract.
  B. If a time for performance is not stated in a contract, the duties are expected to be performed within a reasonable time.
  C. An equitable title is transferred when the deed is signed by the grantor at the closing table.
  D. Liquidated damages are agreed to in advance by the buyer and seller to compensate one party if the other does not live up to the contract.

88. Which of the following is NOT false?

  A. An earnest money deposit is necessary to create a legally binding contract.
  B. The death of the agent will affect the status of listing contracts.
  C. If time is of the essence is found in a contract, then the contract must be performed within the time limit specified.
  D. A contract entered into under duress, undue influence or misrepresentation is void.

89. Because the cost of clean-up and removal of hazardous waste can be greater than the value of the property, an agent is expected to have

  A. a technical expertise in possible hazardous substances.
  B. a technical expertise in the area of asbestos, which is present in so many buildings.
  C. taken a class on how to identify asbestos, because it is present in so many buildings.
  D. a basic knowledge of hazardous substances and be aware of environmental issues in a real estate transaction.

90. The primary objectives of a property manager are to

  A. generate the highest net operating income of the property while maintaining and preserving the owner's investment.
  B. secure tenants by offering the lowest possible rents that the budget allows.
  C. negotiate contracts with service providers that give the manager the most advantageous kickbacks.
  D. cut expenses in any way necessary to generate a profit for the owner.

91. A lease with a definite beginning, a definite ending and no notice is required to terminate the lease is a(n)

  A. estate for years.
  B. periodic tenancy.
  C. estate at will.
  D. estate at sufferance.

92. A tenant entered into a three-year lease that was an estate for years agreement. Upon termination of the lease agreement, the tenant remained in possession of the property. Which of the following is true?

  A. If the landlord accepted payment for another month, the original lease automatically renewed for another term.
  B. The landlord could evict the tenant or treat the holdover tenant as a periodic tenancy.
  C. The tenant had the right to remain in the property because the landlord did not give proper notice.
  D. The tenant had the right to remain in the property because the landlord does not have it rented to anyone anyway.

93. Which of the following is NOT a requirement for a valid lease?
    A. Offer and acceptance
    B. Description of the leased premises
    C. Capacity to contract
    D. An option agreement

94. A property leases for $700 per month, plus 4 percent of all gross sales of more than $350,000. How much were the gross sales if the total rent paid for the year was $14,975?
    A. $414,375   C. $356,375
    B. $164,375   D. $514,375

95. A homeowner purchased a first principal place of residence for $69,000. In the next five years, she made $10,000 worth of improvements. The property sold for $109,000 and a 6 percent commission was paid. Which of the following is true regarding the capital gains?
    A. The adjusted basis is $102,460.
    B. The capital gain is $23,460.
    C. The capital gain is $33,460.
    D. The adjusted basis is $89,000.

96. Which of the following is true regarding the refinancing of property?
    A. A title search is conducted, the property is appraised and the borrower must requalify for the loan.
    B. The general rule of thumb is that a property should be refinanced when there is a 1 percent interest differential.
    C. If the borrowers have divorced, only one party's income will still be considered because only one name is now on the deed.
    D. If the borrowers have divorced, both parties' income will still be considered because both names are on the deed.

97. What is the priority of the following liens?
    A. IRS liens then property taxes
    B. IRS liens then special assessments
    C. First mortgage then property taxes
    D. Property taxes then first mortgage

98. A borrower purchased mortgagee's title insurance on a property. After the final payment was made on the mortgage, a title defect was found. The borrower may have recourse through the
    A. previous owner if a general warranty deed was transferred at the closing.
    B. previous owner if a quitclaim deed was transferred at the closing.
    C. title insurance company because a title policy was secured when the property was purchased.
    D. title insurance company even though a mortgagee's title insurance was secured when the property was purchased.

99. What is the major difference between constructive notice and actual notice?
    A. Constructive notice is direct knowledge while actual notice is legal notice.
    B. Constructive notice is documented at an attorney's office while actual notice is documented through the newspapers.
    C. Constructive notice provides protection because it is recorded by an attorney while actual notice can be recorded by an agent.
    D. Constructive notice is notice that the law presumes we have while actual notice is what a party actually knows.

100. Which of the following is NOT true regarding RESPA?
    A. RESPA requirements apply when a residential purchase is financed by a federally related mortgage loan.
    B. RESPA was enacted to eliminate kickbacks and other referral fees that increase the cost of settlement.
    C. RESPA requires that a good-faith estimate of settlement costs be provided to the buyer within two days of loan application.
    D. The settlement statement must be made available for inspection by the borrower at or before settlement.

ANSWERS

For additional information please refer to the page number in parenthesis.

1. C $37,500 – 25,000 = $12,500

$$\frac{\$750}{\$25,000 \mid 3\%}$$
×

$$\frac{\$625}{\$12,500 \mid 5\%}$$
×

(171)

$750 + 625 = $1,375
$37,500 – 1,375 = $36,125

2. C   Nolan is the only party bound to the contract; therefore it is a unilateral contract. (40)

3. A   20% + 40% = 60%

$$\frac{\$3,600 \div}{\$6,000 \mid 60\%}$$

$$\frac{\$6,000 \div}{\$120,000 \mid 5\%}$$

(168)

4. D   By definition of term loan. (117)
5. B   Ownership in severalty is ownership by one party. (21)
6. B   A deficiency judgment allows a mortgagee to sue for the balance owned when the security for a loan is insufficient to satisfy the debt. (129)
7. B   The Torrens system is a method of registering land, and the Torrens certificate is proof of ownership. (8)
8. B   A title transferred by a quitclaim deed provides no warranties. It transfers whatever interest the grantor has in the property. (95)
9. B   In an open listing, the seller retains the right to sell the property and not pay a commission to the broker. (28)
10. A   The buyer's interest in the property when legal title is held by another party is known as equitable title. (41)
11. B   A deed in trust conveys title to the trustee to manage property for the trustor, but it does not indicate the sale of property. (115)

12. B   A = 50′ × 137′   6,850 × $4.50 = $30,825

$$\frac{\$2,234.81}{\$30,825 \mid 7.25\%}$$
×

(168, 174)

A = 6,850 s.f.

13. A   The buyer owes interest from June 15 through June 30, or 15 days.

$$\frac{\$4,143.75}{\$42,500 \mid 9.75\%}$$
×

$4,143.75 ÷ 360 = $11.51 $11.51 × 15 = $172.65   (179)

14. A   To transfer a title, a deed is signed by the grantors. (96)
15. D   Proof of heirship is not one of the requirements for a valid deed. (96)
16. A   The rental of rooms in an owner-occupied one- to four-family dwelling is exempt from the federal Fair Housing Act. No broker can be used and the owner cannot discriminate in advertising. (146)
17. B   Property managers are usually paid a percentage of the gross income. (169)
18. A   The commission is a debit to the seller on a settlement sheet. (179)
19. B   The sellers owe the remaining month's rent to the buyer. (179)
20. C   RESPA requires the lender to make the proper disclosures. (94)
21. D   A purchase agreement would least likely be recorded at the county recorder's office. (8)
22. B   State laws require that all listed property be advertised through the broker. (156)
23. B   State laws require that parties receive a copy of all contracts they sign. (156)
24. C   If written consent is secured from the seller, all the brokers in the open listing can place signs on the property. (142)

25. D DUST is the acronym to remember the economic characteristics of real estate. Demand, utility, scarcity and transferability make real estate valuable. (18)
26. B By definition of capitalization rate. (14)
27. A Adjustments are made in the amenities of the comparable properties. (13)
28. D The final step in the appraisal process is to reconcile the difference to arrive at the value. (13)
29. B If the property is uninhabitable, the tenant may leave the property. This is known as constructive eviction. (73)
30. A Tenancy at sufferance is created when the tenant refuses to surrender possession of the property upon the expiration of the lease. (70)
31. A By definition of remainder interest. (27)
32. A A fee simple defeasible title is transferred when the real estate is conveyed with specified conditions. (27)
33. B The buyer and/or seller may pay the points in FHA insured loans. (118)
34. B In title-theory states, the lender has title to the property. (115)
35. A The Sherman Antitrust Act and state laws prohibit price fixing. (8)
36. D All are examples of public and private land-use controls. (24)

37. B $$\frac{\$5{,}450.78}{\$198{,}210 \mid 2.75\%} \quad\quad \$5{,}450.78 + 400 = \$5{,}850.78$$
$$\times$$

38. A By definition of net lease.
39. B The landlord's interest is a leased fee interest, while the tenant's interest is a leasehold interest. (69)

40. C $\$6.50 \div 100 = .065$ $\dfrac{\$48{,}240}{\$72{,}000 \mid 67\%}$ $\dfrac{\$3{,}135.60}{\$48{,}240 \mid .065}$ $\$3{,}135.60 \div 12 = \$261.30$ (170)
$$\times \quad\quad\quad \times$$

41. A $$\frac{\$50{,}000 \div}{\$62{,}500 \mid 80\%} \quad\quad (171)$$

42. D Nonjudicial foreclosure does not involve civil action. The lender is allowed to foreclose by advertisement. (129)

43. B

Debit	Credit		$26,360		$65,900 − 26,360 = $39,540
$65,900.00	$39,540.00	$65,900	40%		
395.40		×			
450.00		$395.40		$66,745.40	
$66,745.40	$39,540.00	$39,540	1%	−39,540.00	
		×		$27,205.40	(179)

44. D V = 200′ × 300′ × 12′   720,000 × .79 = $568,880 × 5 = $2,844,000   (184)
V = 720,000 c.f.

45. A Prepaid expenses are a credit to the seller and a debit to the buyer. (179)
46. D Ginnie Mae does not negotiate loans. (119)
47. A A contract not performed within the statutory time period is unenforceable. (41)
48. A To delete a provision in an agreement, the parties should execute a supplement to the purchase agreement. (45)
49. D A broker is required by the law of agency to disclose all material facts to the principal. (47)
50. B 640 ÷ 4 ÷ 4 ÷ 2 = 20 acres (4)
51. D The party who is the procuring cause of the sale should be paid the commission. (28)
52. D An agent cannot accept offers for a seller unless authorized to do so by the seller through a power of attorney or other legal document. (29)
53. A Tenancy in common ownership allows unequal shares of the real estate. (21)

54. B   The signed contract was not received by the buyer within two days and upon the death of the buyer became void. (42)
55. C   Leases for less than one year need not be in writing and are enforceable. (74)
56. C   An acceleration clause in the mortgage allows the lender to call the entire mortgage balance due and payable. (128)
57. D   Religion is a protected status under the federal Fair Housing Act. (145)
58. A   Longworth wants to assure that Mrs. Barclay has released her dower rights to the property. (23)
59. D   By definition of net listing. (28)

60. A $$\frac{\$22,000 \div}{\$275,000 \mid 8\%}$$ (175)

61. C $V = 12' \times 9' \times 8'$ $864 \times \$1.82 = \$1,572.48 \div 2 = \$786.24$ (184)
    $V = 864$ cu.ft.

62. B   The sales contract becomes valid when signed by the buyer and seller. (39)
63. B   By definition of novation. (41)
64. D   A homeowner can rent a spare bedroom and discriminate because of gender. (145)

65. C $$\frac{\$1,540}{\$38,500 \mid 4\%}$$ (172)
    $\times$

66. A   A tenancy at will is a lease for an uncertain duration that is created with the consent of the landlord. (70)
67. B   By definition of datum. (3)
68. D   An agent can work only under the authority of a broker. (152)
69. A   By definition of steering. (145)
70. B   Unless there are unusual circumstances, the date on which the lien was recorded determines priority. (90)
71. A   A management agreement must contain a statement of the owner's purpose. (66)
72. D   By definition of specific performance. (42)
73. B   Count from January 1 through August 12 for 222 days. (179–180)

    $\$743.25 \div 360 = \$2.0645$ $\$2.0645 \times 222 = \$458.32$

74. A   The purpose of the Federal Reserve is to regulate the flow of money by regulating reserve requirements and discount rates. (112)
75. B   The annual net operating income is used to compute the value of the property. (14)
76. B   An IRS lien is a general lien against real and personal property. (91)
77. A   By definition of joint tenancy and tenancy by the entireties. (21)
78. B   When an owner purchases a condominium, the air space is owned in severalty; whereas the land and the improvements on the land are owned by all members in the condominium community as tenancy in common. (20)
79. D   L has been granted a life estate pur autre vie based on the life of M. Should L predecease M, L's heirs inherit the life estate as long as M was alive. (23)
80. C   Only one neighbor is necessary to enforce the deed restrictions through court action. (24)
81. B   A variance may be granted to relieve the harshness of a zoning ordinance. (24)

82. D $100\% - 6\% = 94\%$ $$\frac{\$130,000 \div}{\$138,297.87 \mid 94\%}$$ (168, 184)
    $A = 30' \times 50' = 1,500 \times 2 = 3,000$ s.f. $\times$
    $3,000 \times \$35 = \$105,000$
    $\$105,000 + 25,000 = \$130,000$

83. C   Upon the death of either the principal broker or the seller, the listing is void. (29)
84. A   A listing contract is an executory contract in that something remains to be performed by one or more parties. It is a bilateral contract because all parties are bound to the contract. (40)
85. D   An offer can be rescinded at any time prior to its acceptance. The seller does not have to accept a full price offer, but a commission is due the broker. (44)
86. D   By definition of option contract. (42)
87. C   The legal title is transferred to the buyer at the closing, not equitable title. (113)
88. C   When time is of the essence is stated in a contract, it means that the contract must be performed within the specified time limit. Any party that does not perform within the proper time period is liable for breach of contract. (41)
89. D   Agents are not expected to be experts in the area of hazardous substances, but should have a basic knowledge so all parties in the transaction can make informed decisions. (66)
90. A   The objectives of a property manager are to generate the highest net operating income from a property while maintaining, modernizing and preserving the owner's interest. (67)
91. A   By the definition of estate for years. (70)
92. B   If the tenant remains in possession of the property after the expiration of the lease, the landlord may evict the tenant or accept payment from the tenant and create a periodic tenancy. (70)
93. D   A lease does not have to contain an option agreement to be valid. (70)

94. D $700 × 12 = $8,400 $6,575 ÷ $164,375   (170)
        $14,975 − 8,400 = $6,575 $164,375 | 4%   +350,000
                                                                                         $514,375

95. B $69,000 + 10,000 = $79,000 adjusted basis
        $109,000 − 6% = $102,460 net to seller
        $102,460 − 79,000 = $23,460 capital gains (177)
96. A   When a property is refinanced, a title search is conducted, the property is appraised, the borrower must qualify for the loan and closing costs must be paid. (131)
97. D   Property taxes and special assessments are paid before all other liens. (91)
98. A   If a general warranty deed was given, there may be recourse through the previous owner. (96)
99. D   By definitions of constructive and actual notice. (8)
100. C   The good-faith estimate must be given to the buyer within three days of loan application. (94)

Appendix I

WEB SITE DIRECTORY

Alabama Real Estate Commission
www.arec.state.al.us

Americans with Disabilities Act
www.usdoj.gov/crt/ada/adahom1.htm

American Society of Home Inspectors
www.ashi.com/

Appraisal Foundation
www.appraisalfoundation.org

Appraisal Institute
www.appraisalinstitute.org

Building Owners and Managers Association
www.boma.org

Department of Housing and Urban Development
www.hud.gov/

Department of Veterans Affairs
www.va.gov/

Environmental Protection Agency
www.epa.gov

Fannie Mae
www.fanniemae.com

Federal Emergency Management Agency
www.fema.gov/

Federal Reserve
www.federalreserve.gov

Freddie Mac
www.freddiemac.com

Georgia Real Estate Commission
www.state.ga.us/ga.real_estate/

Ginnie Mae
www.ginniemae.gov

Illinois Office of Banks and Real Estate
www.state.il.us/obr

Internal Revenue Service
www.irs.gov

Institute of Real Estate Management
www.irem.org

Lead Safe USA
www.leadsafeusa.com/

Michigan Board of Real Estate
www.cis.state.mi.us/bcs.re

Missouri Real Estate Commission
www.ecodev.state.mo.us/pr/restate

Montana
**http://www.discoveringmontana.com/dli/
bsd/pol/bus_licensing_boards.htm**

National Association of Exclusive Buyer Agents
www.naeba.com

National Association of Home Builders
www.nahb.com/

National Association of Independent Fee Appraisers
www.naifa.com

National Association of Real Estate Brokers
www.nareb.com

National Association of REALTORS®
www.realtor.com

National Association of Residential Property Managers
www.narpm.com

National Fair Housing Advocate Online
www.fairhousing.com/

Nebraska
www.nol.org/home/nrec/

North Dakota
ddschulz@pioneer.state.nd.us

Real Estate Buyer's Agent Council
www.rebac net

Real Estate News
www.inman.com

Reverse Mortgages
www.financialfreedom.com

South Dakota
www.state.sd.us/SDREC

U.S. Department of Justice, Antitrust Division
www.usdoj.gov/atr

U.S. Farm Service Agency
www.fsa.usda.gov

Wyoming Real Estate Commission
http://realestate.state.wy.us/

Form 8300

(Rev. August 1997)

Department of the Treasury
Internal Revenue Service

Report of Cash Payments Over $10,000
Received in a Trade or Business

▶ See instructions for definition of cash.
▶ Use this form for transactions occurring after July 31, 1997.
Please type or print.

OMB No. 1545-0892

1 Check appropriate box(es) if: **a** ☐ Amends prior report; **b** ☐ Suspicious transaction.

Part I Identity of Individual From Whom the Cash Was Received

2 If more than one individual is involved, check here and see instructions . . . . ▶ ☐

3 Last name **4** First name **5** M.I. **6** Taxpayer identification number

7 Address (number, street, and apt. or suite no.) **8** Date of birth (see instructions) ▶ M M D D Y Y Y Y

9 City **10** State **11** ZIP code **12** Country (if not U.S.) **13** Occupation, profession, or business

14 Document used to verify identity: **a** Describe identification ▶ ....
b Issued by .... **c** Number ....

Part II Person on Whose Behalf This Transaction Was Conducted

15 If this transaction was conducted on behalf of more than one person, check here and see instructions . . . . . ▶ ☐

16 Individual's last name or Organization's name **17** First name **18** M.I. **19** Taxpayer identification number

20 Doing business as (DBA) name (see instructions) Employer identification number

21 Address (number, street, and apt. or suite no.) **22** Occupation, profession, or business

23 City **24** State **25** ZIP code **26** Country (if not U.S.)

27 Alien identification: **a** Describe identification ▶ ....
b Issued by .... **c** Number ....

Part III Description of Transaction and Method of Payment

28 Date cash received M M D D Y Y Y Y

29 Total cash received $ _____ .00

30 If cash was received in more than one payment, check here . . . . ▶ ☐

31 Total price if different from item 29 $ _____ .00

32 Amount of cash received (in U.S. dollar equivalent) (must equal item 29) (see instructions):

a U.S. currency $ _____ .00 (Amount in $100 bills or higher $ _____ .00)
b Foreign currency $ _____ .00 (Country ▶ _____)
c Cashier's check(s) $ _____ .00 Issuer's name(s) and serial number(s) of the monetary instrument(s) ▶ ....
d Money order(s) $ _____ .00
e Bank draft(s) $ _____ .00
f Traveler's check(s) $ _____ .00

33 Type of transaction

a ☐ Personal property purchased
b ☐ Real property purchased
c ☐ Personal services provided
d ☐ Business services provided
e ☐ Intangible property purchased
f ☐ Debt obligations paid
g ☐ Exchange of cash
h ☐ Escrow or trust funds
i ☐ Bail bond
j ☐ Other (specify) ▶

34 Specific description of property or service shown in 33. (Give serial or registration number, address, docket number, etc.) ▶ ....

Part IV Business That Received Cash

35 Name of business that received cash **36** Employer identification number

37 Address (number, street, and apt. or suite no.) Social security number

38 City **39** State **40** ZIP code **41** Nature of your business

42 Under penalties of perjury, I declare that to the best of my knowledge the information I have furnished above is true, correct, and complete.

Signature of authorized official Title of authorized official

43 Date of signature M M D D Y Y Y Y **44** Type or print name of contact person **45** Contact telephone number ( )

For Paperwork Reduction Act Notice, see page 4. Cat. No. 62133S Form **8300** (Rev. 8-97)

Form 8300 (Rev. 8-97) Page **2**

Multiple Parties
(Complete applicable parts below if box 2 or 15 on page 1 is checked)

Part I   Continued—Complete if box 2 on page 1 is checked

3 Last name	**4** First name	**5** M.I.	**6** Taxpayer identification number

7 Address (number, street, and apt. or suite no.)   **8** Date of birth . . ▶ M M D D Y Y Y Y (see instructions)

9 City	**10** State	**11** ZIP code	**12** Country (if not U.S.)	**13** Occupation, profession, or business

14 Document used to verify identity: **a** Describe identification ▶ ----------------------------------
   b Issued by   **c** Number

3 Last name	**4** First name	**5** M.I.	**6** Taxpayer identification number

7 Address (number, street, and apt. or suite no.)   **8** Date of birth . . ▶ M M D D Y Y Y Y (see instructions)

9 City	**10** State	**11** ZIP code	**12** Country (if not U.S.)	**13** Occupation, profession, or business

14 Document used to verify identity: **a** Describe identification ▶ ----------------------------------
   b Issued by   **c** Number

Part II   Continued—Complete if box 15 on page 1 is checked

16 Individual's last name or Organization's name	**17** First name	**18** M.I.	**19** Taxpayer identification number

20 Doing business as (DBA) name (see instructions)	Employer identification number

21 Address (number, street, and apt. or suite no.)	**22** Occupation, profession, or business

23 City	**24** State	**25** ZIP code	**26** Country (if not U.S.)

27 Alien identification: **a** Describe identification ▶ ----------------------------------
   b Issued by   **c** Number

16 Individual's last name or Organization's name	**17** First name	**18** M.I.	**19** Taxpayer identification number

20 Doing business as (DBA) name (see instructions)	Employer identification number

21 Address (number, street, and apt. or suite no.)	**22** Occupation, profession, or business

23 City	**24** State	**25** ZIP code	**26** Country (if not U.S.)

27 Alien identification: **a** Describe identification ▶ ----------------------------------
   b Issued by   **c** Number

Glossary

abandonment. The voluntary and permanent cessation of use or enjoyment with no intention to resume or reclaim one's possession or interest. May pertain to an easement or a property.

abstract of title. A condensed version of the history of title to a particular parcel of real estate, as recorded in the county clerk's records; consists of a summary of the original grant and all subsequent conveyances and encumbrances affecting the property.

abutting. The joining, reaching or touching of adjoining land. Abutting parcels of land have a common boundary.

accelerated depreciation. A method of calculating for tax purposes the depreciation of income property at a faster rate than would be achieved using the straight-line method. Note that any depreciation taken in excess of that which would be claimed using the straight-line rate is subject to recapture as ordinary income to the extent of gain resulting from the sale. See also straight-line method.

acceleration clause. A provision in a written mortgage, note, bond or conditional sales contract that, in the event of default, the whole amount of principal and interest may be declared to be due and payable at once.

accretion. An increase or addition to land by the deposit of sand or soil washed up naturally from a river, lake or sea.

accrued depreciation. The actual depreciation that has occurred to a property at any given date; the difference between the cost of replacement new (as of the date of appraisal) and the present appraised value.

acknowledgment. A declaration made by a person to a notary public, or other public official authorized to take acknowledgments, that an instrument was executed by him or her as a free and voluntary act.

actual eviction. The result of legal action originated by a lessor, whereby a defaulted tenant is physically ousted from the rented property pursuant to a court order. See also eviction.

actual notice. Express information or fact; that which is known; actual knowledge.

adjustable rate mortgage. A mortgage in which the interest rate changes at predetermined intervals. The mortgage has caps or a ceiling that limit the amount it can change at the predetermined intervals.

administrator. The party appointed by the county court to settle the estate of a deceased person who died without leaving a will.

ad valorem tax. A tax levied according to value; generally used to refer to real estate tax. Also called the general tax.

adverse possession. The right of an occupant of land to acquire title against the real owner, where possession has been actual, continuous, hostile, visible and distinct for the statutory period.

affidavit. A written statement signed and sworn to before a person authorized to administer an oath.

agent. One who represents or has the power to act for another person (called the principal). The authorization may be express or implied. A fiduciary relationship is created under the law of agency when a property owner, as the principal, executes a listing agreement or management contract authorizing a licensed real estate broker to be his or her agent.

agreement of sale. A written agreement whereby the purchaser agrees to buy certain real estate and the seller agrees to sell, upon terms and conditions set forth in the agreement.

air lot. A designated airspace over a piece of land. Air lots, like surface property, may be transferred.

air rights. The right to use the open space above a property, generally allowing the surface to be used for another purpose.

alienation. The act of transferring property to another. Alienation may be voluntary, such as by gift or sale, or involuntary, such as through eminent domain or adverse possession.

alienation clause. The clause in a mortgage or deed of trust that states that the balance of the secured debt becomes immediately due and payable at the mortgagee's option if the property is sold by the mortgagor. In effect, this clause prevents the mortgagor from assigning the debt without the mortgagee's approval.

alluvion. New deposits of soil as the result of accretion.

amenities. The tangible and intangible features that increase the value or desirability of real estate.

Americans with Disabilities Act. The ADA is a federal law that became effective in 1992. It is designed to eliminate discrimination against individuals with disabilities by mandating equal access to jobs, public accommodations, public transportation, telecommunications and government services.

amortization. The liquidation of a financial burden by installment payments.

amortized loan. A loan in which the principal as well as the interest is payable in monthly or other periodic installments over the term of the loan.

antitrust laws. The laws designed to preserve the free enterprise of the open marketplace by making illegal certain private conspiracies and combinations formed to minimize competition. Violations of antitrust laws in the real estate business generally involve either price fixing (brokers conspiring to set fixed compensation rates) or allocation of customers or markets (brokers agreeing to limit their areas of trade or dealing to certain areas or properties).

appraisal. An estimate of the quantity, quality or value of something. The process through which conclusions of property value are obtained; also refers to the report setting forth the process of estimation and conclusion of value.

appraised value. An estimate of a property's present worth.

appreciation. An increase in the worth or value of a property due to economic or related causes which may prove to be either temporary or permanent; opposite of depreciation.

appurtenant. Belonging to; incident to; annexed to. For example, a garage is appurtenant to a house, and the common interest in the common elements of a condominium is appurtenant to each apartment. Appurtenances pass with the land when the property is transferred.

arbitration. A means of settling a controversy between two parties through the medium of an impartial third party whose decision on the controversy (it is agreed) will be final and binding.

assemblage. The process of merging two or more parcels of real estate to create one parcel.

assessment. The imposition of a tax, charge or levy, usually according to established rates.

assignment. The transfer in writing of rights or interest in a bond, mortgage, lease or other instrument.

assumption of mortgage. The transfer of title to property to a grantee wherein he assumes liability for payment of an existing note secured by a mortgage against the property; should the mortgage be foreclosed and the property sold for a lesser amount than that due, the grantee-purchaser who has assumed and agreed to pay the debt secured by the mortgage is personally liable for the deficiency. Before a seller may be relieved of liability under the existing mortgage, the lender must accept the transfer of liability for payment of the note.

attachment. The method by which a debtor's property is placed in the custody of the law and held as security pending outcome of a creditor's suit.

attorney-in-fact. The holder of a power of attorney.

attorney's opinion of title. An instrument written and signed by the attorney who examines the title, stating his or her opinion as to whether a seller may convey good title.

automatic extension. A clause in a listing agreement that states that the agreement will continue automatically for a certain period of time after its expiration date. In many states, use of this clause is discouraged or prohibited.

avulsion. The sudden removal of land by natural forces, such as an earthquake.

balloon payment. The final payment of a mortgage loan that is considerably larger than the required periodic payments because the loan amount was not fully amortized.

bargain and sale deed. A deed that carries with it no warranties against liens or other encumbrances, but that does imply that the grantor has the right to convey title. Note that the grantor may add warranties to the deed at his or her discretion.

base line. One of a set of imaginary lines running east and west and crossing a principal meridian at a definite point, used by surveyors for reference in locating and describing land under the rectangular survey system (or government survey method) of property description.

bench mark. A permanent reference mark or point established for use by surveyors in measuring differences in elevation.

beneficiary. 1. The person for whom a trust operates, or in whose behalf the income from a trust estate is drawn. 2. A lender who lends money on real estate and takes back a note and deed of trust from the borrower.

bequest. A provision in a will providing for the distribution of personal property.

bilateral contract. A contract in which each party promises to perform an act in exchange for the other party's promise to perform.

bill of sale. A written instrument given to pass title to personal property.

binder. An agreement that may accompany an earnest money deposit for the purchase of real property as evidence of the purchaser's good faith and intent to complete the transaction.

blanket mortgage. A mortgage covering more than one parcel of real estate, providing for each parcel's partial release from the mortgage lien upon repayment of a definite portion of the debt.

blockbusting. The illegal practice of inducing homeowners to sell their properties by making representations regarding the entry or prospective entry of minority persons into the neighborhood.

blue-sky laws. The common name for those state laws that regulate the registration and sale of investment securities.

branch office. A secondary place of business apart from the principal or main office from which real estate business is conducted. A branch office generally must be run by a licensed real estate broker working on behalf of the broker operating the principal office.

breach of contract. The failure, without legal excuse, of one of the parties to a contract to perform according to the contract.

broker. One who buys and sells for another for a commission. See also real estate broker.

brokerage. The business of buying and selling for another for a commission.

budget loan. A loan in which the monthly payments made by the borrower cover not only interest and a payment on the principal, but also one-twelfth of such expenses as taxes, insurance, assessments and similar charges.

budget mortgage. A mortgage wherein the monthly payment includes principal, interest, taxes, and insurance.

buffer zone. A zone or space between two different use districts. An example of a buffer zone would be a park between a residential district and a commercial district.

building code. An ordinance specifying minimum standards of construction of buildings for the protection of public safety and health.

building line. A line fixed at a certain distance from the front and/or sides of a lot beyond which no structure can project; a setback line used to ensure a degree of uniformity in the appearance of buildings and unobstructed light, air and view.

building restrictions. The limitations on the size or type of property improvements established by zoning acts or by deed or lease restrictions.

bulk zoning. Bulk zoning controls the density of the development on land to avoid overcrowding.

bundle of legal rights. The theory that land ownership involves ownership of all legal rights to the land such as possession, control within the law, and enjoyment, rather than ownership of the land itself.

buydown mortgage. A mortgage in which the interest rate is reduced by paying interest in advance. A temporary buydown is for the initial years of the loan. A permanent buydown is for the life of the loan.

capacity of parties. The legal ability of persons to enter into a valid contract. Most persons have full capacity to contract, and are said to be competent parties.

capital gains. A tax on the profits realized from the sale of a capital asset.

capital investment. The initial capital and the long-term expenditures made to establish and maintain a business or investment property.

capitalization. The process of converting into present value (or obtaining the present worth of) a series of anticipated future periodic installments of net income. In real estate appraising, it usually takes the form of discounting. The formula is expressed:

$$\frac{\text{Income}}{\text{Rate}} = \text{Value}$$

capitalization rate. The rate of return a property will produce on the owner's investment.

cash flow. The net spendable income from an investment, determined by deducting all operating and fixed expenses from the gross income. If expenses exceed income, a negative cash flow is the result.

casualty insurance. A type of insurance policy that protects a property owner or other person from loss or injury sustained as a result of theft, vandalism or similar occurrences.

caveat emptor. A Latin phrase meaning "Let the buyer beware."

caveat venditor. A Latin phrase meaning "Let the seller beware."

certificate of eligibility. A certificate given by the federal government to qualified veterans to show their remaining eligibility for a VA guaranteed loan.

certificate of occupancy. A certificate of occupancy is issued after the building is inspected to make sure it complies with building codes.

certificate of reasonable value. A certificate issued by the Veterans Administration certifying the value, as determined by an approved VA appraiser, of property secured by a VA mortgage.

certificate of sale. The document generally given to a purchaser at a tax foreclosure sale. A certificate of sale does not convey title; generally it is an instrument certifying that the holder received title to the property after the redemption period had passed and that the holder paid the property taxes for that interim period.

certificate of title. A statement of opinion on the status of the title to a parcel of real property based on an examination of specified public records.

chain of title. The succession of conveyances from some accepted starting point whereby the present holder of real property derives his or her title.

chattel. Personal property.

City Planning Commission. A local governmental organization designed to direct and control the development of land within a municipality.

cloud on title. A claim or encumbrance that may affect title to land.

codicil. An addition to a will that alters, explains, adds to or confirms the will, but does not revoke it.

coinsurance clause. A clause in insurance policies covering real property that requires the policyholder to maintain fire insurance; coverage is generally equal to at least 80 percent of the property's actual replacement cost.

collateral. Something of value given or pledged to a lender as security for a debt or obligation.

commercial property. A classification of real estate which includes income-producing property such as office buildings, restaurants, shopping centers, hotels and stores.

commingled property. That property of a married couple which is so mixed or commingled that it is difficult to determine whether it is separate or community property. Commingled property becomes community property.

commingling. The illegal act of a real estate broker who mixes the money of other people with that of his or her own; by law, brokers are required to maintain a separate trust account for the funds of other parties held temporarily by the broker.

commission. The payment made to a broker for services rendered, such as in the sale or purchase of real property; usually a percentage of the selling price of the property.

common elements. Those parts of a property that are necessary or convenient to the existence, maintenance and safety of a condominium, or are normally used in common by all of the condominium residents. All condominium owners have an undivided ownership interest in the common elements.

common law. The body of law based on custom, usage and court decisions.

community property. A system of property ownership based on the theory that each spouse has an equal interest in the property acquired by the efforts of either spouse during marriage.

Community Reinvestment Act. A part of the Housing and Community Development Act passed in 1977. The purpose of the Act is to prevent the practice of redlining and disinvestment by lenders in certain areas of a city.

comparables. The properties listed in an appraisal report that are substantially equivalent to the subject property.

competent parties. Those persons who are recognized by law as being able to contract with others; usually those of legal age and sound mind.

condemnation. A judicial or administrative proceeding to exercise the power of eminent domain, by which a government agency takes private property for public use and compensates the owner.

conditional-use permit. A permit granted which allows the holder to build a special purpose property which is inconsistent with zoning in the area. A conditional permit is generally issued to allow buildings for the good of the public such as hospitals and houses of worship in a residential area.

condominium. The absolute ownership of an apartment or a unit, generally in a multi-unit building, based on a legal description of the airspace that the unit actually occupies, plus an undivided interest in the ownership of the common elements which are owned jointly with the other condominium unit owners. The entire tract of real estate included in a condominium development is called a parcel, or development parcel. One apartment or space in a condominium building or a part of a property intended for independent use and having lawful access to a public way is called a unit. Ownership of one unit also includes a definite undivided interest in the common elements.

conformity. The maximum value is achieved when the property is in harmony with its surroundings.

contribution. The value of any part of the property is measured by its effect on the value of the whole.

consideration. Something of value that induces one to enter into a contract. Consideration may be "valuable" (money or commodity) or "good" (love and affection).

constructive eviction. 1. Acts done by the landlord that so materially disturb or impair the tenant's enjoyment of the leased premises that the tenant is effectively forced to move out and terminate the lease without liability for any further rent. 2. A purchaser's inability to obtain clear title.

constructive notice. Notice given to the world by recorded documents. All persons are charged with knowledge of such documents and their contents, whether or not they have actually examined them. Possession of property is also considered constructive notice that the person in possession has an interest in the property.

contingency. A provision in a contract that requires completion or that a certain event occurs before the contract becomes binding.

contract. An agreement entered into by two or more legally competent parties by the terms of which one or more of the parties, for a consideration, undertakes to do or to refrain from doing some legal act or acts. A contract may be either unilateral, where only one party is bound to act, or bilateral, where all parties to the instrument are legally bound to act as prescribed.

contract for deed. A contract for the sale of real estate wherein the sales price is paid in periodic installments by the purchaser, who is in possession although title is retained by the seller until final payment. Also called an installment contract or a land contract.

contract for exchange of real estate. A contract of sale of real estate in which the consideration is paid wholly or partly in property.

conventional life estate. A life estate created by the grantor rather than by law.

conventional mortgage. A mortgage (loan) where real property is used as security for the payment of the debt and the loan is not insured through FHA or guaranteed by VA.

conventional insured mortgage A mortgage (loan) wherein the borrower has less than a 20 percent down payment. The lender may require the borrower to purchase private mortgage insurance to reduce the lender's risk.

conventional uninsured mortgage. A mortgage (loan) wherein the borrower has a 20 percent or greater down payment and the lender accepts the creditworthiness of the borrower and the property as security for the loan.

conveyance. A written instrument that evidences transfer of some interest in real property from one person to another.

cooperative. A residential multi-unit building whose title is held by a trust or corporation, which is owned by and operated for the benefit of persons living within the building, who are the beneficial owners of the trust or stockholders of the corporation, each having a proprietary lease.

corporation. An entity or organization created by operation of law whose rights of doing business are essentially the same as those of an individual. The entity has continuous existence until dissolved according to legal procedures.

correction lines. Used in the government survey to compensate for the curvature of the earth.

cost approach. The process of estimating the value of a a special purchase property. The formula is reproduction or replacement cost minus depreciation plus land equals value.

counseling. The business of providing people with expert advice on a subject, based on the counselor's extensive, expert knowledge of the subject.

counteroffer. A new offer made as a reply to an offer received, having the effect of voiding the original offer, which cannot be accepted thereafter unless revived by the offeror's repeating it.

covenant of quiet enjoyment. 1. In a deed, this covenant assures that the grantee and his or her heirs have the right to the property free from interference from the acts or claims of third parties. 2. In a lease, this covenant assures the tenants' right of possession without interference from the landlord or third parties.

covenants. A covenant is a promise to do or refrain from an act. The covenants found in a general warranty deed are seizen, encumbrances, further assurance, quiet enjoyment and warranty forever.

cul-de-sac. A dead-end street that widens sufficiently at the end to permit an automobile to make a U-turn.

curable depreciation. When the cost of fixing the property does not exceed the value of the property.

curtesy. A life estate, usually a fractional interest, given by some states to the surviving husband in real estate owned by his deceased wife. Many states have abolished curtesy.

cycle. A recurring sequence of events that regularly follow one another, generally within a fixed interval of time. The cycle of real estate is growth, stability, decline and restoration.

datum. A horizontal plane from which heights and depths are measured.

dba. Doing business as.

debenture. A note or bond given as evidence of debt and issued without security.

debt. Something owed to another; an obligation to pay or return something.

debt service. A borrower's periodic payment, comprised of principal and interest, on the unpaid balance of a mortgage.

decreasing returns. When adding improvements to the land does not produce a proportional increase in the property value.

deed. A written instrument that, when executed and delivered, conveys title to or an interest in real estate.

deed in trust. A three party instrument in which the trustor conveys legal title to the trustee for the benefit of the beneficiary. That trustee has full power to sell, mortgage and subdivide a parcel of real estate. The beneficiary controls the trustee's use of these powers under the provisions of the trust agreement.

deed of reconveyance. The instrument used to reconvey title to a trustor under a deed of trust once the debt has been satisfied.

deed of trust. An instrument used to create a mortgage lien by which the mortgagor conveys his or her title to a trustee, who holds it as security for the benefit of the note holder (the lender); also called a trust deed.

deed restrictions. The clauses in a deed limiting the future uses of the property. Deed restrictions may impose a vast variety of limitations and conditions, such as limiting the density of buildings, dictating the types of structures that can be erected and preventing buildings from being used for specific purposes or from being used at all.

default. The nonperformance of a duty, whether arising under a contract or otherwise; failure to meet an obligation when due.

defeasance. A provision or condition in a deed or in a separate instrument which, being performed, renders the instrument void.

defeasible fee estate. An estate in land in which the holder has fee simple title subject to being divested upon the happening of a specified condition. Two categories: (1) fee simple determinable or special limitation and (2) fee simple subject to a condition subsequent.

deficiency judgment. A personal judgment levied against the mortgagor when a foreclosure sale does not produce sufficient funds to pay the mortgage debt in full.

delinquent taxes. Those unpaid taxes that are past due.

delivery. The legal act of transferring ownership. Documents such as deeds and mortgages must be delivered and accepted to be valid.

delivery in escrow. Delivery of a deed to a third person until the performance of some act or condition by one of the parties.

demand. The willingness of a number of people to accept available goods at a given price; often coupled with supply.

density zoning. The zoning ordinances that restrict the average maximum number of houses per acre that may be built within a particular area, generally a subdivision.

depreciation. 1. In appraisal, a loss of value in property due to all causes, including physical deterioration, functional depreciation and economic obsolescence. 2. In real estate investment, an expense deduction for tax purposes taken over the period of ownership of income property.

descent. The hereditary succession of an heir to the property of a relative who dies intestate.

designated agent. An agent who has been appointed by a broker to act for a specific principal or client.

determinable fee estate. A defeasible fee estate in which the property automatically reverts to the grantor upon the occurrence of a specified event or condition. Also known as special limitation.

devise. A transfer of real estate by will or last testament. The donor is the devisor and the recipient is the devisee.

diminishing returns. The principle of diminishing returns applies when a given parcel of land reaches its maximum percentage return on investment, and further expenditures for improving the property yield a decreasing return.

discount points. An added loan fee charged by a lender to make the yield on a lower-than-market-value FHA or VA loan competitive with higher-interest conventional loans.

discount rate. The rate of interest a commercial bank must pay when it borrows from its Federal Reserve bank. Consequently, the discount rate is the rate of interest the banking system carries within its own framework. Member banks may take certain promissory notes that they have received from customers and sell them to their district Federal Reserve bank for less than face value. With the funds received, the banks can make further loans. Changes in the discount rate may cause banks and other lenders to re-examine credit policies and conditions.

dispossess. To oust from land by legal process.

dominant tenement. A property that includes in its ownership the appurtenant right to use an easement over another's property for a specific purpose.

dower. The legal right or interest recognized in some states that a wife acquires in the property her husband held or acquired during their marriage. During the lifetime of the husband, the right is only a possibility of an interest; upon his death, it can become an interest in land. Many states have abolished dower.

dual agency. This occurs when an agent represents both parties in the same transaction. Both parties are clients.

due-on-sale clause. A clause in a mortgage allowing the lender the right to implement the acceleration clause in the mortgage, if the borrower transfers title to the property.

duress. The use of unlawful constraint that forces action or inaction against a person's will.

earnest money deposit. An amount of money deposited by a buyer under the terms of a contract.

easement. A right to use the land of another for a specific purpose, such as for a right-of-way or utilities; an incorporeal interest in land. An easement appurtenant passes with the land when conveyed.

easement by necessity. An easement allowed by law as necessary for the full enjoyment of a parcel of real estate; for example, a right of ingress and egress over a grantor's land.

easement by prescription. An easement acquired by continuous, open, uninterrupted, exclusive and adverse use of the property for the period of time prescribed by state law.

easement in gross. An easement that is not created for the benefit of any land owned by the owner of the easement but which attaches personally to the easement owner. For example, a right to an easement granted by Eleanor Franks to Joe Fish to use a portion of her property for the rest of his life would be an easement in gross.

economic life. The period of time over which an improved property will earn an income adequate to justify its continued existence.

economic obsolescence. The impairment of desirability or useful life arising from factors external to the property such as economic forces or environmental changes that affect supply-demand relationships in the market. Loss in the use and value of a property arising from the factors of economic obsolescence is to be distinguished from loss in value from physical deterioration and functional obsolescence, both of which are inherent in the property. Also referred to as locational obsolescence or environmental obsolescence.

emblements. Those growing crops produced annually through the tenant's own care and labor, and which he or she is entitled to take away after the tenancy is ended. Emblements are regarded as personal property even prior to harvest, so if the landlord terminates the lease, the tenant may still re-enter the land and remove such crops. If the tenant terminates the tenancy voluntarily, however, he or she is not generally entitled to the emblements.

eminent domain. The right of a government or municipal quasi-public body to acquire property for public use through a court action called condemnation, in which the court determines that the use is a public use and determines the price or compensation to be paid to the owner.

employee status. One who works as a direct employee of an employer. The employer is obligated to withhold income taxes and Social Security taxes from the compensation of his or her employees. Also see independent contractor.

employment contract. A document evidencing formal employment between employer and employee or between principal and agent. In the real estate business, this generally takes the form of a listing agreement or management agreement.

encroachment. A fixture, or structure, such as a wall or fence that invades a portion of a property belonging to another.

encumbrance. Any lien such as a mortgage, tax or judgment lien, an easement, a restriction on the use of the land or an outstanding dower right, that may diminish the value of the property.

Equal Credit Opportunity Act. The ECOA is a federal act which prohibits discrimination by lenders on the basis of race, color, religion, sex, national origin, age, or marital status in any aspect of a credit transaction.

equalization. The raising or lowering of assessed values for tax purposes in a particular county or taxing district to make them equal to assessments in other counties or districts.

equitable lien. A lien which arises out of common law, wherein the parties have agreed in writing that a certain property will be held as security for a debt.

equitable right of redemption. The right of a defaulted borrower to redeem her or his property before foreclosure upon full payment of the outstanding debt as well as accrued interest and related costs prior to the foreclosure.

equitable title. The interest held by a vendee under a contract for deed or a sales contract; the equitable right to obtain absolute ownership to property when legal title is held in another's name; and an insurable interest.

equity. The interest or value that an owner has in a property over and above any mortgage indebtedness.

erosion. The gradual wearing away of land by water, wind and general weather conditions; the diminishing of property caused by the elements.

errors and omissions insurance. An insurance that protects brokers from loss due to errors, mistakes, and negligence.

escalation clause. A clause found in a mortgage or lease that allows the payment to adjust over the life of the mortgage or lease.

escheat. The reversion of property to the state in the event the owner thereof dies without leaving a will and has no heirs to whom the property may pass by lawful descent.

escrow. The closing of a transaction through a third party called an escrow agent, or escrowee, who receives certain funds and documents to be delivered upon the performance of certain conditions in the escrow agreement.

estate for years. An interest for a certain, exact period of time in property leased for a specified consideration.

estate in land. The degree, quantity, nature and extent of interest that a person has in real property.

estate in severalty. An estate owned by one person.

estoppel certificate. A legal instrument executed by a mortgagor showing the amount of the unpaid balance due on a mortgage and stating that the mortgagor has no defenses or offsets against the mortgagee at the time of execution of the certificate. Also called a certificate of no defense.

ethical. Conforming to professional standards of conduct.

eviction. A legal process to oust a person from possession of real estate.

evidence of title. A proof of ownership of property, which is commonly a certificate of title, a title insurance policy, an abstract of title with lawyer's opinion or a Torrens registration certificate.

exchange. A transaction in which all or part of the consideration for the purchase of real property is the transfer of like-kind property (that is, real estate for real estate).

exclusive-agency buyer agency agreement. A buyer brokerage agreement wherein the broker is entitled to a payment only if he or she locates the property the buyer purchases. The buyer can find property without the services of the agent.

exclusive agency listing. A listing contract under which the owner appoints a real estate broker as his or her exclusive agent for a designated period of time to sell the property on the owner's stated terms for a commission. However, the owner reserves the right to sell without paying anyone a commission by selling to a prospect who has not been introduced or claimed by the broker.

exclusive buyer agency agreement. An exclusive agency agreement wherein the buyer is legally bound to compensate the agent whenever the buyer purchases a property of the type described in the contract.

exclusive-right-to-sell listing. A listing contract under which the owner appoints a real estate broker as his or her exclusive agent for a designated period of time to sell the property on the owner's stated terms and agrees to pay the broker a commission when the property is sold, whether by the broker, the owner or another broker.

executed contract. A contract in which all parties have fulfilled their promises and thus performed the contract.

execution. The signing and delivery of an instrument. Also, a legal order directing an official to enforce a judgment against the property of a debtor.

executory contract. A contract under which something remains to be done by one or more of the parties.

executrix. The female designated in a will to handle the estate of the deceased. The probate court must approve any sale of property by the executrix.

executor. The male designated in a will to handle the estate of the deceased.

expenses. The short-term costs that are deducted from an investment property's income, such as minor repairs, regular maintenance and renting costs.

expressed contract. An oral or written contract in which the parties state their terms and express their intentions in words.

familial status. A protected class under federal Fair Housing law. A landlord cannot refuse to rent to the head of the household with minor children or to a pregnant woman.

Federal Fair Housing Act. The term for the Civil Rights Act of 1968 that prohibits discrimination based on race, color, sex, religion or national origin in the sale and rental of residential property.

Federal Home Loan Bank System. A system created by the Federal Home Loan Bank Act of 1932 to provide for a central reserve credit system for savings institutions engaged in home mortgage finance (predominantly savings and loans). The system is divided into 12 federal home loan bank districts with an FHLB in each district. The FHLBs maintain a permanent pool of credit to maintain liquidity of members or to provide means for mortgage lending when local funds are insufficient. Three sources of funds are available for the operation of the FHLB: (1) capital stock, (2) deposits of member institutions and (3) consolidated obligations sold on the market. When member associations need funds, they obtain money by borrowing from FHLB. The FHLB Board supervises the system. The board is composed of three members appointed by the President of the United States with the advice and consent of the Senate.

Federal Home Loan Mortgag77e Corporation. A mem-ber of the secondary mortgage market that primarily buys conventional loans.

Federal Housing Administration (FHA). A federal administrative body created by the National Housing Act in 1934 to encourage improvement in housing standards and conditions, to provide an adequate home financing system through the insurance of housing mortgages and credit and to exert a stabilizing influence on the mortgage market.

federal income tax. An annual tax based on income, including monies derived from the lease, use or operation of real estate.

Federal National Mortgage Association (FNMA). "Fannie Mae" is the popular name for this federal agency that creates a secondary market for existing mortgages. FNMA does not loan money directly, but rather buys VA, FHA and conventional loans.

Federal Reserve banks. The government controls banks located in each of the 12 Federal Reserve districts, established by the Federal Reserve Act of 1913. The Board of Governors, working closely with the President and the U.S. Treasury, controls the Federal Reserve. The Federal Reserve system (through the 12 central banks) supervises and examines members' commercial banks; clears and collects checks drawn on commercial banks; and may influence the cost, supply and availability of money.

fee simple absolute. The highest form of ownership recognized by law. Also known as fee simple or ownership in fee.

fee simple defeasible with a special limitation. Also known as a fee simple determinable estate. An estate created with a special limitation. Title would automatically revert back to the grantor or the grantor's heirs if the estate ceased to be used for the special limitation.

fee simple estate. The maximum possible estate or right of ownership of real property continuing forever. Sometimes called a fee or fee simple absolute.

fee simple subject to a condition subsequent. A defeasible fee estate in which the grantor reserves right of reentry to the property when the condition of ownership is violated.

FHA appraisal. A Federal Housing Administration (FHA) evaluation of a property as security for a loan. Includes study of the physical characteristics of the property and surroundings; the location of the property; the prospective borrower's ability and willingness to repay a loan; and the mortgage amount and monthly payments.

FHA loan. A loan insured by the FHA and made by an approved lender in accordance with the FHA's regulations.

fiduciary relationship. A relationship of trust and confidence, as between trustee and beneficiary, attorney and client and principal and agent.

financing statement. See Uniform Commercial Code.

first mortgage. A mortgage that creates a superior voluntary lien on the property mortgaged relative to other charges or encumbrances against same.

fixture. An article that was once personal property, but has been so affixed to real estate that it has become real property.

floor area ratio (FAR). The FAR indicates the relationship between a building area and land, or the relationship between the square footage of the building and the square footage of the land.

forcible entry and detainer. A summary proceeding for restoring to possession of land one who is wrongfully kept out or has been wrongfully deprived of the possession.

foreclosure. A legal procedure whereby property used as security for a debt is sold to satisfy the debt in the event of default in payment of the mortgage note or default of other terms in the mortgage document. The foreclosure procedure brings the rights of all parties to a conclusion and passes the title in the mortgaged property to either the holder of the mortgage or a third party who may purchase the realty at the foreclosure sale, free of all encumbrances affecting the property subsequent to the mortgage.

formal will. A will written by an attorney, with two subscribing witnesses, and with necessary language. Such a will may appoint the executor of the estate as independent agent and avoid the necessity of a bond.

fractional sections. An oversized or undersized section that is not exactly one mile by one mile is a fractional section; used only in the government or rectangular survey.

fraud. A misstatement of a material fact made with intent to deceive or made with reckless disregard of the truth, and which actually does deceive.

freehold estate. An estate in land in which ownership is for an indeterminate length of time, in contrast to a leasehold estate.

front feet. A unit of linear measurement of the side of a property that faces the street.

functional obsolescence. The impairment of functional capacity or efficiency. Functional obsolescence reflects the loss in value brought about by factors that affect the property, such as overcapacity, inadequacy or changes in the design. The inability of a structure to perform adequately the function for which it is currently employed.

future interest. A person's present right to an interest in real property that will not result in possession or enjoyment until some time in the future, such as a reversion or right of reentry.

gap. A defect in the chain of title of a particular parcel of real estate; a missing document or conveyance that raises doubt as to the present ownership of the land.

general agent. A party authorized to perform all acts of the principal's affairs within the continued operation of a particular job or business.

general contractor. A construction specialist who enters into a formal construction contract with a landowner or master lessee to construct a real estate building or project. The general contractor often contracts with several subcontractors specializing in various aspects of the building process to perform individual jobs.

general lien. A lien on all real and personal property owned by a debtor.

general partnership. See partnership.

general tax. See ad valorem tax.

general warranty deed. A deed that states that the title conveyed therein is good from the sovereignty of the soil to the grantee therein; no one else can claim the property.

GI-guaranteed mortgage. See VA loan.

government lot. Those fractional sections in the rectangular (government) survey system that are less than one full quarter-section in area.

Government National Mortgage Association (GNMA). Ginnie Mae," a federal agency and division of HUD that operates special assistance aspects of federally aided housing programs and participates in the secondary market through its mortgage-backed securities pools.

graduated lease. A lease which provides for periodic step increases in the rental payments.

graduated payment mortgage. A loan in which smaller payments are made in the early years and larger payments at some predetermined time. This may create negative amortization.

grant. The act of conveying or transferring title to real property.

grant deed. A type of deed that includes three basic warranties: (1) the owner warrants that he or she has the right to convey the property; (2) the owner warrants that the property is not encumbered other than with those encumbrances listed in the deed; and (3) the owner promises to convey any after-acquired title to the property. Grant deeds are popular in states that rely heavily on title insurance.

grantee. A person to whom real estate is conveyed; the buyer.

granting clause. That portion of the deed that states the grantor's intention to transfer title and type of ownership interest conveyed.

grantor. A person who conveys real estate by deed; the seller.

gross lease. A lease of property under which a landlord pays all property charges regularly incurred through ownership, such as repairs, taxes, insurance and operating expenses. Most residential leases are gross leases.

gross rent multiplier (GRM). A figure used as a multiplier of the gross rental income of a property to produce an estimate of the property's value.

ground lease. A lease of land only, on which the tenant usually owns a building or is required to build his or her own building as specified in the lease. Such leases are usually long-term net leases; a tenant's rights and obligations continue until the lease expires or is terminated through default.

growing-equity mortgage. A loan in which the monthly payments increase, with the increased amount being applied directly to the outstanding principal balance; and thus decreasing the loan term.

guaranteed sale plan. An agreement between broker and seller that if the seller's real property is not sold before a certain date, the broker will purchase it for a specified price.

guardian. One who guards or cares for another person's rights and property. A guardian has legal custody of the affairs of a minor or a person incapable of taking care of his own interests, called a ward.

habendum clause. The deed clause beginning "to have and to hold" that defines or limits the extent of ownership in the estate granted by the deed.

heir. One who might inherit or succeed to an interest in land under the state law of descent when the owner dies without leaving a valid will.

highest and best use. That possible use of land that will produce the greatest net income and thereby develop the highest land value.

holdover tenancy. A tenancy whereby a lessee retains possession of leased property after his or her lease has expired and the landlord, by continuing to accept rent from the tenant, agrees to the tenant's continued occupancy as defined by state law.

holographic will. A will that is written, dated and signed in the handwriting of the maker, and that does not need to be notarized or witnessed to be valid.

homeowner's insurance policy. A standardized package insurance policy that covers a residential real estate owner against financial loss from fire, theft, public liability and other common risks.

homeowner's warranty program. An insurance program offered to buyers by some brokerages, warranting the property against certain defects for a specified period of time.

homestead. The land, and the improvements thereon, designated by the owner as his or her homestead and, therefore, protected by state law from forced sale by certain creditors of the owner.

HUD. The Department of Housing and Urban Development, which regulates FHA and GNMA.

implied contract. A contract under which the agreement of the parties is demonstrated by their acts and conduct.

implied grant. A method of creating an easement. One party may be using another's property for the benefit of both parties; for example, a sewer on a property.

improvement. 1. Improvements on land—any structure, usually privately owned, erected on a site to enhance the value of the property; for example, buildings, fences and driveways. 2. Improvements to land—usually a publicly owned structure, such as a curb, sidewalk or sewer.

income approach. The process of estimating the value of an income-producing property by capitalization of the annual net income expected to be produced by the property during its remaining useful life.

increasing returns. When increased expenditures for improvements to a given parcel of land yield an increasing percentage return on investment, the principle of increasing returns applies.

incurable depreciation. The cost of fixing the property will be more than the increase in value or the corrections are not physically possible.

indemnification. An agreement to compensate someone for a loss.

independent contractor. One who is retained to perform a certain act, but who is subject to the control and direction of another only as to the end result and not as to how he or she performs the act. Unlike an employee, an independent contractor pays for all his or her expenses, income and Social Security taxes, and receives no employee benefits. Many real estate salespeople are independent contractors.

index lease. A lease in which the rental payment is tied to some agreed upon index, such as the Consumer Price Index or the Wholesale Price Index.

industrial property. All land and buildings used or suited for use in the production, storage or distribution of tangible goods.

installment contract. See contract for deed.

installment sale. A method of reporting income received from the sale of real estate when the sales price is paid in two or more installments over two or more years. If the sale meets certain requirements, a taxpayer can postpone reporting such income to future years when his or her other income may be lower.

insurable title. A title to land that a title company will insure.

insurance. The indemnification against loss from a specific hazard or peril through a contract (called a policy) and for a consideration (called a premium).

intangible property. Personal property that cannot be physically "touched," such as stock or lease.

interest. A charge made or paid by a lender for the use of money.

interim financing. A short-term loan usually made during the construction phase of a building project, often referred to as a construction loan.

inter vivos trust. A living trust created by an owner during his or her lifetime.

intestate. The condition of a property owner who dies without leaving a will. Title to such property will pass to his or her heirs as provided in the state law of descent.

invalid. In regard to contracts, it means having no legal force or effect.

invalidate. To render null and void.

investment. Money directed toward the purchase, improvement and development of an asset in expectation of income or profits. A good financial investment has the following characteristics: safety, regularity of yield, marketability, acceptable denominations, valuable collateral, acceptable duration, required attention and potential appreciation.

involuntary lien. A lien that is placed on the property without the consent of the owner.

IRS tax lien. A general, statutory, involuntary lien on all real and personal property owned by a debtor.

joint tenancy. The ownership of real estate between two or more parties who have been named in one conveyance as joint tenants. Upon the death of a joint tenant, his or her interest passes to the surviving joint tenant or tenants by the right of survivorship.

joint venture. The joining of two or more people to conduct a specific business enterprise. On the one hand, a joint venture is similar to a partnership in that it must be created by agreement between the parties to share in the losses and profits of the venture. On the other hand, it is unlike a partnership in that the venture is for one specific project only, rather than for a continuing business relationship.

judgment. The official decision of a court on the respective rights and claims of the parties to an action or suit. When a judgment is entered and recorded with the county recorder, it usually becomes a general lien on the property.

judgment clause. A provision that may be included in notes, leases and contracts by which the debtor, lessee or obligor authorizes any attorney to go into court to confess a judgment against him or her for a default in payment. Also called a cognovit.

judicial sale. A type of foreclosure in which the lender enforces the acceleration clause in the mortgage and files a suit to foreclose on the property.

laches. An equitable doctrine used by courts to bar a legal claim or prevent the assertion of a right because of undue delay, negligence or failure to assert the claim or right.

land. The earth's surface extending downward to the center of the earth and upward infinitely into space.

land contract. The seller finances the property instead of a traditional lender. The seller holds title until final payment is made.

landlocked. Property that does not have access to a public road to enter (ingress) or leave (egress) the land. This situation may create an easement by necessity.

latent defect. A hidden defect in the property.

law of agency. See agent.

lawyer's opinion of title. See attorney's opinion of title.

lease. A contract between a landlord (the lessor) and a tenant (the lessee) transferring the right to exclusive possession and use of the landlord's real property to the lessee for a specified period of time and for a stated consideration (rent). By state law, leases for longer than a certain period of time (generally one year) must be in writing to be enforceable.

leased fee interest. The landlord's retained interest in the leased property is the leased fee interest.

leasehold estate. A tenant's right to occupy real estate during the term of a lease, generally considered to be a personal property interest.

leasehold interest. The tenant's interest in the leased property is the leasehold interest.

legal description. A description of a specific parcel of real estate sufficient for an independent surveyor to locate and identify it. The most common forms of legal description are: rectangular survey, metes and bounds, and lot, block (plat) and subdivision.

lease option. This lease gives the tenant the option right to purchase the property within or at the end of the lease.

lease purchase. The tenant leases property for a period of time with the intention of purchasing it.

legal life estate. A life estate created by law; dower, curtesy and homestead.

legality of object. An element that must be present in a valid contract. All contracts that have for their object an act that violates the laws of the United States, or the laws of a state to which the parties are subject, are illegal, invalid and not recognized by the courts.

legatee. A person who receives personal or real property under a will.

lessee. The tenant who leases a property.

lessor. One who leases property to a tenant.

leverage. The use of borrowed money to finance the bulk of an investment.

levy. To assess; to seize or collect. To levy a tax is to assess a property and set the rate of taxation. To levy an execution is to seize officially the property of a person to satisfy an obligation.

license. 1. A privilege or right granted to a person by a state to operate as a real estate broker or salesperson. 2. The revocable permission for a temporary use of land—a personal right that cannot be sold.

lien. A right given by law to certain creditors to have their debt paid out of the property of a defaulting debtor, usually by means of a court sale.

lienee. The party whose property is subject to a lien.

lienor. The party holding the lien right.

lien theory state. A state in which the mortgage gives the mortgagee the right to place a lien on the property and the mortgagor retains title to the property.

life estate. An interest in real or personal property that is limited in duration to the lifetime of its owner or some other designated person.

life tenant. A person in possession of a life estate.

liquidated damages. An amount predetermined by the parties to a contract as the total compensation the aggrieved party will receive should the other party breach the contract.

liquidity. The ability to sell an asset and convert it into cash at a price close to its true value.

lis pendens. Latin for "action pending" and is recorded to give constructive notice that an action affecting the property (lawsuit) has been filed, but a judgment has not been decreed. A lis pendens notice renders the property unmarketable.

listing agreement. A contract between a landowner (as principal) and a licensed real estate broker (as agent) by which the broker is employed as agent to sell real estate on the owner's terms within a given time, for which service the landowner agrees to pay a commission.

listing broker. The broker in a multiple listing situation from whose office a listing agreement is initiated, as opposed to the selling broker, from whose office negotiations leading up to a sale are initiated. The listing broker and the selling broker may, of course, be the same person. See also multiple listing.

littoral rights. 1. A landowner's claim to use water in large lakes and oceans adjacent to his or her property. 2. The ownership's rights to land bordering these bodies of water up to the high-water mark.

loan-to-value. The relationship between the amount of a loan and the appraised value of a property. It is expressed as a percentage of the appraised value.

lock-in clause. 1. The lender's agreement to lock-in an interest rate for a specified time period. 2. A condition in a promissory note that prohibits prepayment of the note.

lot-and-block description. A description of real property that identifies a parcel of land by reference to lot and block numbers within a subdivision, as identified on a subdivided plat duly recorded in the county recorder's office.

management agreement. A contract between the owner of income property and a management firm or individual property manager outlining the scope of the manager's authority.

marketable title. A good or clear saleable title reasonably free from risk of litigation over possible defects; also called a merchantable title.

market-data approach. That approach in analysis which is based on the proposition that an informed purchaser would pay no more for a property than the cost to him of acquiring an existing property with the same utility. This approach is applicable when an active market provides sufficient quantities of reliable data that can be verified from authoritative sources.

The approach is relatively unreliable in an inactive market or in estimating the value of properties for which no real comparable sales data are available. It is also questionable when sales data cannot be verified with principals to the transaction. Also referred to as the market comparison or direct sales comparison approach.

market price. The actual selling price of a property.

market value. The highest price that a property will bring in a competitive and open market under all conditions requisite to a fair sale. The price at which a buyer would buy and a seller would sell, each acting prudently and knowledgeably, and assuming the price is not affected by undue stimulus.

master deed. A document that legally establishes the condominium regime. It is referred to as a condominium declaration and fully describes each unit and common elements as well as specific essential elements of ownership that govern its operation.

master plan. A master plan provides the guidelines for the future development of a community.

mechanic's lien. A statutory lien created in favor of contractors, laborers and materialmen who have performed work or furnished materials in erecting or repairing a building.

metes-and-bounds description. A legal description of a parcel of land that begins at a well marked point and follows the boundaries, using direction and distances around the tract back to the place of beginning.

mill. One-tenth of 1¢ (.001). Some states use a mill rate to compute real estate taxes; for example, a rate of 52 mills would be .052 tax for each dollar of assessed valuation of a property.

millage rate. A property tax rate obtain[ed] dividing the total assessed value of property in the tax district into [the] amount of revenue needed by the [dis]trict. This millage rate is then ap[plied] assessed value of each property [ ] to determine individual taxes.

ministerial acts. Acts performed b[y] a consumer that are informativ[e] do not rise to the level of activ[e] such as responding to inqui[ries] erty's price range or providi[ng]

misrepresentation. To represe[nt] an untrue idea of a prop[erty] plished by omission or concealment of a material fact.

money judgment. A court judgment ordering payment of money rather than specific performance of a certain action. See also judgment.

money market. Those institutions—such as banks, savings and loan associations and life insurance companies—whose function it is to supply money and credit to borrowers.

month-to-month tenancy. A periodic tenancy; the tenant rents for one period at a time. In the absence of a rental agreement (oral or written), a tenancy is generally considered to be month to month.

monument. A fixed natural or artificial object used to establish real estate boundaries for a metes-and-bounds description.

mortgage. A conditional transfer or pledge of real estate as security for a loan. Also, the document creating a mortgage lien.

mortgage banker. A firm or individual who originates loans for sale to other investors.

mortgage broker. A mortgage broker is a firm or person who brings borrowers and lenders together, and the finders' fee is normally paid by the lender, but could be paid by the borrower.

mortgage lien. A lien or charge on a mortgagor's property that secures the underlying debt obligations.

mortgagee. The lender who receives a pledge from a borrower to repay a loan.

mortgagor. One who, having all or part of title to property, pledges that property as security for a debt; the borrower.

multiple listing. An exclusive listing (generally, an exclusive-right-to-sell) with the additional authority and obligation on the part of the listing broker to distribute the listing to other brokers in the multiple-listing organization.

al ordinances. The laws, regulations and enacted by the governing body of a ality.

ssion. The act of putting an end to a mutual agreement of the parties.

tization. A loan in which the loan eases with each payment rather ing because the payment amount t to cover the interest.

essness and inattentiveness re-ion of trust. Failure to do what

net income. The gross income of a property minus operating expenses (not including debt service).

net lease. A lease requiring the tenant to pay not only rent, but also all costs incurred in maintaining the property, including taxes, insurance, utilities and repairs.

net listing. A listing establishing a price, which must be expressly agreed upon, below which the owner will not sell the property and at which price the broker will not receive a commission; the broker receives the excess over and above the net listing price as commission.

nonconforming loan. A loan that does not meet secondary market standards.

nonconforming use. A use of property that is permitted to continue after a zoning ordinance prohibiting it has been established for the area. Also, a use of property that is not conforming to current zoning because of a change in zoning, such as property being used for residential purposes, but currently zoned commercial.

nonhomogeneity. A lack of uniformity; dissimilarity. As no two parcels of land are exactly alike, real estate is said to be unique or nonhomogeneous.

nonjudicial foreclosure. Also known as foreclosure by advertisement because it is a foreclosure procedure where the lender does not have to involve the courts.

nonrecourse loan. A loan in which the property being pledged as collateral is the sole security for the loan. The borrower cannot be held personally liable for the note.

notarize. To certify or attest to a document, as by a notary.

notary public. A public official authorized to certify and attest to documents, take affidavits, take acknowledgments, administer oaths and perform other such acts.

note. An instrument of credit given to attest a debt.

notice of abandonment. An instrument filed to release a recorded declaration of homestead.

novation. Substituting a new contract for an old one and the release of liability.

obligor/promisor. The borrower in a note.

obligee/promisee. The lender in the note.

obsolescence. To be obsolete; as used in appraising the loss of value because it is outdated or less useful.

offer and acceptance. The two components of a valid contract; a "meeting of the minds."

officer's deed. A deed by sheriffs, trustees, guardians and the like.

one hundred-percent-commission plan. A salesperson compensation plan whereby the salesperson pays his or her broker a monthly service charge to cover the costs of office expenses and receives 100 percent of the commissions from the sales that he or she negotiates.

open buyer agency agreement. A nonexclusive agency contract between a broker and a buyer wherein the buyer may enter into similar agreements with an unlimited number of brokers; the broker is paid who locates the property the buyer purchases.

open-end mortgage. A mortgage loan that is expandable by increments up to a maximum dollar amount, all of which is secured by the same original mortgage.

open listing. A listing contract under which the broker's commission is contingent upon the broker's producing a ready, willing and able buyer before the property is sold by the seller or another broker; the principal (owner) reserves the right to list the property with other brokers.

open mortgage. An open mortgage is a mortgage without a prepayment clause. FHA insured and VA-guaranteed mortgages are open mortgages.

option. The right to purchase property within a definite time at a specified price. No obligation to purchase exists, but the seller is obligated to sell if the option holder exercises right to purchase.

optionee. The party that receives and holds an option.

optionor. The party that grants or gives an option.

ownership. The exclusive right to hold, possess or control and dispose of a tangible or intangible thing. Ownership may be held by a person, corporation or political entity.

package mortgage. A method of financing in which the loan that finances the purchase of a home also finances the purchase of certain items of personal property, such as a washer, dryer, refrigerator, stove and other specified appliances.

participation financing. A mortgage in which the lender participates in the income of the mortgaged venture beyond a fixed return, or receives a yield on the loan in addition to the straight interest rate.

partnership. An association of two or more individuals who carry on a continuing business for profit as co-owners. Under the law, a partnership is regarded as a group of individuals, rather than as a single entity. A general partnership is a typical form of joint venture, in which each general partner shares in the administration, profits and losses of the operation. A limited partnership is a business arrangement whereby the operation is administered by one or more general partners and funded by limited or silent partners who are by law responsible for losses only to the extent of their investment.

party wall. A wall that is located on or at a boundary line between two adjoining parcels for the use of the owners of both properties.

patent defect. A defect that can be found by normal inspection of the property.

payee. The party that receives payment.

payor. The party that makes payment to another.

percentage lease. A lease commonly used for retail property in which the rental is based on the tenant's gross sales at the premises; often stipulates a base monthly rental plus a percentage of any gross sales above a certain amount.

periodic estate. An interest in leased property that continues from period to period—week to week, month to month or year to year.

personal property. Those items, called chattels, that are not classified as real property; tangible and movable objects.

physical deterioration. A reduction in utility resulting from an impairment of physical condition. For purposes of appraisal analysis, it is most common and convenient to divide physical deterioration into curable and incurable components.

plat. A map of a town, section or subdivision indicating the location and boundaries of individual properties.

plat book. A record of recorded subdivisions of land.

plottage. The value that is created when two or more tracts of land are merged into a single, larger one.

point. A unit of measurement used for various loan charges. One point equals one percent of the amount of the loan. See also discount points.

point of beginning. The starting point of the survey situated in one corner of the parcel in a metes-and-bounds legal description. All metes-and-bounds descriptions must follow the boundaries of the parcel back to the point of beginning.

police power. The government's right to impose laws, statutes and ordinances to protect the public health, safety and welfare, including zoning ordinances and building codes.

power of attorney. A written instrument authorizing a person (the attorney-in-fact) to act on behalf of the maker to the extent indicated in the instrument.

premises. The specific section of a deed that states the names of the parties, recital of consideration, operative words of conveyance, legal property description and appurtenance provisions.

prepayment privilege clause. The statement of the terms upon which the mortgagor may pay the entire or stated amount of the mortgage principal at some time prior to the due date.

prepayment penalty. A charge imposed on a borrower by a lender for early payment of the loan principal to compensate the lender for interest and other charges that would otherwise be lost.

prescription. The right or easement to land that is acquired by adverse possession or "squatter's rights." It must be acquired under certain conditions as required by law.

price fixing. See antitrust laws.

primary mortgage market. See secondary mortgage market.

principal. 1. A sum lent or employed as a fund or investment, as distinguished from its income or profits. 2. The original amount (as in a loan) of the total due and payable at a certain date. 3. A main party to a transaction—the person for whom the agent works.

principal meridian. One of 35 north and south survey lines established and defined as part of the rectangular (government) survey system.

principle of conformity. The appraisal theory stating that buildings that are similar in design, construction and age to other buildings in the area have a higher value than they would in a neighborhood of dissimilar buildings.

principle of substitution. The appraisal theory that states that no one will pay more for a property than the cost of buying or building a similar property; or, in the case of investments, the price of a substitute investment.

priority. The order of position or time. The priority of liens is generally determined by the chronological order in which the lien docu-

ments are recorded; tax liens, however, have priority even over previously recorded liens.

private mortgage insurance (PMI). Insurance written by a private company (not government) that protects a lender against loss if a borrower defaults.

probate. The formal judicial proceeding to prove or confirm the validity of a will.

procuring cause. The effort that brings about the desired result. Under an open listing, the broker who is the procuring cause of the sale receives the commission.

progression. When a small structure is placed in an area of larger more expensive structures, the value of the smaller structure will increase.

property management. The operation of the property of another for compensation. Includes marketing of space; advertising and rental activities; collection, recording and remitting of rents; maintenance of the property; tenant relations; hiring of employees; keeping proper accounts; and rendering periodic reports to the owner.

property tax. Those taxes levied by the government against either real or personal property. The right to tax real property in the United States rests exclusively with the states, not with the federal government.

proprietary lease. A lease given by the corporation that owns a cooperative apartment building to the shareholder, giving the shareholder (tenant) the right to occupy one of the units.

proration. The proportionate division or distribution of expenses of property ownership between two or more parties. Closing statement prorations generally include taxes, rents, insurance, interest charges and assessments.

prospectus. A printed advertisement, usually in pamphlet form, presenting a new development, subdivision, business venture or stock issue.

public utility easement. A right granted by a property owner to a public utility company to erect and maintain poles, wires and conduits on, across or under his or her land for telephone, electric power, gas, water or sewer installation.

pur autre vie. A term meaning for the life of another. A life estate pur autre vie is a life estate that is measured by the life of a person other than the grantee.

purchase-money mortgage. A note secured by a mortgage or deed of trust given by a buyer, as mortgagor, to a seller, as mortgagee, as part of the purchase price of the real estate.

pyramiding. Obtaining additional investment prop-erty by borrowing against the equity of existing investments.

qualification. The act of determining the prospect's needs, abilities and urgency to buy and then matching these with available properties.

quiet enjoyment. A covenant in a deed that the title being given is good against third parties.

quiet title lawsuit. A suit to clear up any defects or clouds on a title.

quitclaim deed. A conveyance by which the grantor transfers whatever interest he or she has in the real estate without warranties or obligations.

range. A strip of land six miles wide, extending north and south and numbered east and west according to its distance from the principal meridians in the rectangular survey system (government survey method) of land description.

ready, willing and able buyer. One who is prepared to buy property on the seller's terms and is ready to take positive steps to consummate the transaction.

real estate. Land; a portion of the earth's surface extending downward to the center of the earth and upward infinitely into space, including all things permanently attached thereto, whether by nature or by man; any and every interest in land.

real estate broker. Any person, partnership, association or corporation who sells (or offers to sell), buys (or offers to buy) or negotiates the purchase, sale or exchange of real estate, or who leases (or offers to lease) or rents (or offers to rent) any real estate or the improvements thereon for others and for a compensation or valuable consideration. A real estate broker may not conduct business without a real estate broker's license.

real estate investment trust (REIT). Trust ownership of real estate wherein a group of individuals purchases certificates of ownership in the trust, which purchases property and distributes the profits back to the investors free of corporate income tax.

Real Estate Settlement Procedures Act (RESPA). The federal law ensuring that the buyer and seller in a real estate transaction have knowledge of all settlement costs when the purchase of a one- to four-family residential dwelling is financed by a federally related mortgage loan.

Federally related loans include those made by savings and loans; insured by the FHA or VA; administered by HUD; or intended to be sold by the lender to an agency.

reality of consent. An element of all valid contracts. Offer and acceptance in a contract are usually taken to mean that reality of consent is also present. This is not the case if any of the following are present, however: mistake, misrepresentation, fraud, undue influence or duress.

real property. Real property, or real estate as it is often called, consists of land, anything affixed to it as to be regarded as a permanent part of the land, that which is appurtenant to the land and that which is immovable by law.

REALTOR®. A registered trademark term reserved for the sole use of active members of local REALTOR® boards affiliated with the National Association of REALTORS®.

receiver. The court-appointed custodian of property involved in litigation, pending final disposition of the matter before the court.

reconciliation. The final step in the appraisal process, in which the appraiser reconciles the estimates of value received from the market-data, cost and income approaches to arrive at a final estimate of market value for the subject property.

recording. The act of entering or recording documents affecting or conveying interests in real estate in the recorder's office established in each county. Until recorded, a deed or mortgage generally is not effective against subsequent purchases or mortgage liens.

recovery fund. A fund established in some states from real estate license funds to cover claims of aggrieved parties who have suffered monetary damage through the actions of a real estate licensee.

rectangular survey system. A system established in 1785 by the U.S. government, providing for surveying and describing land by reference to principal meridians and base lines.

redemption period. A period of time established by state law during which a property owner has the right to redeem his or her real estate from a foreclosure or tax sale by paying the sales price, interest and costs. Many states do not have mortgage redemption laws.

redlining. The illegal practice of some institutions of denying loans or restricting their number for certain areas of a community.

regression. When a large structure is placed in an area of smaller, less expensive structures, the value of the larger structure will decrease.

release. To relinquish an interest in or claim to a parcel of property.

reliction. When water recedes, new land is acquired by reliction.

relocation service. An organization that aids a person in selling a property in one area and buying another property in another area.

remainder. The remnant of an estate that has been conveyed to take effect and be enjoyed after the termination of a prior estate, such as when an owner conveys a life estate to one party and the remainder to another.

remainder interest. A third party who has a future ownership interest in the property upon the death of the life tenant. See life estates.

rent. A fixed, periodic payment made by a tenant of a property to the owner for possession and use, usually by prior agreement of the parties.

rent control. The regulation by the state or local government agencies restricting the amount of rent landlords can charge their tenants.

rent schedule. A statement of proposed rental rates, determined by the owner or the property manager, or both, based on a building's estimated expenses, market supply and demand and the owner's long-range goals for the property.

replacement cost. The cost of construction at current prices of a building having utility equivalent to the building being appraised but built with modern materials and according to current standards, design and layout. The use of the replacement cost concept presumably eliminates all functional obsolescence, and the only depreciations to be measured are physical deterioration and economic obsolescence.

reproduction cost. The cost of construction at current prices of an exact duplicate or replica using the same materials, construction standards, design, layout, quality of workmanship, embodying all the deficiencies, superadequacies and obsolescences of the subject building.

rescission. The termination of a contract by mutual agreement of the parties.

reservation in a deed. The creation by a deed to property of a new right in favor of the grantor. Usually involves an easement, life estate or a mineral interest.

restriction. A limitation on the use of real property, generally originated by the owner or subdivider in a deed.

reverse annuity mortgage. A form of mortgage wherein the lender makes periodic payments to the borrower, using the borrower's equity in the home as security. The loan is repaid upon the sale of the property.

reversion. The remnant of an estate that the grantor holds after he or she has granted a life estate to another person; the estate will return or revert to the grantor; also called a reverser.

reversionary right. An owner's right to regain possession of leased property upon termination of the lease agreement.

rezoning. The process involved in changing the existing zoning of a property or area.

right of survivorship. See joint tenancy.

riparian rights. An owner's rights in land that borders on or includes a stream, river, lake or sea. These rights include access to and use of the water.

sale and leaseback. A transaction in which an owner sells his or her improved property and, as part of the same transaction, signs a long-term lease to remain in possession of the premises.

sales comparison approach. Also known as the market approach to appraising. It is used to appraise residential property or vacant land that will be used for residential purposes. It is based on the principle of substitution.

sales contract. A contract containing the complete terms of the agreement between buyer and seller for the sale of a particular parcel or parcels of real estate.

salesperson. A person who performs real estate activities while employed by, or associated with, a licensed real estate broker.

sandwich lease. The lessee's interest in a sublease is the sandwich lease.

satisfaction. A document acknowledging the payment of a debt.

secondary mortgage market. A market for the purchase and sale of existing mortgages, designed to provide greater liquidity for mortgages; also called the secondary money market.

section. A portion of a township under the rectangular survey system (government survey method). A township is divided into 36 sections numbered 1 to 36. A section is a square with mile-long sides and an area of 1 square mile or 640 acres.

security deposit. A payment made by the tenant that the landlord holds during the lease term and that may be kept wholly or in part on default or destruction of the premises by the tenant.

selling broker. See listing broker.

separate property. The real property owned by a husband or wife prior to their marriage.

severance. The process of changing real property to personal property.

servient tenement. The land on which an easement exists in favor of an adjacent property (called a dominant estate); also called a servient estate.

setback. The amount of space local zoning regulations require between a lot line and a building line.

severalty. The ownership of real property by one person only, also called sole ownership.

shared appreciation mortgage. A type of participation mortgage in which the lender shares in the appreciation of the mortgage property, when the property is sold.

situs. The personal preference of people for one area over another, not necessarily based on objective facts and knowledge.

sole ownership. See severalty.

special agent. A party authorized to perform with limited authority given by the principal.

special assessment. A tax or levy customarily imposed against only those specific parcels of real estate that will benefit from a proposed public improvement, such as a street or sewer.

special warranty deed. A deed in which the grantor warrants or guarantees the title only against defects arising during the period of his or her tenure and ownership of the property and not against defects existing before that time, generally using the language, "by, through, or under the grantor but not otherwise."

specific lien. A lien affecting or attaching only to a certain, specific parcel of land or piece of property.

specific performance suit. A legal action brought in a court of equity in special cases to compel a party to carry out the terms of a contract. The basis for an equity court's jurisdiction in breach of a real estate contract is the fact that land is unique and mere legal damages would not adequately compensate the buyer for the seller's breach.

sponsoring broker. A duly licensed real estate broker who employs a salesperson. Under law,
the broker is responsible for the acts of his or her salespeople.

squatter's rights. Those rights acquired through adverse possession. By "squatting" on land for a certain statutory period under prescribed conditions, one may acquire title by limitations. If an easement only is acquired, instead of title to the land itself, one has title by prescription.

statute of frauds. The part of a state law that requires that certain instruments, such as deeds, real estate sales contracts and certain leases, be in writing in order to be legally enforceable.

statute of limitations. That law pertaining to the period of time within which certain actions must be brought to court.

statutory lien. A lien imposed on property by statute, such as a tax lien, in contrast to a voluntary lien that an owner places on his or her own real estate, such as a mortgage lien.

statutory right of redemption. In some states, defaulted borrowers have the statutory right of redemption, which allows them to buy back their property after the foreclosure sale by paying the sales price, interest, and costs.

steering. The illegal practice of channeling home seekers to particular areas, either to maintain the homogeneity of an area or to change its character in order to create a speculative situation.

stigmatized property. A property is considered stigmatized or undesirable because of events that have occurred on the property.

straight-line method. A method of calculating depreciation for tax purposes, computed by dividing the adjusted basis of a property less its estimated salvage value by the estimated number of years of remaining useful life.

strict foreclosure. A foreclosure procedure in which the lender secures title and all equity to the property.

subagent. An agent of an agent. The broker is the agent of the principal. The salesperson is a subagent of the principal.

subcontractor. See general contractor.

subdivision. A tract of land divided by the owner, known as the *subdivider*, into blocks, building lots and streets according to a recorded subdivision plat, which must comply with local ordinances and regulations.

subletting. The leasing of premises by a lessee to a third party for part of the lessee's remaining term. See also assignment.

subordination. A relegation to a lesser position, usually in respect to a right or security.

subrogation. The substitution of one creditor for another, with the substituted person succeeding to the legal rights and claims of the original claimant. Subrogation is used by title insurers to acquire rights to sue from the injured party to recover any claims they have paid.

substitution. An appraisal principle that states that the maximum value of a property tends to be set by the cost of purchasing an equally desirable and valuable substitute property, assuming that no costly delay is encountered in making the substitution.

suit for possession. A court suit initiated by a landlord to evict a tenant from leased premises after the tenant has breached one of the terms of the lease or has held possession of the property after the lease's expiration.

suit for specific performance. A legal action brought by either a buyer or a seller to enforce performance of the terms of a contract.

suit to quiet title. A legal action intended to establish or settle the title to a particular property, especially when there is a cloud on the title.

summation appraisal. An approach under which value equals estimated land value plus reproduction costs of any improvements, after depreciation has been subtracted.

supply. The amount of goods available in the market to be sold at a given price. The term is often coupled with demand.

surety bond. An agreement by an insurance or bonding company to be responsible for certain possible defaults, debts or obligations contracted for by an insured party; in essence, a policy insuring one's personal and/or financial integrity. In the real estate business, a surety bond is generally used to ensure that a particular project will be completed at a certain date or that a contract will be performed as stated.

survey. The process by which boundaries are measured and land areas are determined; the on-site measurement of lot lines, dimensions and positions of buildings on a lot, including the determination of any existing encroachments or easements.

syndicate. A combination of two or more persons or firms to accomplish a joint venture of mutual interest. Syndicates dissolve when the specific purpose for which they were created has been accomplished.

tacking. Combining successive periods of property use; associated with adverse possession claims.

tangible property. Property that can be seen and touched.

taxation. The process by which a government or municipal quasi-public body raises monies to fund its operation.

tax deed. An instrument, similar to a certificate of sale, given to a purchaser at a tax sale. See also certificate of sale.

taxes. A compulsory contribution required by the government from persons, corporations and other organizations, according to a law, for the general support of the government and for the maintenance of public services.

tax lien. A charge against property created by operation of law. Tax liens and assessments take priority over all other liens.

tax rate. The rate at which real property is taxed in a tax district or county. For example, in a certain county, real property may be taxed at a rate of 56¢ per dollar of assessed valuation.

tax sale. A court-ordered sale of real property to raise money to cover delinquent taxes.

tenancy at sufferance. The tenancy of a lessee who lawfully comes into possession of a landlord's real estate, but who continues to occupy the premises improperly after his or her lease rights have expired.

tenancy at will. An estate that gives the lessee the right to possession until the estate is terminated by either party; the term of this estate is indefinite.

tenancy by the entirety. The joint ownership, recognized in some states, of property acquired by husband and wife during marriage. Upon the death of one spouse, the survivor becomes the owner of the property.

tenancy in common. A form of co-ownership by which each owner holds an undivided interest in real property as if he or she were sole owner. Each individual owner has the right to partition. Unlike a joint tenancy, there is no right of survivorship between tenants in common.

tenant. One who holds or possesses lands or tenements by any kind of right or title.

tenement. Everything that may be occupied under a lease by a tenant.

termination (lease). The cancellation of a lease by action of either party. A lease may be terminated by expiration of term; surrender and acceptance; constructive eviction by lessor: or option when provided in lease for breach of covenants.

termination (listing). The cancellation of a broker-principal employment contract; a listing may be terminated by death or insanity of either party, expiration of listing period, mutual agreement, sufficient written notice or the completion of performance under the agreement.

term mortgage. A nonamortized loan in which the borrower makes periodic interest payments to the lender and the principal balance is due upon maturity. Also known as a straight mortgage.

testamentary trust. A trust created through a will after a property owner's death.

testate. Having made and left a valid will.

testator. A male will maker.

testatrix. A female will maker.

time is of the essence. A phrase in a contract that requires the performance of a certain act within a stated period of time.

time-share estate. A fee simple interest in an interval ownership of property for a specified time period. The owner's occupancy is limited to the time period purchased.

time-share use. The right to use and occupy the property for a certain number of years. A time-share use may be conveyed by a lease or license.

title. The legal evidence of ownership rights to real property.

title insurance. Insurance that is designed to indemnify the holder for loss sustained for reason of defects in a title, up to and including the policy limits.

title-theory states. A state in which a security instrument gives the mortgagee the title to the property.

Torrens system. A method of evidencing title by registration with the proper public authority, generally called the registrar. Named for its founder, Sir Robert Torrens.

township. The principal unit of the rectangular (government) survey system. A township is a square with 6-mile sides and an area of 36 square miles.

township lines. The lines running at six-mile intervals parallel to the base lines in the rectangular (government) survey system.

trade fixtures. The articles installed by a tenant under the terms of a lease and removable by

the tenant before the lease expires. These remain personal property and are not true fixtures.

transaction broker. A person who represents neither party in a transaction. Both parties are treated as customers.

trust. A fiduciary arrangement whereby property is conveyed to a person or institution, called a trustee, to be held and administered on behalf of another person, called a beneficiary.

trust deed. An instrument used to create a mortgage lien by which the mortgagor conveys his or her title to a trustee, who holds it as security for the benefit of the note holder (the lender); also called a deed of trust.

trustee. One who as agent for others handles money or holds title to their land.

trustee's deed. A deed executed by a trustee conveying land held in a trust.

trustor. A borrower in a deed of trust; a grantor in a deed in trust.

Truth-in-Lending Act. Also known as Regulation Z, this act requires the lender to disclose the true cost of credit to individual borrowers for certain types of loans. It also regulates the advertisement of creditors.

unconventional mortgage. An unconventional mortgage (loan) is backed by the government to reduce the lender's risk. Examples: FHA insured loans and the VA guaranteed loans.

unenforceable contract. A contract in which neither party can sue the other to force performance, such as a contract missing the signature of the person authorized to perform.

undivided interest. See tenancy in common.

Uniform Commercial Code (UCC). A codification of commercial law adopted in most states that attempts to make uniform all laws relating to commercial transactions including chattel mortgages and bulk transfers. Security interests in chattels are created by an instrument known as a security agreement. Article 6 of the code regulates bulk transfers—the sale of a business as a whole, including all fixtures, chattels and merchandise.

unilateral contract. A one-sided contract wherein one party makes a promise in order to induce a second party to do something. The second party is not legally bound to perform; however, if the second party does comply, the first party is obligated to keep the promise.

unity of ownership. The four unities that are traditionally needed to create a joint tenancy—

unity of title, unity of time, unity of interest and unity of possession.

universal agent. An agent that represents a principal in all activities; such as someone given full power of attorney.

useful life. In real estate investment, the number of years a property will be useful to the investors.

usury. The practice of charging more than the rate of interest allowed by law.

valid contract. A contract that complies with all the essentials of a contract and is binding and enforceable on all parties to it.

valid deed. An enforceable deed that has a competent grantor and grantee, consideration, conveyance, legal description of land, signature of grantor, acknowledgment, delivery and acceptance.

valid lease. An enforceable lease that has the following essential parts: lessor and lessee with contractual capacity; offer and acceptance; legality of object; description of the premises; consideration; signatures; and delivery. Leases for more than one year must also be in writing.

VA loan. A mortgage loan on approved property made to a qualified veteran by an authorized lender and guaranteed by the Department of Veterans Affairs to limit possible loss by the lender.

variance. The permission obtained from zoning authorities to build a structure or conduct a use that is expressly prohibited by the current zoning laws; an exception from the zoning ordinances.

vendee. The buyer or purchaser.

vendor. The seller.

voidable contract. A contract that seems to be valid on the surface, but may be rejected or disaffirmed by one of the parties.

void contract. A contract that has no legal force or effect because it does not meet the essential elements of a contract.

voluntary lien. A lien that is created intentionally by the property owner, such as a mortgage.

voluntary transfer. See alienation.

waiver. The intentional or voluntary relinquishment of a known claim or right.

warranty deed. A deed in which the grantor fully warrants good clear title to the premises. Used in most real estate deed transfers, a warranty deed offers the greatest protection of any deed.

warranty of habitability. In a lease, this warranty requires the landlord to keep the property in good condition, that is to maintain the property, equipment and to comply with state and local codes.

waste. An improper use or an abuse of a property by a possessor who holds less than fee ownership, such as a tenant, life tenant, mortgagor or vendee. Such waste generally impairs the value of the land or the interest of the person holding the title or the reversionary rights.

will. A written document, properly witnessed, providing for the transfer of title to property owned by the deceased, called the testator.

wraparound mortgage. A method of refinancing in which the new mortgage is placed in a secondary, or subordinate, position. In essence, it is an additional mortgage in which another lender refinances a borrower by lending an amount over the existing first-mortgage amount without disturbing the existence of the first mortgage.

writ of attachment. Action taken by a creditor wherein the court retains custody of the property while a lawsuit is being decided, thus preventing the debtor from transferring unsecured real estate before a judgment is rendered. This ensures that the property will be available to satisfy the judgment.

writ of execution. A court order that authorizes and directs the proper officer of the court (usually the sheriff) to sell the property of a defendant as required by the judgment or decree of the court.

year-to-year tenancy. A periodic tenancy in which rent is collected from year to year.

zoning ordinance. An exercise of police power by a municipality to regulate and control the character and use of property.

Index

Instructions for Installing and Using the CD-ROM

Dearborn™ Real Estate Education has added a computer-based training CD-ROM with 100 practice questions to your *Guide to Passing the AMP Real Estate Exam*, 3rd Edition. It is located in the plastic sleeve on the inside back cover of the textbook.

There are three main topic areas contained in the CD-ROM: (1) Tutorial; (2) 50-Question Salesperson Practice Exam; (3) 50-Question Broker Practice Exam.

Installing the CD-ROM

Remove the Dearborn™ Real Estate Education CD-ROM from the plastic sleeve on the inside back cover of the book. Exit all other Windows programs that you may have running before you begin this procedure.

1. Insert the CD-ROM in your CD-ROM drive.
2. Double-click on the **My Computer** icon on your desktop. A window will open and your computer's drive icons will appear.
3. Double-click on the drive containing the CD icon. A window will open to display the **setup.exe** file.
4. Double-click **setup.exe** and follow the installation instructions.

Setup

Setup displays a **Welcome** screen that informs you which program you are about to install. Click on **Next** to begin installing the program, or click on **Cancel** to exit Setup.

The next screen introduces you to the contents and features of your Dearborn™ Real Estate Education CD-ROM program. Click on **Next** to continue with this installation, or click on **Cancel** to exit Setup.

Once the installation is complete, **Setup** will inform you that the setup procedure is complete. To exit Setup, click on **Finish**, or hit [**Enter**].

Starting the CD-ROM Program

When you have successfully installed the CD-ROM, go to 1) Start; 2) Programs; 3) Real Estate Exams; 4) AMP Exams. This will open the application.

Student Logon Screen

You are now ready to log on to your Dearborn™ Real Estate Education CD-ROM program. The first time you log on, the **Student Logon** screen appears. Type in an **ID number**. The ID number must be nine digits in length and should be easy to remember, such as your Social Security number. **You will be required to type it in exactly the same way each time you log on.** Use the [**Tab**] key to move to the next blank field. Then type in your name [**Tab**], then type your last name. Click **OK** when you are done. You will be asked to enter this information a second time to verify that you have typed it correctly.

Continue entering information as it is requested, including company name, address, location, and division. If these fields do not apply, please enter an **X** in each field. Use the [**Tab**] key to move to the next blank field. **PLEASE NOTE: THE DAYTIME TELEPHONE NUMBER MUST BE TEN DIGITS IN LENGTH** in order to log on successfully. You must enter information in **EACH** field in order to log on successfully.

Future Study Sessions

The next time you enter your CD-ROM program, click on the **Real Estate Exams** icon. The **Student Logon** screen will appear. If you have previously logged on, you need only enter your ID number again, hit [**Enter**], and the remaining information will automatically appear.